REMEMBER WHEN...?

REMEMBER WHEN...?

By

John Tigges

Produced in the United States of America
by BQW Publishing House in conjunction with Paintbrush Press

ISBN # 1-878406-14-0

INTRODUCTION
by
Tom Gifford, aka...
Jazzbo of Old Dubuque

You lucky folks! You are about to spend several hours in the company of Dubuque's own Doctor of Nostalgia, otherwise known as John Tigges. John is also known as the local guru for would-be writers interested in learning the rudiments of their craft. He regularly turns out, as well as his own novels, writers who manage to get published. Ask him, he'll tell you more about the hot new manuscript he's found than he will about his own work. Down deep, I have the feeling that that glimmering moment of discovery, the realization he's dealing with an undiscovered writer who may be just about to be discovered, is his greatest pleasure.

But the John Tigges awaiting you here is the relentless searcher, the determined sleuth in pursuit of Dubuque's past. He's most interested in the days some folks can still remember--it's history, sure, but not out of touch. Living history, so to speak. When Wyatt Earp went to Hollywood to advise on the making of western movies he was part of the living history of his era and when he died, Tom Mix cried. Well, John Tigges is a kind of advisor on the Dubuque that once was. He remembers a lot of it, dating from Depression days. And what he doesn't remember, he goes to work to find out.

He's a lifelong Dubuquer, educated at Holy Ghost, Loras Academy and College. His father, an auctioneer, a farm implement salesman and a county supervisor.

He had the gift of gab and a good deal of cleverness that showed up in his son. To wit, when Dad Tigges decided he wanted to be a county supervisor, an elective post, he knew there was only one way he could get himself elected, he stripped off His Republican identity and ran as a Democrat! And won!

Gift of gab. John tottered off to Chicago as a young man to work as a standup comic in nightclubs. "Making a complete fool of myself," he recalls now. "When I worked my way through the audience--seemed like it took a couple of days--I came back to Dubuque, tail between my legs, but a dazed grin on my kisser. I had seen the Great World and I'd made a couple of people laugh. Then I had a stroke of luck. I met this girl named Kathy Johnson from Bernard, Iowa. We were both working at Roskek's in '53. I was selling hardware and she was in ladies' lingerie--no wait, that was an old joke. Well, I could see right away she wasn't anything like hardware. We got married, of course."

He's an accomplished violinist. In fact, he has continued his comedy career in more recent years doing his impression of Jack Benny, including playing Jack's theme song, "Love in Bloom." Those who have seen his extravaganza have described it in these terms:

"I'll tellya, I never seen nothin' like it!"--Clark from Peosta.

"I was amazed!"--Betty from Massey Station.

"It's quite an act, I'll tell you that!"--Godfrey from Balltown.

"First time such a thing's ever been seen in these parts."--Bub from Dubuque.

"My old coon hound Zoroaster, he yowled right along with the fiddle playin'."--Hal from Maquoketa.

Yessiree, Bob. You don't get reactions like that by accident, my friends. We can only hope that John can be coaxed into yet another performance.

He tells the story of how he helped Dr. Parviz Mahmoud, Clark Stevens, M.D. and Dr. Doy Baker co-found the Dubuque Symphony Orchestra while he was working at John Deere, "doing as little as possible," he claims. It's a complicated story. Did the Symphony thing in his spare time, so to speak. You have to hear him tell it. He can be pretty convincing.

After co-founding the Symphony, he went on from John Deere to the world of insurance. That was when he wrote Ravel's *Bolero* and Beethoven's Fifth. No, no, that was just a test, students. He absolutely did not write *Bolero* and it was Johnny Walker's Fifth, not Beethoven's. Don't want you falling asleep during this priceless introduction. I mean that literally. Priceless. You wouldn't believe how much I'm getting paid for this. And John told me I actually get to keep the shovel.

Turned out he needed some insurance himself because in 1973 he fell ill, somehow contracting a rare tropical disease which blended the symptoms of beriberi and St. Vitus Dance. What a day. The townsfolk capered and romped and the Drum and Bugle Corps played the big march thingie from *Aida*. It was a day to remember. John, however, was less enthusiastic about the whole thing. Sick abed. Feeling rotten. He wanted no part of making medical history.

But did this keep our good man down ?

No way. The dad-blamed fool recovered. His work was not yet done. In fact, his life's work was only just beginning. Because while he couldn't work, he started writing. And as we writers love to hear people say: "Why don't you go to work and stop this writing!" To her dying day, my mother always looked at me a trifle suspiciously, ignoring my best sellers and Book Of the Month Club selections, and remarked, "Yes, yes, I know, but what do you actually do for a living?"

"Well, look at it this way," Tigges says today, "I was laid up, couldn't go out and earn an honest day's wage, there was nothing else to do. Nothing to keep my mind busy. You can only watch so much television and then St. Vitus Dance and beriberi become something to look forward to. That's when you know you watched too much TV. And I discovered I really enjoyed writing. I sold the first few things I wrote, and now, let's see, I've written 21 novels, two books on railroads, some biographies...and over 2,000 articles." This in a little over 20 years. Not bad for a standup comic/violin playing/insurance salesman!

In 1976 he started teaching adult creative writing at NICC, which was then NITI, and he continued the writing course until 1997, when he "retired." He still coaches writing classes in his home and he can never include all those who want to join. In 1982, he inaugurated the Sinipee Writers Conference and it has been a Dubuque area staple ever since, housed over the years at the University of Dubuque, Clarke College, and now permanently at Loras College. While he presided over his last such conference this past spring he was pleased to learn that a writing scholarship has been named in his and Kathy's honor and that the annual Sinipee writers contest will henceforth be called the John Tigges Writing Competition.

It was in 1991 that he staked his claim to being Dubuque's Nostalgia King, when he approached the Dubuque *Telegraph Herald* about doing what has become his monthly "Remember When" page, a compilation of which makes up the bulk of this book, along with short stories and God only knows what else. We can only hope and pray there's nothing actually subversive coded into these pages. Let's face it, like my dear friend and relentless humiliation, Guy Fortescue, John Tigges is capable of just about anything. Believe me when I say I assume no responsibility for any young minds derailed in these pages.

In addition to the writing groups he coaches in his home, he also visits writers' conferences all over the area. Just this year, he has spread the word at Madison and Rhinelander, Wisconsin, conferences. He tends to devote most of his coaching to the nuts and bolts of getting the words properly arranged on the page, getting the story told, getting the characters in and out of the room. He does not delve deeply, say, into the juxtaposition of water images and crucifixion symbols. All to the good, sez I.

At the very moment I write, he has in various stages of completion, a novel about terrorism, a horror novel, and a western. You name it, he can write it.

But always, whether coaching or editing some aspiring writer's manuscripts or writing his own books, he is never far from the history of the town where he's made his stand, so to speak. Present him with a question about the The Old Mill ice cream parlor out on Central, or the movies you used to see at the long gone Capitol and Varsity theaters...and off you'll go on a wild and exhilarating and loving ride down through the years, and Old Dubuque will come alive again.

You're going to love this book. Take it from Jazzbo.

FOREWORD

When the opportunity presented itself to write the nostalgic column, "Remember When...?" I jumped at the chance. While it would appear that fiction has been my mainstay in 27 novels, the truth of the matter is that my nonfiction output far surpasses that in the number of articles and books I have written. Over 2,000 articles and a couple three history books.

But why a column such as "Remember When...?"

While many people today are convinced they had rotten childhoods and were mistreated among other things, I had a wonderful, memorable childhood. I had loving parents and one sister who was loving, too, when we weren't fighting like cats and dogs, which of course is an undeniable right to siblings. I had friends back then and still number three even today as good friends. One of 60 years duration, Fred Uthe, one of 59, Bob Knopp and one of 58, Bob Hantelmann. Best part is, we're still speaking after all those years.

Still, writing a column that reflects on times gone by can be either a dirge or howling success. I like to think that "Remember When...?" falls into the latter category. If people were interested enough to make over 350 telephone calls in three days, when one man wanted to know the whereabouts of a tavern of which he had a picture but couldn't find its location, it means there were at least that number of people who had read that particular column. Is that good? I don't know. People call me with ideas and talk about days gone by in general and thank me for writing the warm, "fuzzy" memories of yesteryear.

Since 1991, when the column made its first appearance in *Over 49 News and Views,* a *Telegraph Herald* monthly supplement, I've had three "corrections" directed my way. One of them, from Dubuque's only grouch (he didn't have the courage to sign his name), didn't read the column carefully enough, since I had stated I was referring to Main Street as it had been in 1940, '41, '42 and so on. He chastised me, whipping me mightily with a typewriter ribbon, demanding I do better research. His corrections referred to Dubuque's Main Street of the 1920s. Another from a good guy, began by ripping me apart but then the humor of his message came through and I called him. He had had a ball at my expense and we both had a good laugh over his "put on or down" letter. The third was legitimate and pointed out that I had referred to a wrong type of plane used by Billy Mitchell to prove that an airplane could sink a battleship. Not one letter but three--and they were all complimentary beyond pointing out the boo-boo. Not too bad for some 74 columns.

The articles in this book have appeared over the years and point out different aspects of maturing in Dubuque, how Dubuque was in the past, how the FBI found an Al Capone still right here in "River City"--ah--I mean Dubuque.

The short stories included are, if for no other reason, fiction relief. But then some of them are nostalgic in nature and won't hurt a thing--I guess. The four Christmas stories, I understand, had the copy editor weeping a bit. At least she told me that.

At any rate, I hope that this stroll along the streets of Dubuque's past will jostle your own memories of growing up and bring back pleasant thoughts you haven't enjoyed for a while.

A wise man, (it could have been Tom Gifford for all I know) once said something to the effect that: "How can you know where you're going if you don't know where you came from?" Or something like that. Happy reading.

The Author

The following articles appeared in various issues of *Over 49 News & Views;*
"A Nose For Booze"; "Stars of Dubuque"; "Mystery of the Treasure Trove"; "He Was Only 19"

The following articles appeared in various issues of *Julien's Journal:*
"That First Thanksgiving"; "There Was a Time..."; "Those Were the Days My Friend"

The following short stories appeared in various issues of *Julien's Journal:*
"In Memoriam"; "Happy Anniversary"; "The Big Event"; "A Measure of Success"; "All Hallowed Eve"; "Just Like Daddy's"; "The Good Thief"

The following short stories are copyrighted by John Tigges:
" An Act of Kindness"; "Incident on Hartness Street"

Dedication
To every Dubuquer, native born and import, who has ever made a contribution to make our city the wonderful place it is. And to my parents, John and Madonna Tigges who gave me a wonderful childhood.

JANUARY

Remember when in the old days, once the holidays were over and January stared everyone in the face and it seemed as if spring were something that would never arrive? Remember that? Well, nothing's changed. It's still that way. January--cold weather-- head colds--cold automobiles. Yuck! Everything's cold in January, except maybe some warm memories of growing up in the '20s, '30s, '40s, '50s and even in the '60s.

Remember when every kitchen had a little wire basket soap saver? Tiny pieces of bar soap, too small to use as hand soap anymore, were put in the basket and the wire lid was closed. When that little device was swished back and forth in warm or hot water--voila!--instant soapy water. Today, those little slivers of soap wind up in the toilet or the wastebasket.

Remember when every kitchen had a metal box to hold wooden matches? The box usually hung close to the stove, since the stove burners and oven had to be lit by hand. Remember when emptying the tray of water from beneath the icebox was the balancing act of the day? It was not a wise thing to act up along about the time your mother or father was carrying it to the sink to dump. Remember the ice man and his truck, or horse and wagon, if you're old enough? Remember his ice pick? Every house had one and it was used to chip off ice to put in a drink or whatever. Remember hot, July days and the wonderfully cool, delicious drops of water dripping down your throat from a chip of ice he either gave you or you "accidentally found" on the back of the truck?

Remember when kerosene stoves with two or three burners could be converted into an oven? A flimsy metal box with a windowed door was placed over one or two of the burners depending on the size of the oven. Hey, it baked good cakes and pies. You just had to watch it like a hawk or it might get too hot and the pastry or whatever was inside would be ruined.

Remember when automobile windows would frost up in the winter? There were little storm windows that could be put on the back and side windows to make certain frost wouldn't form and the driver could see to the sides and to the back, through the rearview mirror. Boy, modern science at it's best. Remember the little fans that were used to keep the windshield clear? My dad had a real strange device that was made of fabric and had a flexible hose on it. The large end was fitted over the heater that was added to the car (in other words, a heater was not standard equipment), and the hose was hooked to the windshield by means of a suction cup and bracket. The hot air would be directed to the windshield through the hose, thus clearing off the glass. Of course everyone in the car nearly froze. But heck, that didn't matter. People were tougher back then--it seems.

Remember when ski jumping was a big, I mean a *BIG* fad in Dubuque? There were two jumps: a really high one that was off to the right at the bottom of Peru Road, along the lane that led to Leo Martin's cottage. Leo would in time become sheriff of Dubuque County. The Peru Road jump was a rickety skeleton and didn't look too safe, at least to my 9-year-old chicken-hearted eyes. The second jump was located on West 32nd Street. For whatever reason, this sport died out during World War II. When the war was over, it never regained the following it had in the '30s and very early '40s.

Remember when right after the Julien Dubuque Bridge opened, the old "high" bridge or wagon bridge was torn down? That old bridge was a lot more scary than the Eagle Point Bridge. Maybe it was the sound of tarred-over planks that had worked loose, slapping loudly on the roadway, when cars drove over them.

Not a comforting sound. Not unlike the Eagle Point Bridge, which had an angled "dog leg" to the left when driving east, the "high" bridge had an almost 90 degree turn to the right, when driving to East Dubuque. After that turn, the road descended to Sinsinawa Avenue along the bluff through which the Illinois Central Railroad tunnel had been bored.

Remember when Archie and Edith Bunker sang the theme song for "All In The Family," and they came to the part that went: "...Gee, our old LaSalle ran great..." Do you Remember the LaSalle automobile? It was a beauty that looked a whole lot like other cars of the '30s. But it had distinctive chrome trim and well, I guess one of the things we're going to recall are automobiles that are no longer with us.

There was the Graham automobile. This one, in it's last years, sported square headlights, as I recall. And there was the Auburn, a truly beautiful auto that seemed to cater to people of distinction to some degree.

The Hudson Terraplane had a small airplane for a hood ornament. I remember our neighbor in the north end had one. I coveted the airplane--not the car--just the hood ornament.

The depression did away with a lot of the names. Probably the most prominent name to go was the Duesenberg. It's a Duesy, came from that car and they were that. I read an article about that make of car and learned that no two were ever exactly alike. Even if you wanted one just like your friend's, they would talk you out of the idea and have some of your personality put into it. Now, that's a class act. Imagine. Making automobiles unique "works of art" that reflected the personality of the owner.

The Pierce Arrow with its stunning streamlining and the Marmon, which was miles ahead of the competition with innovations, some of which are still waiting to be reintroduced. An example of that technology would be the electric shift that was located on the dash.

The Willys car, was a strong candidate for a means of transportation that would last virtually forever. I saw a Willys heading out Rhomberg Avenue one evening about 25 years ago, and I followed it. When the driver parked it, I pulled in behind and got out to take a look at that "antique." The interior was all leather and smelled great. The driver and I chatted and he told me the car was given a ring job and complete overhaul every 100,000 miles. I asked him how many times he had done that to the motor and he replied, "The next ring job will be the sixth." Detroit doesn't build 'em like that anymore.

The Hudson Terraplane was mentioned before as having gone the way of other nice cars. Well, the entire Hudson line is no longer with us. The Nash and Desoto have left us with only memories and who didn't lust after a 1948 Tucker Torpedo? A great car, built with ideas that were so numerous some simply dribbled out the exhaust pipe. A magnificent car that, had Detroit and one of the big three seen fit to design and market, would still be with us today.

But...

Remember when your parents got their first electric refrigerator? Some called it an electric ice box, which I guess is proper terminology. The old wooden ice box was gone with its dripping pan and in its place stood a white box trimmed with shiny pot metal handles and hinges. Wow. Our first at home was a Stewart Warner and Mom and Dad bought it from Otto Dunbar. In later years, Otto and his wife went into the grocery business on the corner of 24th and Jackson Boulevard. Yes, Jackson really is a boulevard. Today, the building is still there but it has been remodeled into an apartment.

Remember when back in the '30s and '40s, when it was too cold to go outside and play, the indoor games were hauled out. Games such as Royal Rummy, Monopoly, Old Maid, checkers, both regular and Chinese. Pop some corn and the kids in the family were set for the evening. Another pastime my sister, Phyllis and I used to enjoy was "drawing." There were and still are six years difference in our age, so when I was six, she was twelve and many times she had to be almost coerced into this artistic endeavor. We'd get some of my dad's old sale bills from past auctions he'd already cried, and draw pictures to our heart's content. Animals, people, houses, trains, airplanes. It was sort of like having television that didn't move. Our imaginations took over and our artistic ability to whatever degree we did or didn't have, supplied the rest.

And Remember when, over 55 years ago, if a young man became eligible for the draft, he headed with his family to the Illinois Central Depot--or the Milwaukee--or the Chicago Great Western--and said good-bye amid tears. Once the train came in and he boarded, his next destination was whichever camp he had been assigned to for his basic training. It was, in a way, getting a ticket to World War II and the seats were fine. Front row center for most of the GIs who left Dubuque to fight in the "big one."

Here's a bunch of memory zingers to jog your recollections right back to the good ol' days.

Remember when going to the grocery store and wanting to purchase some canned pork and beans, you had choices like Hurff pork and beans and Naas pork and beans?

Remember when there were such brands of crackers as Liberty Bell Graham Crackers (2-lb. box 18¢) or Liberty Bell Salted Crackers (2-lb. box 15¢)?

Instead of Quaker Oats, one could purchase Banner Oatmeal. And do you Remember Crystal White Soap (6 bars for 23¢)?

Do you Remember when Break O'Morn Coffee sold for 15¢ a pound? How about brand names, such as Hills, Butternut or Chocolate Cream Coffee? One pound 28¢ or a two pound can for 53¢? A box of Shredded Wheat for one thin dime?

Remember when Marquette Coal sold for $6.50 a ton? You need some? Call Linehan and Molo. There phone number is 53. Yes. That's right. Just two numbers.

Remember when Conlon Motor Company, who sold and serviced Desoto and Plymouth automobiles, were located at 880 Locust Street? Their phone number was 881.

Hey, how about recalling Grunrow refrigerators and do you remember Servel gas refrigerators?

Do you remember when a person in search of a new automobile, could go shopping on Iowa at Sixth Streets? What sort of automobile would the shopper be looking for at that spot? Ford? Chevrolet? Dodge? If you said Chevrolet, you'd be right. Hurry on down to your Chevrolet dealer and see the beautiful new 1936 models which have just arrived. Now the big question. In 1935, who was the dealer for Chevrolet in Dubuque? Wrong if you said Bird, even though they operated at the same location later on. If you said Mathey, you said right. Take a bow.

Okay. The same type question about Nash automobiles. Same year, 1935. Who was the dealer for Nash and Lafayette automobiles in Dubuque and where were they located? The dealer was Engel and they were located on Iowa at 13th.

Remember when, after getting a spot on a favorite dress or pants, the soiled garment was sent to Apple's Crystal Clean. Not Cleaners but Clean. They were at Sixth and Central and in 1935 had already given Dubuque over 50 years of service. Gone, but not completely forgotten.

Remember when Dubuque had two Plymouth dealers? It's a fact. In addition to the Conlon operation on Locust, Kassler Motor Company sold Plymouth and Chrysler cars to the Dubuque public from their location at Fifth and White Streets.

There's no way we can leave out the Ford distributor, Universal Car & Tractor out of this memory jogger. Remember when, in 1935, if you wanted a V-8, one you drove instead of drinking, there was one available for under $2,000 at Universal? Go get one or a dozen at those prices with today's dollars.

Remember the name of the dairy that sold Meadow Gold Products in Dubuque back in the '30s and '40s? Iowa Dairy, and they were located for years in the 2100 block on Central Avenue. There was another dairy operating back then, out of a group of buildings at Seventh and Washington Streets. Remember it? Years after the dairy went out of business, a person could still read Sanitary Dairy in fading letters on the side of the corner building.

Remember when, if the man of the house wanted a new suit and maybe wanted a really good suit, maybe even a Hart, Schaffner & Marx, where would he have gone back in the '30s and '40s? That place was around up into the '50s and maybe even the '60s. Well, the home of Hart, Schaffner & Marx was the Hub on Main Street.

Who could forget the Erie Cafe with its good, clean, home-cooked food and snappy service? And what about Rath's, Dubuque's premiere Market on Central at 12th. Back in the '30s that must have been on the northeast or southeast corner where there are school playgrounds today.

Remember when Dubuque had *THREE* Plymouth dealers in 1935? Yes. There were actually three of them. Conlon and Kassler, the aforementioned dealers, and Frank Fluckiger had the third dealership. Fluckiger sold Dodges and Plymouths from his location at 450 Central Avenue.

Remember when there was a Dubuque Fire and Marine Insurance Company?

Remember when there was a restaurant on Main Street called the Euqubud Cafe?

Remember when National Tea had a market on Main Street?

Remember when I said I had a bunch of memory zingers to jog your recollections?

Have I done it?

Remember when there was a radio program entitled ? "I Love A Mystery?" Sure you do. With Doc, Jack and Reggie? Well, I love a mystery, too, the way Dick Brandenburg of Epworth, Iowa does. Back in October of the year we just finished, Dick contacted me and gave me the photo of a tavern, which allegedly was someplace in Dubuque at one time. On the back of the original photo the following information appears: Papa October 20, 1922 Peter Pals.

Now, both Dick and I feel the date is wrong because in the photo, the date on the place's license is 1908. Other signs that can be read under powerful magnification are: the Banquet Beer sign, which was made by the Dubuque Brewing and Malting Company. Right above that sign is the notice posted that the bar is a Union Bar. To the right of the Union bar sign is the posted closing time. Are you ready for this? 9:30 p.m. That's when everyone went home, the place was swept out and made ready for the next day's business. To the right of that sign and just to the right of the younger bartender is a sign that defies explanation. It reads: Bell Rings One / Minute Before/ Curtain Rises. Now, what do you suppose that means? Could there have been a curtained off stage that doesn't show in the picture? Above that mysterious sign, a mounted golden eagle holds dominion over the room. The bar had electric lights, sold cigars and even provided a bar towel for the customers, as evidenced by the one hanging in front. What do you suppose the brass cuspidors were used for?

The five customers all appear as if it might be winter outside and they're simply having a "quick one" on the way home or someplace else. The laws and ordinances against having an animal in such a place were either not yet written or were totally ignored because of the little terrier-type pooch standing there as if it didn't have a care in the world. The ceiling is tin with a design impressed in it and the floor looks in pretty good shape.

Does anyone remember when this bar operated, other than in 1908, (or 1922) and where it might have been located? One more clue. The first name on the license looks as if it might be William.

Remember when Walgreen's Drug Store downtown had two entrances? One was on Main Street and the other was on Eighth Avenue, although at the time, I think it was just Eighth Street. Do you remember the business it "wrapped around," so to speak? The one on the corner? You flunk the test if you said The Union Cigar Store. That was between

Seventh and Eighth Streets on Main Street, east side. If you said it was Whelan's United Cigar Store, you win the prize, although I have no idea as to what that might be. A person could get a shoe shine in one of about six chairs and I say a person because some women patronized the shoe shine boys there. During clement weather, the newsstand outside was loaded with magazines, newspapers and what have you.

Remember when little boys with portable shoe shine stands roamed downtown, charging a nickel or a dime for a shine? I know of one guy at least who remembers, because he did it, didn't you, Allan?

Remember when the Maid Rite that closed some time ago on 11th Street began business in a Quonset-type hut, set on a slab of concrete across the alley from where the restaurant eventually wound up doing business?

Remember when the Girls' Club existed on the third floor of the fire station at Ninth and Iowa Streets? Across Ninth, the YMCA operated and across from the fire station on Iowa, the Boys' Club was open for business?

Remember when Tenenbaum's Supermarket was located right next door to the Iowa Liquor Store? Then, another supermarket opened on the north end of that block? Kroger's. Remember? Right where the Mercantile bank is today. Tenenbaum's and the Iowa Liquor store were wiped out in a fire in 1962 or thereabouts. Mercantile, then called The First National Bank, built their current building and Kroger's left town after being in Dubuque only a short time.

And finally, we have a bit of poetry. It's a bit of Americana, long since gone from the highways and byways of our country. Beneath this stone/ Lies Elmer Gush/ Tickled to death/ By his shaving brush/ Burma Shave. They were around for about 40 years and with the advent of our interstate system, they slowly disappeared from the countryside.

Remember when George Ketoff ran the High School Store right across the street from Dubuque Senior High during the '30s? Take a look at the menu he offered the students and anyone else who stopped in for a quick snack. Ray Grutz, an old neighbor of mine from the north end wrote to me and sent the accompanying ads. Ray can't recall what the "400" for five cents was. Do any of you remember what it was? He thinks it might have been a soft drink.

Remember when Edwards Style Shop operated on the southeast corner of Seventh and Main Streets? Look at those prices in the ad. Wow. How

about the Fuhrman Triller Company that operated on the northwest
corner of Ninth and Central Avenue? Remember it? And the prices in
both ads were not sale prices but your ordinary- everyday- stop- in- and-
buy-right-now prices. Take note of the suede leather jackets and the fact
that some of the leathers involved were ostrich and sharkskin--and at a
price of only $6.95. Today that $6.95 might get you into an ostrich farm
to take a look at one of the big birds.

And just to refresh your memories on Fuhrman-Triller, the owners
were: Frank A. and Fred W. Fuhrman and John O. Triller. That store
always had that smell peculiar to clothing. So did J.C.Penney's basement
when the men's clothing department was located there.

The manager, Bob Berkley, did me a tremendous favor in 1942.
During the Christmas Rush, he had control of J.C. Penney's temporary
toy department and that year, one, count it, one, Lionel train set came in
from the warehouse where it had languished since the previous year. My
mother, Madonna Tigges, knew I wanted one for Christmas and she
quickly put a dollar down and had the set laid away, paying a dollar
whenever she went downtown. When all six of the dollars necessary to
buy the train set, were paid, she brought it home and hid it until that
magical day. While I don't have the original set, I do have a duplicate
that I operate on my Marx layout.

Joe "Kayo" Wareham called the other day and recalling Christmas
memories, told me about the Junior Musicale that he, Bobby Gribben and
Jack Rhomberg sang in as a trio. They were sort of managed by Arnie
Stierman, one of the announcers at KDTH. In 1940, that trio of voices
blended together coast-to-coast. Bobby Gribben went on to local fame as
a disc jockey at KDTH, Jack Rhomberg wound up singing "Old Man
River" when Loras College produced *Show Boat* and Joe emulated his
brother, Dave, by playing basketball.

Here's something for you--a Burma Shave rhyme. Famous last words/
About lights that shine/ He won't dim his, so/ I won't dim mine.

MYSTERY OF THE TREASURE TROVE

Did someone bury more than $80,000 on a Dubuque bluff overlooking the Mississippi River? Research indicates that Tom Kelly, a recluse miner might have done just that before he died in 1867.

Arriving with other miners, adventurers and tradesmen in 1829, Kelly became one of Dubuque's first citizens when the Black Hawk Treaty was ratified in 1833 and Iowa's first city was founded. By 1843, he had purchased 30 acres of lead-rich bluff land. With the aid of one employee, Dan Ryan, Kelly sunk shafts and brought lead to the surface.

When he was able to afford it, he sent for his widowed mother, brothers and sister, all of whom had remained in Ireland, and he established them in a home of their own . However, Kelly chose to remain on his bluff, segregated from his family and the community.

Since no local outlet existed for the ore being mined in Dubuque, the lead was transported to the nearest smelter in St. Louis. The rafts, barges or keel boats, which had carried the lead, were sold along with the ore. After enjoying "big city" life in St. Louis for a while, the miners would return upriver on a packet boat, repeating the process the next year.

In about 1853, Kelly began finding St. Louis' diversions a little too tame and longed for some real adventure. Considering his solitary nature, it's hard to understand why he wanted to travel to New York City. But he did, carrying with him, the proceeds of his year-long labors.

Dressed in his coarse mining clothes, Kelly attracted curious stares from the more sophisticated New Yorkers. One man in particular seemed drawn to him, following Kelly wherever he went. Fearful of being robbed and without provocation the Dubuquer shot the stranger dead. Arrested, tried and convicted, Kelly found the confinement of jail too much for his outdoor nature and succeeded in escaping. Stripped of his gold, he returned weeks later to Dubuque, walking all the way.

Apparently the loss of his money in New York warped his mind to the point of acting hostile toward everyone--except Ryan. The only show of generosity on his part was a purchase of an elaborate gravestone for his mother who died in 1856.

Shortly after his return to Dubuque, Kelly traveled to Rockdale, where he had the local blacksmith make a chest of iron. The box's measurements were two feet, 10 inches long, 22 inches wide and eight inches deep.

In early 1867, Kelly scratched his hand on a rusty nail but, owing to his miserliness, did not seek medical attention immediately. When he did, he learned that blood poisoning had spread through his arm and shoulder. Nothing could be done to check the infection. When he returned to his cabin, he summoned his sister and brothers to his blufftop home above St. Raphael's Cathedral challenging them, "If ye want it, look ye for it!" Tom Kelly died May 16, 1867.

His total estate amounted to $66.93 in cash, tools, 60 tons of ore and 30 acres of land. No bank accounts. No hidden money in the cabin. No maps. And no iron chest.

People began swarming over the bluffs looking for the gold almost before Kelly was cold in his Linwood Cemetery grave. Several years passed before a boy, with the appropriate name of Peter Fortune, found $1,200 in gold coins. Another trove of treasure was found by a George Ellis, who accidentally uncovered $1,800 in gold pieces.

Then in 1871, two boys, Otto Geiger and John Becke, dug a pit in which to build a fire for warmth, while tending cattle.

Not far under the surface of the ground, they found a small chest, 8 inches by 5 inches by 4 inches, which contained $10,000 in gold coins. Each discovery of buried money caused a stir among the townspeople and launched another short-lived search for the bigger metal chest.

Nothing more was found until 1914, when a city reservoir was built on the edge of what had been Kelly's property. This time a tin can, containing $400 in silver coins bearing the dates of 1856 to 1860, was uncovered by the workmen.

Since the small chest, with 160 cubic inches capacity, held $10,000, the larger chest with 5,984 cubic inches, could have held 37.4 times more, or $374,000. Naturally, it isn't known if the chest was full, or if it contained gold, silver or a combination of the minted coins.

Considering the price of lead ore in the 1800s, Kelly could easily have handled $200,000 during his mining days. Since he spent little on himself, and considering the worth of his estate, what happened to the money he did earn? Allowing one half for living and business expenses, which is considerably more than Kelly would have spent on himself, there would be about $100,000 missing. Subtract the $13,400 found in smaller caches, and the "Rockdale chest" could be holding $86,000. Remember, outside of the $66.93 in cash, not one red cent turned up other than that which was uncovered by chance. The thought of what the gold content would be worth on the inflated market of today is mind-boggling. And what would numismatists give to get their hands on rare collectibles such as these coins?

Today, the land is privately owned and treasure hunting is not allowed. Even if it were, the lead ore still in the bluffs would probably confuse electronic gear.

Someday, someone may accidentally uncover the chest and end the legacy of mystery that Tom Kelly left to Dubuque.

The mysterious bar that defied identification (contributed)

Three ads
from the 1930s
(contributed)

FEBRUARY

Remember when Duke Strazinsky rode his Milwaukee Road locomotive to glory? October 1934, brought to an end Duke's half century of service with that railroad. It seems when doing a little research on this gentleman, one finds he was one helluva man.

Duke was at the throttle of a rescue train that dashed north to save two men and a little girl who had been mangled in a dynamite explosion. A young target shooter's stray bullet had detonated 150 pounds of explosives in a quarry shack near Specht's Ferry. Twelve miles of twisting, light rail separated the train with medical supplies, doctors and nurses aboard, from the victims. The posted speed limit was 40 mph on the fastest of stretches that paralleled the Mississippi. Duke, decked out in his Sunday best, pulled open the throttle and 32 minutes later, slammed to a screeching stop. Within minutes, Duke, the medical people and the patients roared back to Dubuque in reverse.

The effort brought Duke Strazinsky nationwide acclaim. On June 7, 1904, it was Duke Strazinsky at the throttle of a special train that carried the Liberty Bell on it's way to the St. Louis World's Fair.

Duke, after 50 years with the railroad, rode his train to glory, as the old railroading expression states, when his locomotive struck a broken rail near Guttenberg and the train rolled down an embankment.

Remember when once the laundry was washed, it had to be hung out on the line to dry--even when the temperature might be well below freezing? When enough time had elapsed, the freshly laundered, stiff-as-a-board shirts, long johns, snuggies, socks and pants were brought inside to thaw. That had to be the freshest-smelling laundry in the entire world--bar none--and I defy anyone to make their weekly wash smell that good today with all the modern conveniences at their disposal.

Remember when swinging in an old tire swing was the epitome of fun? If there happened to be a tree in the yard, and there were kids who regularly slept inside the house each night, and the head of the house, Papa, had access to an old tire, there would be such a swing in the yard before long.

Remember when the only name in sleds was Flexible-Flyer? Once the snow fell and the hills and streets of Dubuque were covered, the Flyers came out of the basements, and garages and attics, and their owners were whisked down the hills for an adventure few children today could even imagine. We'll talk about sled riding in Dubuque again--believe me.

Remember when the first valentine was sent? Of course you don't. No one alive today does. But in 1847, on February 14, Esther Howland of Worcester, Massachusetts, received one from a long-time but not forgotten admirer. Esther picked up on the idea and within a matter of years she had set up a business that flooded the country, if not the world, with lacy hearts and touching verses of undying love. In a few years, she was running a business earning in excess of $100,000 per year. There's money in those syrupy verses, I tell you.

Remember when I ran a few Burma Shave signs? How about another for the road? (What an awful pun!) The answer to/ A maiden's prayer/ Is not a chin/ Of stubby hair/ Burma Shave!

Remember when, way back in the '30s and '40s, when most houses in Dubuque and similar cities, were heated with coal. Sure, some were heated with wood but the issue at hand has to do with handling icy sidewalks. If Mother Nature didn't see fit to have it rain and then freeze, thus making ice, and in turn icy sidewalks and then streets, kids would make a sliding pond, usually on the sidewalk in front of their own house. That's right. Right where pedestrians were supposed to walk.

Assuming the consistency of snow was proper for stamping it down and then making a few slides over it, the area soon became glassy smooth and slicker than anything you can think of in comparison. And these neat slides, anywhere from 10 feet to maybe 25, would last until someone sprinkled ashes from their furnace all over the full length. Sure, anyone could walk on the ice with ashes all over it. Some people sure didn't give a horse's hoot about kids having any fun. And the same went for Interstate Power Company when they'd send out Cinderella, the old Mack bus that had been converted to sprinkle ashes on the bus routes, loaded with ashes from the I.P. power house, to cinder the best sliding hills in the city. Oh, well. Kids had the best and the worst, I guess, even back then.

Remember when, if your schoolground had a hill of any size, it was paramount to find a piece of cardboard to utilize as a sled? Recess periods and noon hours were filled with flying down the hill on that little hunk of paper. As an old northend Holy Ghoster, I remember sliding from the top of the hill, immediately to the north of the driveway that ran past the north side of Holy Ghost Church. Then, there was no school building to stop such silly notions as sliding down that hill. Instead, the precarious climb was made to the top and taking in a deep breath, the slider sat down quite unceremoniously on his (it was the boy's playground, after all) butt, making certain the cardboard was between it and the icy hill. The next 4-6 seconds zipped by so fast the slider was hardly aware that Central Avenue was the width of a sidewalk away. And, the times were such that some guy had to be a hero and that guy was Jim Rupp. Jim could go down that hill, are you ready, on his leather-soled boots, standing as though he were on skis. I still don't know how he did it, and I don't recall ever seeing him take a spill.

Remember when, on Sunday afternoons, some of the theaters featured new movies? A run of Sunday, Monday and Tuesday was about normal. Then Wednesday and Thursday, a new double feature would move into the theater and Friday and Saturday saw the same thing happen. The Avon, Strand and State, as second run movie houses, changed the most frequently. The Grand and Orpheum as first run theaters, didn't change quite as often, while the two neighborhood theaters, the Capitol and the Varsity, also ran features that had already been shown downtown.

Remember when, taking your date to the Hollywood Grill on Fifth and Main was the "in" thing to do? An order of fries, a malt or coke to wash

'em down and music from the Seeburg juke box set the atmosphere to
stare into your date's eyes and dream about the future--like the next day
when you maybe had a test in school and should have been home
studying for it. There were other sites that were much like the
Hollywood on Main Street. Remember Diamond's and the Triangle?
Boy, those places could get crowded after a basketball game. If the
Duhawks, Spartans, Gubs, CoDukes or Rams won, the air was one of
festivity. If they lost, the pain passed quickly and a festive air soon filled
the night.

Remember when Valentine's Day rolled around during the years you
were in school? If you were lucky, your teacher had a box covered with
paper red hearts and a slot to accept the valentines you were going to
send to your friends and "secret love." Naturally, the high point came
when the box was opened and one or two of the students were appointed
mail carriers and the cards were handed out. It's strange to think that,
while today so-called child experts state that such things put children on
the defensive and the whole thing is nothing but a popularity contest,
such thoughts seldom ran through children's minds B.C.E (that's Before
Child Experts). You gave to the kids you liked and received from your
friends. And, to play it safe, it was wise to give every one in the room a
card.

Remember when, during the winter nights, despite the down side of
the '30s, families still gathered wherever the radio was and listened to
comedians such as Jack Benny, and Fred Allen, Edgar Bergan and
Charlie McCarthy? Mystery shows such as "Inner Sanctum" and "The
Shadow "? A game of checkers or Chinese checkers could be played
while listening to your favorite program or the family could work on a
jigsaw puzzle. A lot of people started hobbies such as butterfly mounting
or stamp collecting.

Remember when there was such a thing as free entertainment in the
home? It was called radio. And, yes, it actually was free--the use of it,
that is. Naturally, one had to first purchase a radio and plug it into an
electrical outlet. And of course the electricity that was used to operate
the radio was a cost to the owner. But only pennies. There was no
charge for the actual entertainment that blasted out of the speaker. And
of course, the same is true today. Sponsors who pick up the cost of radio
disc jockeys today and the cost of, let's say Jack Benny's program,
expected the listener to try their product. If a person did buy a box of

Jello or two or later on a pack of Lucky Strike cigarettes, both of which were Jack Benny's sponsors at one time or another, that person gave a bit of a profit to the sponsor and enabled the next program and the next and so on to be heard. Of course the consumer came out ahead--I think. It was the consumer's idea to purchase a sponsor's product and have the use of it while at the same time be able to hear Jack Benny.

Remember when during any one week, a radio owner and his or her family could tune into Major Bowes' Amateur Hour ("Around and 'round she goes, and where she stops nobody knows."), "Gangbusters," "The Lone Ranger," "The Hermit," "The F.B.I. in Peace and War," "Gunsmoke," "Have Gun, Will Travel." Yes, the last two also started on radio before moving to television.

Remember when ice cream came on sticks (I know they still do) and there might be a prize indicated on the stick once you had eaten the ice cream? If the word "free" appeared on the wooden stick, another ice cream bar was yours for the asking. Now, there was a deal. Those freebies were few and far between but hope sprung eternal while a kid's tongue slurped away at the Popsicle, Dreamsicle or Fudgesicle.

Remember when Dixie Cups were around and a pretty low-cost hobby was collecting the pictures of movie stars that appeared on the inside lid. There was a small amount of ice cream, usually vanilla but strawberry and chocolate were also available, in a small cardboard cup. A wax-paper-like liner kept the picture free from the ice cream and furious trading would ensue if one star or another would appear that was already in someone's collection. ("I'll give you two Jane Withers for one Ken Maynard. Com'on. Whaddaya say?")

Remember when a kid could buy a candy bar for a nickel or three for a dime?

Remember when that nickel or dime might be the pay for "taking care of a load of kindling"? Kindling? What's that? Well, way back when, when furnaces in homes were more like a musical instrument that had to be "played" to coax the maximum amount of heat from to warm the house, coal fires were started with kindling. Loads of end pieces and curved pieces from the furniture, window sash and door factories and so on would be purchased for a nominal amount of money and unceremoniously dumped in front of a house, to be left there until the boys or girls of the house got home from school. It was written someplace, I believe, that only kids were allowed to do that job--never adults. At any rate, if there was a coaster wagon around, it would be loaded and pulled to the open basement window. Each piece was thrown inside. Then another load was brought and so on. Doesn't sound too bad, does it? But then, the kids had to go inside and re-pile it away from below the window. So triple handling of each piece seemed to be the order of the day. The different shaped blocks of wood gave countless hours of enjoyment to children who didn't have much in the way of toys and such "big" building blocks allowed great skyscrapers and mighty forts to be constructed. Those blocks became whatever the imagination of a child of the '30s wanted them to be. Parts for a house. A railroad train connected with bits of string for couplers. In the '30s, a kid was lucky if he or she had two or three toys to call their own. But kindling blocks could be used to supplement playthings anytime.

Remember when a picture of a turn-of-the-century saloon, which had been furnished by Dick Brandenburg, appeared in January's chapter. I opened a can of worms. If nothing else, that little exercise proved that at least 347 people read "Remember When...?" That's right. I had almost 350 phone calls and I'm sorry to say that none of the suggestions made, really identify the tavern in question. And no, it's not a contest and no, I don't, nor does Dick, know where it is located.

We truly thought that someone would know without a doubt. But there are too many questions concerning the tavern names submitted. As far as can be determined none of them was the bar pictured.

After putting the picture under strong magnification, I concluded there would have to be at least two corroborating pieces of evidence. Either on-premises entertainment from a stage with a curtain or a location very close to the Orpheum (or Majestic as it was called way back when) or the Grand theaters' or some theater. The reasoning was that darned sign: "Bell rings one minute before curtain." Of all the tavern names submitted (48 to be exact), only one was known to have entertainment on premises. That was Budde's or Buddy's Bar in Cascade in the first part of the 20th Century. A man called, telling me that he had talked with old timers and they recalled there had been at one time, show girls who had danced on a stage at that particular bar. But when I asked if there was a golden eagle mounted above the mirrors in the center of the back bar, he said he didn't know but would ask his sources. The fact the tavern has been sold and it's equipment taken away doesn't help much. The Cascade nominee was struck from the list.

Another tavern that drew a couple of dozen call votes from Dyersville, concerned the Palace Bar. The same floor and the bar and back bar were "identical" to the one in the picture, made everyone who called believe that it might be "the one." Someone who had operated that tavern in the past, called but wasn't certain if there were any mounting holes in the back bar for the stuffed raptor. Plus the fact, he believed there wasn't a theater close enough to get from the Palace to the theater in under a minute for the next act.

The third and last candidate to go down the tubes, was the basement room at Jerry Turner's Instant Replay. That particular room had the most calls for any of the Dubuque entries. I spoke with Jerry and he told me he'd do some checking. He called back on Thursday after the picture was published and told me he could see no evidence of holes or repaired holes on the back bar. The floor was the same as in the picture and as far as he could tell, the bar was very similar to the one in the photo. He also said a man named William Mauring owned the bar at one time in 1902. Remember when I wrote in the column that the name on the license appeared to be "Willam"? Eerie stuff, huh? But no nearby theater or evidence of a one-time stage in the room and no eagle over the bar. Away went the Instant Replay.

I thought it might have been in the building next to the Majestic, which was in 1914 and later, a cafe. There are two pictures in the *Telegraph Herald's Dubuque, the Birthplace of Iowa*, of the cafe on page 22 and page 89. But as I recall there was a wooden floor in that room, not a black and white tile one.

On Page 86 of the same book, there is a photo of Bristram Brothers' Saloon at 506 Main Street in Dubuque. It was around 1912 and shows a bar setup with the glass cigar case at the end toward the photographer, just like the mystery photo. Well, almost. The back bar pillars are different and there are ceiling lights. The mirrors in the back bar are framed differently as well. But I'm willing to bet a nickel that Metz Manufacturing Company built all of those bars and back bars that everyone thought might belong in their mystery tavern candidate. Why would I be willing to make such a risky wager? Because someone who called, told me that the Dubuque Malt and Brewing Company, who brewed Banquet Beer, would actually give them a Metz bar and back bar arrangement if they sold their leading product, Banquet Beer, for five years. As a result, that mystery isn't solved, and I'm throwing in the bar towel.

Remember when Ray Grutz brought up the question as to what a "400" was in January's chapter? Well, after 63 phone calls and several letters, I know. It was a chocolate drink manufactured by the Sanitary Dairy, which was located at 60 East Seventh Street. Thick chocolate syrup on the bottom and milk on top. The customer had to shake it to mix it into the drink. Cost all of a nickel and came in a half pint glass bottle that had the same lines as the old-fashioned quart milk bottle.

In that same column, I made mention of Fuhrman and Triller Men's Clothing store. One man I should have mentioned, because I remember him well, working there part time, is Art Rooney. Art worked for the railroad (the Milwaukee if I remember correctly or was that your dad, Art?) and sold my parents a few winter jackets for me along with winter caps and blue jeans and what have you. All right they were called overalls in those days even if they were belted at the waist.

Considering the fact that it is February, it's time to reflect more about St. Valentine's Day and all the love and kisses and flowers and candy that go with that particular observation.

Valentines started their trips through the mail in 1847. And they didn't always mean love 'n' stuff. Friendship was expressed through the cards in the earlier days up until probably the 1920s or '30s, before going love full time. However, those concerned with wooing wooing the man or woman of their desire sent poetry that would make a stop sign blush, when one considers the times.

That would send a turn-of-the-century young miss awhirl. How about this one?

REALIZATION

Met, with bliss!
Snatched a kiss!
Now she's mine
Own Valentine

That would send a turn-of-the-century young miss awhirl.

TO MY VALENTINE
None could love you better
Now or anytime
Than the one who sends this letter
With violets and Valentine

They were decked with Cupid and his love filled arrows and bow, lace and most of the time the letters of the verse and figures thereon, were embossed.

Along the lines of love and friendship, one of the biggest "fads" if I dare call collecting autographs in a small book a fad, was just that. I have my mother's, with autographs of her in-laws and five of her grandchildren. While there was no elegant verse written, the love seemed to come through nevertheless, especially from the five grandchildren.

Another thing that started out in a completely different way was the calling card. Today, sales personnel, business men and business women, teachers and even one author I know, uses calling cards.

In the late 1800s, the calling card had nothing but a name such as J.T. Heiberger, on it as per my grandfather's calling card in the photo. Note the bouquet covering his name along with the brief but succinct message: *With fond love for thee*. I'm sure my grandmother, Susan Jarding was the recipient of that one.

As some of you know, I collect old books and in a few cases, rare books. In two such old books, I ran across three of the old calling cards. The one with the dove sitting among peonies and black-eyed Susans(?), carries a message: *Friendship increases your happiness.* Beyond the dove and the flowers is the name: Rosa E. Hofferd.

The card with the hands holding the script, which reads:

Summer may change to winter
Flowers may fade and die
But I shall ever love thee
While I can heave a sigh
hides the name: Laura M. Kuen

The one with the white flower and remnants of silk feathers on the left side reads: *All my best wishes are for thee.* Beneath the fold-out flower is Lizzie M. Kuen. Sisters?

Not being an expert on these cards I would guess they date from the late 1880s or '90s. My mother's calling card, which bears only her name, Madonna J. Heiberger, would have been printed about 1921 when she was 21 years of age. I have the brass printing plate for her brother's calling card and would conclude that a person had the printer engrave the card. After printing a supply, the printer gave the plate to the owner, who would bring it in when a new supply was needed. Just speculation.

A NOSE FOR BOOZE

My quest for the story on the federal raid on the Corn Belt Building is complete.

After hearing from Mary Burris Post, the rest was easy. Mrs. Post's father, Forest "Frosty" Burris conducted the raid, and this dear lady gave me the track to run on by nailing down the date within ten days in 1929. A big thank you, Mary, and I hope you enjoy the article about the raid.

While driving north on Jackson Street one day in June, 1929, Forest "Frosty" Burris, resident federal investigator in charge of the Dubuque FBI office, smelled something that he shouldn't have. Fumes from fermenting mash.

Someone was operating a still nearby. He turned around and retraced his route. When he passed the Corn Belt Building, he slowed and looked up at the imposing Victorian structure. The Corn Belt Packing Company had closed down in the recent past and someone must have set up a still inside the building. Before it was known as the Corn Belt Building, the structure on the northeast corner of 30th and Jackson Streets housed the Dubuque Malting Company. Today, it is known as the H&W Motor Express Company.

Along with his partner H.H. Kirschman, Burris began surveillance duty that wasn't long in producing evidence the ol' factory Burris had first sniffed out.

They had learned that there was an egg candling and seperation operation ostensibly operating in a part of the former packing house. They continued their watch for a few days and noticed railroad cars that should have been carrying eggs to market in Chicago were heading out of Dubuque on westbound trains. Then, too, a carload or two of sugar came in to be unloaded. Something new, perhaps? Sugared eggs?

On Sunday night, June 23, 1929, the two intrepid agents along with Chicago-based agent, Clarence Gelhausen and Fort Dodge, Iowa agent Frank Wilson, climbed on to the roof of a two-story section of the packing company buildings. After stealthily searching for a couple of hours, they found a third story window that, unlike the other doors and windows, wasn't barred. They entered after quietly braking a pane of glass.

Making their way through the stygian blackness and not being able to use any sort of light themselves, the federal agents found a heavily barred door and opened it. Later, after many more barred doors and obstacles, they opened a door and found a shaft of light from overhead. Then the light went out and came on again. The agents tensed and waited to see what was going on. A man's legs suddenly appeared while he climbed a ladder.

Making their way through the stygian blackness and not being able to use any sort of light themselves, the federal agents found a heavily barred door and opened it. Later, after many more barred doors and obstacles, they opened a door and found a shaft

The agents took into custody and arrested Al Kramer, 40, who gave his place of residence as Duluth, Minnesota. Using his exit hole as an entrance, they climbed up and into a room and found the still they knew had to be there. In that room they found 1,000 gallons of 188 proof alcohol, 40,000 gallons of mash in seven giant vats, 225 pounds of Fleischman yeast, 5,000 empty gallon cans, electrical ventilator equipment, electric compression pumps, a 3,000 gallon cooker and its attendant coils and distilling equipment, a modern steam boiler that was hooked up to Key City Gas Company lines by means of a five inch main, and a huge quantity of empty egg crates that were used for shipping out the finished product. In a storeroom adjacent to the still room, the agents found 80,000 pounds of sugar.

The egg crates were used to ship the full gallon cans out of Dubuque and to the thirsty public. It didn't take long for the agents to determine that this was no ordinary still. A sophisticated vacuum system allowed the coils to carry the liquid corn through the system much more rapidly--producing between 1,000 and 2,500 gallons of liquor per day. Agents valued the equipment at over $50,000.

Had Kramer gotten away undetected, the still in all likelihood would have gone undetected. Had they known, all the agents would have to have done was pick up a wooden match stick near the elevator door, stick it into a certain small hole near the elevator and push. A bell would have sounded upstairs and with the correct code, the way would have been paved for the Feds. But they didn't know about the match stick or the codes.

Then Kramer heard a funny noise, he elected to take one of the many escapes from the building, and was tackled by the agents in a coincidental meeting.

During their investigation, the agents discovered how the still could operate around the clock and not be seen by neighbors. The only rooms used by the bootleggers were rooms that had no windows. From the condition of the rooms, the still had not been in operation for much more than 15 days, according to Burris, who led the raid.

There were means of escape from the still, other than the one used by Kramer that Sunday night. Several chutes made for quick escapes to the ground level. Unfortunately for Kramer, he used the ladder that night instead.

Several weeks earlier, a privately-owned Ford Tri-Motor plane had landed at the Dubuque Air Port on City Island carrying some suspicious looking men.

It was said by Burris's daughter, Mary Burris Post, that her father believed the still was part of Al Capone's operation, but he was never able to prove it. Nine years old at the time of the raid, Mary Post recently said her father and the other agents involved in the raid had to stand guard on the premises of the still around the clock. The head honchos, or "big shots" as Post referred to the ranking officials in the alcohol and tobacco departments of the government, weren't able to come to Dubuque until sometime after the Fourth of July. She fondly recalled "eating potato salad at a picnic on the roof of the building on the Fourth of July, 1929, and...shooting our fireworks up there because dad couldn't leave his post."

Post also related how the gas meter had been read every day by someone from the Key City Gas Company, making it probable that "someone at the gas company had to know" what was going on in the building.

MARCH

Remember when Crystal Lake Cave was about the only tourist attraction around, outside of Eagle Point Park once it was completed in the 1930s?

This cave, one of Mom Nature's more beautiful pieces of work, was discovered in 1868 on farmland south of Dubuque, along what is today U.S. 52. It was opened in an official way in 1880, but didn't become a genuine tourist attraction until 1932, when signs went up along highways and byways, and electric lights were installed. With the steady, even glow of incandescent lights, the true beauty of the cave became evident. On a trip to the Black Hills with my parents and sister back in the early '50s, I can recall going through a cave that was bland by comparison.

I can remember sitting in front of a bandstand down at Crystal Lake Cave, one day back in the late '30s or early '40s, listening to Sheriff Tom Owens and His Cowboys, whooping it up with their

Western music. That far back it wasn't yet referred to as Country 'n' Western. I do remember hearing for the first time "The Beer Barrel Polka" at one of those "cave shindigs." Nice memories.

Remember when Sanitary Dairy still used horse-drawn wagons to deliver milk, chocolate milk, their yummy orange drink and other dairy products? My great uncle, John "Buddy" Butlett, drove for that dairy. Back then, my uncle and a lot of other milkmen delivered milk in glass bottles, with three or four inches of cream on top of the milk. Before use, the bottle was either shaken to mix the cream and milk or the cream was carefully poured off for baking or for coffee.

My uncle would fill up his wire basket with milk bottles and other dairy items for delivery and leave the horse and wagon at one end of the block. He'd walk and deliver the milk, picking up empty bottles set out the night before on the back step or whatever. When his supply of products was gone and his basket full of empties, he simply walked back to the street and whistled. Instead of my uncle walking to the horse and wagon, the horse and wagon came to him.

Once Sanitary Dairy became fully de-horsed or mechanized, whichever you prefer, he mentioned to my dad once that no matter how much he whistled "that damned truck" would not come to him.

Remember when the song, "Milkman, Keep Those Bottles Quiet" hit the charts across the country ? I don't recall the words right off but the song told the story of some "night owl" who just got to bed when the milkman showed up and rattled a few bottles.

Remember when Aunt Het graced the front page of the *Telegraph Herald*? "Aunt Het" was a one-panel cartoon written and drawn by Robert Quillen. Publisher's Syndicate supplied it to the *TH*, and virtually every day the old woman, Aunt Het, would offer some sage advice or bit of philosophy. An example: "I knew it wouldn't last. These wild women always fall in love with the easy-going kind they can't have a good time with."

Remember when Officer James "Gentleman Jim" Corbett was the presiding "mayor of Main Street" while he walked his beat at Main and Eighth? Jim was a nice guy who had the time of day for just about everybody from toddler to tippler, although the last one received a little different type of attention. Remember the police officer who preceded him on that beat? He was a pretty large man.

Here's one for the road: His face was loved/ By just his mother/ He Burma-Shaved and now--/ Oh, Brother!

'Tis the month of Saint Patrick and His Day. Aye and that's the day that all men and women are of the *auld sod,* or wish they were. All of the old traditional songs are sung and so are the newer ones such as "McNamara's Band," wherein Clancy lowered his boom. Sure and it's enough to make one wonder if perhaps the renowned Mr. Clancy might not have been patterned after Dubuque's own Rocky Ryan. Let's investigate, shall we?

Rocky Ryan had a reputation as a fighter, a sometime thug if the case demanded, a love for the sauce of St. Patrick's Day and available to anyone who wanted to hire a pair of fists. Now, I could go on and on about Rocky but I'll simply give you a news story word for word that appeared in the *Dubuque Daily Times,* April 6, 1858.

"Yesterday the notorious bully and desperado known as 'Rocky Ryan,' was conspicuous at several of the voting places, employed in his usual demonstrations of ruffianism. He endeavored to vote at the Second Ward polls, but was repulsed by the intrepid challengers. He then visited the First Ward and for some time abused, used and blackguarded the citizens there. As he has for a long time set our police at defiance he was allowed to go away unmolested, and soon after got into a row with Constable Nagle, whom he beat and mangled in a shocking and perhaps fatal manner. Officers Carpenter and Swivel soon after arrived at the spot and attempted to arrest Ryan when a confederate of the latter named Borlan, drew a six-shooter on them. Ryan picked up two rocks, and bid them (the officers) defiance. Detective Carpenter drew his pistol and would have shot him had not a citizen interfered. Ryan and his confederate started for the levee, with the police on his trail.   Sheriff Hayden started down Main Street to head them off. As he reached Second Street he met them, and on attempting to arrest Ryan, Borlan placed his pistol at the sheriff's head and swore by his Maker if he (the sheriff) advanced a step he (Borlan) would blow his (the sheriff's) brains out. The Sheriff being unarmed, was obliged to desist for the time; he however followed them into Dublin, where other confederates assisted in putting the law in defiance. Meantime, one or two of the police came up, and the sheriff stationed them to prevent his (Rocky's) escape while he (the sheriff) went off for a posse, but Ryan fled with Borlan in the direction of the furnace."

Rocky Ryan and Borlan were both arrested and sentenced to six months in the county jail but the arrest must have been something. It took six to seven officers and sheriff's deputies to   subdue the high-spirited lad. Victor McLaughlin, the actor, would have been great in the role of a movie *Rocky Ryan*.

Enough of Rocky and his exploits. Remember when there were chewing gums such as Clove, Black Jack and Beeman's California Fruit Chewing Gum on the market?

Remember when a popular "bulk" candy was orange slices? And how about circus peanuts that were as big as a six-year-old's fist and tasted like bananas with the consistency of stale marshmallows? And taffy apples from any number of confectioners in Dubuque? And who made the absolute best--the VERY best popcorn in town--BAR NONE? Why, Browne's, of course. Yeah. Yumm!

Remember when, usually early in March, the snow along the street gutters would turn to ice, and water, thawing going on all over the place, flowed to the nearest sewer opening. Remember dropping a piece of paper, or a match stick into that "raging torrent" and then following it to the sewer grate? What adventures raced through our minds while we "manned" that "boat" or "raft"?

Remember when the snow was just about gone and a simple stick would be used to draw a circle in the damp earth? The show down! That's what it was! Yeah! And for "keeps," too. Yeah! Marbles! No funchin'! Lose your turn if you do. Do you remember your favorite shooter? I had a yellow one that looked for all the world just like a hard-boiled egg yoke. A little smaller but the right color. On occasion I would make it "stick" and get another shot. Marbles owned by a young"sharpshooter," were the measure of a kid's wealth back then. Hell! Who had money? But marbles??? Ah, an entirely different concept.

Remember when girls would be jumping rope? And kids of all sizes and ages would go roller skating? And they didn't go to some fancy indoor rink, although they were around. No sir. The sidewalks were used and while smooth floors in an indoor rink could give you a burn if you fell, the sidewalks were absolutely unforgiving. Take a fall? Bleed! Steel wheels on concrete were the surest sound to tell everyone that spring was just around the corner if not already arrived.

Remember when there were such things as milk routes in town? We had quite a few dairies at one time. Oakland, Sanitary, Iowa Dairies, Armour Creameries (although I think that they only bought milk and shipped it out of town), Dubuque Co-op Dairy Marketing Association, Treanor's Dairy Products, Brookside and later on Meadow Gold and Hilldale Dairy. Today, we have one. But we're recalling the days when there were many and quite a few of those had horsedrawn milk wagons.

I was visiting with Cy Behr on the phone and we reminisced some about those days. Horses were pretty darn smart and got to know the routes almost as well as the milkmen themselves.

Cy reminded me that after World War II started and gas was rationed, the dairies abandoned their gas-powered dairy trucks for the old reliable horsedrawn milk wagons. In fact, I remember my great uncle John "Buddy" Butlett and how happy he was when the horses came back for service during the war.

Today, with all the dairies just a memory for those who remember them, it's good to know there are a few of the old-timers still left. Cy Behr, was 91 years old this month and is one of the two original horse-drawn milk wagon drivers still with us. The other is Clem Welch, who was 91 this fall. Cy started for Iowa Dairies in 1926, and Clem started driving and delivering milk in 1928. Clem and Cy meet with four other milkmen who drove teams during World War II once a month for breakfast. It must have been nice to take eight quarts of milk in round glass bottles, and a tray with butter, cottage cheese and other dairy products and start delivering. A milkman could go to three, four or even five or six houses with that much milk and stuff. Now, if the milkman was driving a truck, he'd have to walk back to the vehicle, drive a short distance and repeat the whole process. Not with a good team of horses. When he finished delivering at the fifth or sixth house, he'd walk out to the curb and lo and behold, there was his team and wagon, waiting for him. If the team wasn't that well-trained, then a simple whistle would bring them to the waiting milkman. Nice, huh?

Remember the Spring and Fall job of rolling up the rugs and taking them outside to hang on the line? Then, they were beaten with a wire rug beater or maybe the kitchen broom. That was one job, usually assigned to the kids in the family, and it was absolutely no fun, until you started beating the tar out of your worst enemy (if you had one) or your least favorite teacher or maybe even Adolf Hitler or Il Duce or Hirohito when World War II was raging. It never ceased to amaze me how the clouds of dust would billow out, and I always thought we were a relatively clean family. My mother vacuumed the rugs on a regular basis, so it must have been the coal furnace. But the rugs and carpets were beaten until there wasn't a puff of dirt left in them. Then, it was back inside and they were put in place until the next go-round. Thank heavens for wall-to-wall carpeting, right?

Remember when (I think I might be in trouble with the spelling of the next word) *sheenies* came around every so often? For those of you too young to remember them, they were rag men, or junk men or tin-can men, who bought such things from housewives for a few cents. They usually had a produce wagon and a horse that pulled them around to the different neighborhoods. Normally older men who either needed a shave or wore a beard to avoid that routine of shaving, they wore old, dirty clothing since they never knew what they might encounter as purchases during the course of a day. I'll say this much. When a kid misbehaved and his mother said, "You'd better be good or the sheeny will get you," the kid shaped up right now.

Remember when you were a kid and caught a "bad chest" cold? Some of the home remedies used were enough to make a person a "Social J. Outcast" with anyone who came close to the sick bed. Remember mustard plasters? They seemed to burn like crazy and when it was time to take the plaster off, most of the chest skin came right along with it. How about having goose grease rubbed in after that? The smell was bad enough but when it came time to clean it off, alcohol was used and seemed to chill the sick one right to the backbone. And if those weren't bad enough, how about getting steamed? I don't mean angry. I mean having a temporary tent rigged over the sick bed and having some medication added to the water. It was heated on a hot plate until it cooked enough to make steam. At least the smell wasn't that bad, but it is a wonder a kid with a cold survived the treatment.

Remember when there were "gangs" in almost every part of Dubuque? The "northend" had several. The "point" area had theirs. There were gangs of kids in the south end of Dubuque. There were gangs in the "flats" and gangs on Loras Boulevard and any neighborhood a person could mention. And those were good "gangs" that roamed around. They did nothing destructive and usually played softball in the summertime or built cars out of orange crates and had races if there was a steep enough hill around. Of course there wasn't that much automobile traffic in the '20s, '30s and '40s.

Take for example a couple of the "gangs" in the northend. The one pictured, shows eight boys showing off their home-made car complete with enclosed cab. The picture was taken around 1937. Times were still tough but by using their imagination and ingenuity, they came up with an above average toy. The picture was taken behind Larry Wilgenbusch's barber shop in the 2900 block of White Street. A few doors away from Larry's Barber Shop, Hans Zurcher operated his butcher shop. Note the sign on the side of the car: Buy your meats at Zurcher's Meat Market, 2920 Central Avenue. Some time after the picture was taken, Earl "Mac" McDonald bought Zurcher's business and opened a confectionery shop complete with lattice work and wire ice cream parlor chairs and tables, on the south half of the building and a butcher shop/grocery store on the north half. The building still stands today and is right across from Holy Ghost Church.

Back to that picture. I knew almost all of those "gang members," including Roger Broessel who provided the photograph. The littlest guy in the photo is Milt Weiser who, with his twin brother, Melvin, was in my First Communion class. We received the sacrament on their birthday--May 28, 1939. We got Monday off and I recall that our two car garage was in the process of being built. It cost my dad $300 for a 20' by 20' building. Now there was a deal.

But the kids hung out together and played ball and created their own toys and didn't get in trouble and wouldn't it be nice if the same thing could be said about gangs today?

Remember when housewives wore aprons? Half ones that covered the front from the waist down and tied in the back. Others had broad shoulder straps and covered the entire front with a tie in the back. Some simply slipped over the head and could be frilly with fancy piping along the edges. The last ones tied in back as well. I can't recall the last time I saw an apron on anyone other than in a tool shop or on TV with "Blondie" or "Leave It to Beaver."

Remember going to Humke's Bakery or to Sutter's or to any of the others in Dubuque to buy the weekly supply of baked goods? The products were wrapped in white paper and tied with a string. Today, everything has to be sealed against this, that and the other thing to "protect" the public. Somehow, people from those times managed to survive without all that "protection."

Here's a couple of Burma Shave rhymes to stir your memory. Hardly a driver/ Is now alive/ Who passed on hills/ at 75/ Burma Shave. And then: Don't stick your/ Elbow out so far/ It might go home/ In another car/ Burma Shave.

Remember when I mentioned that Joe "Kayo" Wareham and I reminisced a bit on the telephone and he told about his group singing coast to coast on the radio? (January) I heard from one of the other singers--Bob Gribben. Bob is currently living in Orlando, Florida. He hasn't seen Kayo in ages, to quote Bob. He said in his letter there were originally six half-pints-of-melody, and that Joe was the first to audition. In time Arnie Stierman found six more and brought the group to 12 members. Bob still has newspaper clippings of what was then a big event. They were paid in chocolate malts and vanilla wafers.

And there are coincidences every day. For example: Bob thought I should mention the Elks Building that once stood on the northwest corner of Seventh and Locust. Wouldn't you know it? Judy Reilly and I had been talking and she promised to send me the latest copy of *The Little Dublin News*, that included a picture of that same building, which was a gorgeous piece of architecture. Bob also recalled the time the Iowa officers raided the Elk's state convention and confiscated all the booze, upsetting the meeting in a BIG way. Of course that was when Dubuque was supposed to be dry like the rest of the state.

Bob also said to say "hello" to Phyllis for him. So, "Hello, Phyllis."

I also received a letter from an 84 year-old youngster, Don Ahrendt, who likes to draw, using the characters in J.R. Williams' comic panel "Bull of the Woods," for models. Now that's one way to stay young.

I was surprised to hear from an old friend I used to date in high school, Damaris Brauer Eichman. She sent me a paper her older sister had written while attending the University of Dubuque on which she received an A+. Her English professor, who was a (pay attention Gifford) HARVARD man as her sister said, wrote that it was one of her best pieces up to that time. The essay concerned the bells and whistles of Dubuque.

I received a letter from Darlene Zahina Manders, whose father was Clarence Zahina. Clarence was a mainstay on the band circuit for many years and he, his accordion and orchestra wowed many a dance floor full of people.

And although Bob Gribben is one of my most far-flung readers, Mary Keas of Alexandria, Virginia dropped me a line again, wanting to know if I had ever written about Genz's Store, Joe Baule's Store, Strayers, Stampfer's and Roshek's Department Stores and Levi's?

Elmer Schwers of 640 Fremont Avenue, practically a neighbor of mine, sent in the following Burma Shave rhyme: Cattle crossing/ Means go slow/ That old bull/ is some cow's beau/ Burma Shave. Yeah. I love it, Elmer.

And Art Rooney dropped me a card, "...just to set the record straight." Art worked full time at Fuhrman Tiller from 1933 to 1943. Then he worked on the Milwaukee Road from 1943 until 1975. His dad also worked for the Milwaukee. I don't think I did that bad considering I was pulling his work history out of my childhood memory of him.

Remember when I mentioned coincidences earlier? I received a note from Al Birch out on Mud Lake. He ran across a couple of my dad's campaigning cards from the 1954 election for County Supervisor 1955 term. Remember Mary Keas's question about some of the stores that once existed in Dubuque including Joe Baule's Variety Store? Well, guess who my dad's opponent was in the race for the supervisor's seat? Right. Joe Baule.

STARS OF DUBUQUE

How many movie/television actors and actresses can you name,
who at one time in their lives had a tie to Dubuque in some way?
One? Margaret Lindsay? Sure she was born and raised right here in
the Key City. Two? Don Ameche? Don Ameche attended Columbia
Academy (later Loras College). Three? If you can add Kate Mulgrew
to your list, you're doing well. This native Dubuquer has had her
own TV series, starred on the big screen and almost nailed Sam
Malone on TV's "Cheers," with a marriage contract.

Are there more? You bet! A fourth name for your list is Joe Frisco,
who started his marvelous career in Dubuque, dancing and singing
in front of theaters, shortly before the turn of the century. More? Of
course. How about Tony Danza of television fame? He attended
one year at the University of Dubuque and not much else is known
of his brief tenure here. Ben Murphy, who gained his initial fame on
TV's "Alias Smith and Jones," attended Loras College for one year.
One more for the road, so to speak. Tom Cunliffe, a character actor,
was just beginning to make some inroads into the tough business of
movies and television when he passed away.

There's more and we'll mention them in passing but let's take a
closer look at some of these thespians of the silver screen.

Margaret Kies left Dubuque and her home on Melrose Terrace in
1930, and after a one year stay at the Academy of Dramatic Arts in

New York City, was dismayed to learn that Hollywood was primarily interested in foreign actors and actresses. Along with several friends, including a Charles Summings, Margaret went to England to become "British." During their six month stay, they learned British history, landmarks, customs and acquired a very definite English-speaking accent. Confident they could pass as English men and women, they returned to the U.S. not as Margaret Kies and Charles Summings but as Margaret Conway and Blade Stanhope. Shortly after they arrived in New York, they changed their names once more. Blade Stanhope became Robert Cummings and Margaret chose the first name she found on a list furnished by her manager--Lindsay.

Margaret "clicked" in Hollywood and soon found herself working with George Arliss on *Voltaire*. While working on *Paddy, The Next Best Thing*, she and Janet Gaynor became fast and inseparable friends. She appeared with Leslie Howard and Doug Fairbanks Jr. in *Captured* and Paul Muni and Bette Davis in *Bordertown*.

Linked romantically with William Powell in the early '30s, Margaret was systematically paired by the press with many other famous leading men during her career. She never married. A shame! Other films in which she played the romantic or female lead, were *G-Men* with James Cagney, *Green Light* with Errol Flynn, and *Hell's Kitchen* starring Ronald Reagan. In the movie *Jezebel,* she played a secondary role to Bette Davis and Henry Fonda, and was magnificent as Hepzibah Pyncheon in *The House of Seven Gables* opposite Vincent Price and George Sanders.

She went back to New York and Broadway in the mid '40s, knowing her career as a romantic lead was over and following several successful plays, moved to TV where she appeared on several different dramatic showcases.

Tammy and the Doctor was her last film in 1964, and Margaret passed away at the age of 70.

The late Don Ameche remained handsome and suave whenever he appeared in movies until the day he died. Listing *Cocoon* and *Trading Places* as two recent works, this man who played Alexander Graham Bell began his acting career in Dubuque, Iowa at Columbia Academy and College. Bypassing an almost-desired career as an attorney, Ameche eventually wound up in radio, which he says was responsible for making him a star. He appeared with Edgar Bergan and Charley McCarthy on the original "Chase and Sanborn Hour." "First Nighter," "Don Ameche's Real Life Stories" and the role as the henpecked husband in the still popular comedy skit, "The Bickersons."

Some movies starring Don Ameche are: *Ramona, In Old Chicago, Alexander's Ragtime Band, Swanee River, The Story Of Alexander Graham Bell, Moon Over Miami, Heaven Can Wait, So Goes My Love* and the list goes on and on.

Married to a Dubuque girl, Honore Prendergast, the Ameches raised four sons and adopted twin daughters.

Kate Mulgrew used to wow local audiences when she appeared on stage in Wahlert High School plays and musicals. While working part time at WDBQ, she was asked to join the cast of several radio dramas produced by the staff of that radio station. She attended one year at Clarke College and one year at New York University, taking up acting as her profession at that time. She gained attention with her role in the soap opera, "Ryan's Hope," played the title role on television's "Mrs. Columbia," portrayed the title role in "Mother Seton," and had the leading role in "The Manions of America."

Shortly after her role of Rachel Manion, Kate signed to star in Mary Higgins Clark's *A Stranger Is Watching*, which featured Rip Torn and Barbara Baxley. Following that effort, Kate appeared in *Tristram and Isolt* that starred the late Richard Burton andGeraldine Fitzgerald. Kate played the role of Isolt, the Irish princess whose father married her to King Mark, the role played by Richard Burton.

During the 1981-82 season, she played Regina Hubbard in *Another Part of the Forest*, during which time she met Robert Egan, of the Seattle Repertory Theater, whom she married July 31, 1982 at Resurrection Church in Asbury. Kate is still very active in theater and acting, and stars in *Star Trek: Voyager.*

A comedian's comedian is probably the best way to describe Joe Frisco. Born Louis Joseph on a farm near Rock Island, Illinois in 1890, Joe moved with his family to Dubuque some eight or nine years later. His formal education stopped when he hit the Key City, finding work as a bellhop at the Old Bijou Annex, later called the Belmont Hotel, where vaudeville performers stayed while in

Dubuque. Hoping to break into show business, Joe would perform a tap dance routine in front of the Grand Theater or the Bijou. Wouldn't you know it? Jake Rosenthal, the Bijou manager caught his act and signed him to a contract.

Pairing up with another hoofer, Andrew Coffee, they created their act, "Coffee and Doughnuts." Anything but successful, the duo made just enough to starve. During the time he was hoofing for next to nothing, Joe spotted the logo for the Frisco Railroad and decided it had a nice ring to it. Loretta McDermott, a shimmy dancer, was Joe's second partner in show business. Sophie Tucker introduced the pair to New York at Resinweber's Cabarets. They were booked over the Keith theater circuit following that smashing debut.

His Frisco Schuffle, a wild and crazy dance routine, allowed him to survive once vaudeville faded and died. He played supper clubs on both coasts and ultimately made his way to Hollywood. Once he made it in the big time, he refused to work for less than $1,500 per week. His inability to handle money was a source of unending jokes that he used in his routine and most of them wound up in the trade newspapers.

His stuttering delivery seemed to make any joke he told that much more funny, even at the I.R.S. office. A friend of his bemoaned the fact that he was behind on his tax payments. Joe stood and walked over to the manager of the office. "D-d-don't bo-bo-bo-ther him, si-si-sir." The manager knew Frisco and that he himself was far behind in payments. "What about his payments, Joe?" he asked. "Ju-ju-just put them on my ta-ta-tab." In 1932, Joe starred in *The Gorilla* and his last movie was *The Sweet Smell of Success*, which starred Burt Lancaster and Tony Curtis. There were many in between. Frisco died of cancer February 17, 1958 in Hollywood.

Bob Kaliban spent a lot of time in American living rooms, exploiting his acting ability on such shows as "Car 54, Where Are You?," "The Doctors," "The Patty Duke Show," plus others. He has done "voice overs" on TV commercials and appeared as the little old toymaker who hustled Remco Toys. Who played the first Ronald McDonald on TV? Bob Kaliban, that's who.

Bob attended Loras College, graduating in 1955. During his tenure there, he appeared in *Finian's Rainbow, Brigadoon* and other

Bob attended Loras College, graduating in 1955. During his tenure there, he appeared in *Finian's Rainbow, Brigadoon* and other productions, directed by Father Karl Schroeder. He married Patricia Spaight, a Clarke College graduate.

And Kaliban had a way of turning up in the most unlikely places. For several seasons, he played the role of Cookie Man in the ads on TV and captained the row boat that showed up at one time or another in nearly everyone's toilet tank, as the "Ty-D-Bol Man."

During the time that CBS produced "Radio Mystery Theater," in the 1970s, Bob had the occasion to be heard in more than one role on that program.

Karen Morrow, a 1958 graduate of Clarke College, was born in Chicago and raised in Des Moines. She came to Dubuque to attend Clarke College and was involved in Loras productions as well as those at her own college. While performing in the musicals at Loras, she met and worked with Eugene Loring of Hollywood. He believed she had "something" going for her. After she graduated, she went to Tinsel Town and worked further with Loring until her money ran out. She tried teaching, for which she had been trained, but found it not to her liking. After making the "big" decision, she had the lucky break to be the only resident performer in a big professional open-air production of *South Pacific*. To make matters even better, she had the lead role.

From Milwaukee and *South Pacific* she made her way to New York and had such good auditions she knew she would make it. Role after role in stage productions came her way and she found herself moving toward TV, as well. She appeared with Sid Caesar, Jim Nabors, Red Skelton, Dinah Shore, Merv Griffin, Mike Douglas, Johnny Carson and the list goes on and on. Her first professional appearance in Des Moines came in 1966 when she starred in *How to Succeed in Business Without Really Trying*. Don Ameche was also in the cast.

Tom Cunliffe's career began in Iowa and he settled in Dubuque for several years after a successful tour of duty with the Old Creamery Theater group. He was heard on several WDBQ productions of horror and whimsy, his distinct, gravelly voice standing out from the others. When the movie *On The Right Track* was filmed in Chicago, Tom landed the role of good guy/heavy who chased Gary Coleman all over Union Station. A lead-in role on "Hill Street Blues," brought him even wider attention. Then, just when his star was seemingly zooming to its zenith, Tom Cunliffe died.

Tony Danza, spent a short tenure at the University of Dubuque and left, virtually unnoticed as far as any acting ability was concerned. A former pugilist in real life, he fit the role of a TV pugilist in "Taxi." Since then he has starred in "Who's the Boss," and is doing some producing on television as well.

Ben Murphy, who attended Loras College in 1960-61, rose to fame on the TV series, "Alias Smith and Jones," in the early '70s. In 1983, he was one of the featured actors in the mini-series, "The Winds of War." Murphy was born in Illinois and after his short stay at Loras, transferred to Loyola of New Orleans.

And finally, Vern Stierman, who along with Arnie Stierman, was an announcer on Dubuque's KDTH. While there, both he and Arnie played in radio dramas produced by the station. But it was Vern's golden voice that brought him to the job of narrator for the movie *The Legend of Boggy Creek*.

Well, there you have it. Dubuque's contributions to the world of acting and make believe. Who knows who the next one will be?

APRIL

Remember when during World War II, about 1943 or '44, a B-24 Liberator bomber was forced to land at the airport on City Island? How the pilot landed that plane, (actually a bigger wingspan than the B-17, Flying Fortress) is still a legend among those who remember. The plane was disassembled and shipped out of town on the Milwaukee Railroad.

Remember when a boy could go to Armstrong's Bowling Alley, or to Dr. Pepper Bowling Alleys or Sacred Heart's Bowling Alleys among others and set pins for a little extra spending money? If the bowler or bowlers had a good night and were a little flush with extra money, a couple of quarters or fifty cent pieces were slid down the alley.

Remember when ladies had sewing circles? It was a great way to socialize and remain "proper" in those days. World War II pretty much knocked such circles askew and they never did come back. Another thing that the ladies did was hold a quilting "bee." I can remember the framework set up in our living room more than once and half a dozen of my mother's friends coming in and putting together a quilt. Nice, warm and fuzzy memories.

Remember when Collier Magazine was delivered door to door as well as being available at the newsstand? I had such a route and the incentive the "boss" used to get me to take on the route was a small first aid kit, which I still have. Isn't it strange what will motivate people? The magazine sold for 10¢ and, if I remember correctly, every fourth sale was mine. I built a pretty good route and had almost 75 or 80 customers. That gave me in the neighborhood of $2.00 a week. Not bad for a nine year old kid in 1941.

Remember when companies that sold such commodities as soft drinks or cigarettes, hired sky-writing pilots to fill the blue skies with such messages as: Drink Pepsi Cola or Drink Cola Cola or Smoke Lucky Strike Cigarettes? A person could get a real crook in his or her neck, gawking at the plane which was nothing more than a dark pin point at the end of a smoking pen. It would take most of an hour or so to write the message in the sky.

Remember when there might be as many as two, three or four parties on one telephone line? It was frustrating if a person had to make a call that was sort of important, and one of your "parties" was on the line. On the other hand, a person could stay abreast of everything that was going on in the lives of those other subscribers. Of course, the receiver had to be lifted very carefully or the talking parties would hear the click. In rural areas, there was a device known as a rubber neck, that allowed the receiver to be lifted, but not far enough to have the mouthpiece activated, and there was no click. As a result, the one doing the extracurricular listening in, could not be heard and the news was received with open ears.

Ah, Spring! My very "favoritest" time of the year. Everything is awakening and being born again. The flowers bloom anew. The grass turns green. The leaves sprout on trees. The birds return, singing their territorial while mating and building nests. It's the rebirth of nature and the most glorious time of the year, and I love it.

Keeping all those idyllic thoughts in mind let's do some remembering.

Remember when Easter Sunday was the "rebirth" of people? I'm not referring to the religious aspect, although that certainly played an important role in Christianity. I'm recalling the way people used to deck themselves out for services on Easter Sunday. Women usually wore a new dress or suit if Easter happened to be earlier than usual. New shoes. New gloves. A new hat or Easter bonnet if you want to call it that.

Remember when every department store had a millinery department? Remember when there were millinery stores that specialized in hats? All gone now but surely something that would be more than welcome back. While the meaning of words and such were not the usual bailiwick of "Remember When...?", but of " What's The Difference?" a word column written by yours truly for the *Telegraph Herald*, I want to point out the meaning of milliner. I think it's interesting. The word milliner comes from the Italian word *Milaner*, an inhabitant of Milan, Italy and in time referred to one who imported silks and ribbons from Milan. The first definition of milliner is a person who designs, makes, trims or sells women's hats, headdresses and so on. As a kid, when I got stuck going shopping with my mother and she wanted to try on a few hats, I was bored out of my gourd.

But the word milliner held a fascination for me. Why was a milliner one who sold hats? Why not a hatter? Or a hat fitter? Or something like that? Well, now we know, don't we.

Remember the 1934 Chrysler Airflow? Now there was a car that set my heart racing. It's a shame it wasn't better received but I guess in a way, it was the Edsel of the '30s. Or would it be more proper to say that the Edsel was the Airflow of the '50s?

Remember when one of the surest signs of Spring was your father bringing out his "sailor" straw hat for examination? Would it be fit to wear one more season? Or was a new one called for? I remember my dad going through this Spring ritual. I also remember the softer straw hat, which he purchased one Spring, that reminded one more of a Panama hat than a straw one. Today? Who wears a hat?

Remember when the surest sign of Spring-time for a kid was getting rid of his or her long underwear? And the attendant long brown or black stockings that went with that torturous piece of clothing? To this day I hate any reference to a trap door--from a trap-door spider to a mystery wherein a trap door plays a vital part. Try to recall the glorious feeling of freedom you enjoyed when your bare legs could feel air flowing around them once more. Long underwear and the winter willies were gone.

Remember when girls and boys had their own style bicycle? I mean, a girl wasn't supposed to ride a boy's bike because it wouldn't be proper. A boy, in the same way, wouldn't be caught dead on a girl's bike for fear of being seen and razzed by his friends. Having had only a sister and no brother, I inherited few if any toys from my big sister. The only thing I can recall is the wagon and sled I used as a boy. Thank god, those things were generic. We couldn't afford a new wagon so my dad painted the old one gray with red trim. He even put my initials on both sides--J.T.T. Wow! Customized wheels at the age of seven. As far as the sleds were concerned, I believe there were two. A neighbor man had built a bob sled, miniature size of course, for his daughter or granddaughter and while constructing it, made a second one for my sister. Darn thing fell apart in the garage during the summer months. It was neat to look at but not to use. Besides, who was going to pull it? The other sled was more to my liking and, while it was short, about three feet long, it carried me down many hills in Dubuque, giving me just the right amount of thrills and chills and spills.

Remember when every neighborhood had a corner grocery store? Well, all right, sometimes it wasn't on the corner but in the middle of the block. In those days, not everyone had an automobile or, dare I go back that far (?), a horse and buggy, to go to the stores down town . Today, it's nothing to jump into your car and tool out to Eagles or Econofoods or Hy-Vee or Aldi and get whatever you need. Of course there are quite a few convenience stores peppered around town, too. But there was something special about those old grocery stores. They had their own smell--one made up of just about every food product in the store and when combined, they were readily recognizable by nose, even by a person who was blindfolded. Usually the neighborhood grocery store was run by the owner and his wife. On occasion a third person would be employed to help operate the business.

Remember when drug stores had an ice cream fountain? That meant there was a soda jerk behind the counter and he (sometimes she) could make the most delicious concoctions on the face of the earth. The smell of ice cream and syrups, intermingling with the bouquet of cosmetics and odors of drugs, gave the neighborhood drug store, a smell all its own , just like the grocery store had its own . If you want to smell an old time drug store, there are one or two around with the ice cream fountain and all. I believe there's one in Strawberry Point, Iowa and one in Bellevue, Iowa. Go inhale and be transported back in time, for one breath's worth of memories that are virtually extinct today.

Remember when there were grocery stores on Main Street here in Dubuque? By chance do you recall how many there were, say, during the early '40s? Were there three? Seven? Eight? Eleven? I'll give the answer later along with the names of each.

Remember when there were *four* bridges spanning the Mississippi River, linking Dubuque with Wisconsin and Illinois? In fact there were two times when this was true. Just recently, when the four lane bridge opened and before the Wisconsin High Bridge was torn down. Then, going back in time, in 1943, when the Julien Dubuque Bridge opened and before the Wagon Bridge was torn down, we had four. The High Bridge and Illinois Central Railroad Bridge, along with the two just mentioned, made four.

Remember when there was a ballroom in Center Grove? How about the one in Lower Balltown? And don't forget Moonlight Gardens. We'll talk more about Centergrove later on in the book.

Remember when, 'long about this time of year thoughts of baseball season would rise to the surface of your mind? Remember sitting at the Dubuque Athletic Field before it was called Petrakis Park, watching the local team play? I could have said teams and included those of the high schools and colleges because every once in a while, they had a night game there, too. Remember the Illinois Central "Land of Corn" coming through behind center and left fields about 8:30 in the evening? Remember troop trains going through during World War II?

Remember when I gave you a test earlier? Well, the answer is seven actual grocery stores plus one meat market and one fruit store. In order, from the south end of Main: Beck's Food Market, 351 Main; Main Street Fruit Store, 552 Main; Jack Solomon's Grocery (later Jack's Super Market), 555 Main; Wertz Grocery

Store, 770 Main; National Tea Company, 898 Main; Brothers
Meat Market, 920 Main; Schweitering Grocery Store, 1005 Main;
The Orange Store, 1079 Main; and Pusateri's Grocery Store, 1098
Main. In some respects, LoBianco's Main Street Fruit Store was
just as much if not moreso a grocery store, but you can call them
whatever you want. Those were the stores on Main Street. Any idea
how many taverns there were? We'll do a bar count later on. You
might be amazed.

Here's a bunch of recollections that I hope will evoke some fond
memories. Remember when a person could travel from Dubuque to
Omaha, Nebraska, via The Milwaukee Road for under $10.00? It
was $9.00. Now that's what I call traveling "right." And one could
do it in around six hours and 45 minutes. That was in 1950. A
person left Dubuque at 2:00 p.m., changed trains at Green Island,
and headed west on the Midwest Hiawatha. The train arrived in
Omaha, Nebraska at 8:45 p.m. The round trip cost a whopping
$16.20. I know you can't travel that way anymore but it was a
thrill, whipping across Iowa on that train.

Remember when (going back to The Milwaukee Road for a quick
recall), the Chicago, Milwaukee & St. Paul Railway operated from
its 45-acre compound of yards and shops and was the biggest
employer in Dubuque for many, many years. Not the river boats or
the boat builders but one railroad. And there were three others
working in the area at the same time. Not as big in Dubuque as
The Milwaukee but railroads nevertheless, and those four were
probably the largest employers for many years to come in a
collective sense.

Remember when (I'm on a railroad kick, it seems) Dubuque had
four beautiful railroad depots? Did you know you can still see
them? Exact scale models of them are on display on the third floor
museum of the Welcome Center at the Ice Harbor. Go down and
take a look at them and see what was destroyed.

Remember when Walnettoes were a big treat? Chocolate-flavored
wax baskets with a few jelly beans and not much else in them went
for a penny. What the heck, you could chew for hours on the basket
if you didn't have any gum. If you didn't have the penny or gum,
you could always chew a hunk of tar, which whitened the teeth like
nothing on the market today. How about wax bottles with half a
swallow of some sort of flavored water inside? Bite off the end,

chug down the juice (?) and chew the bottle. Then there was licorice from the licorice factory formed into all sorts of shapes. A rectangular piece shaped like a plug of tobacco--a stick of bitter licorice shaped somewhat like a cigar--strips with toys imprinted in them so the purchaser could press out a doll, a carriage, a flat iron (you do remember flat irons?), carpenter tools or boys' toys--cars, airplanes, trains, and what have you. Most of each cost one cent. Once the toys were eaten, the remaining strip with all of the weird-shaped openings could be devoured. Nothing went to waste. Eat candy today and it all goes to "waist," if you remember this stuff.

Remember when that beautiful licorice smell mixed in with baking bread from Trausch's Bakery and fresh sawdust from the many wood-working factories.

Remember when, in the spring of the year, hills and vacant lots in Dubuque, were burned off to get rid of the dead grass and weeds, to allow new growth. Today, we can't burn a leaf, much less a hillside. People tended those fires and on rare occasions, if one got out of hand, the fire department was called. But that seldom happened.

Remember when Post's Corn Toasties, then Post's Toasties came in red and yellow/orange boxes? In the '30s, I believe the boxes were waxed and had no inner liner. Mickey Mouse, Pluto, Horace Horsecollar, Clarabelle Cow and other Disney creations roamed the back panel in cartoon stories.

Remember some of the great cars that disappeared during the Great Depression or right before World War II? The Hupmobile? The Marmon? The Graham? Hudson's Terraplane? (Neat car.) The Cord? The Duesenberg? And those came to mind without any research. Of course, once World War II was won by the Allies, every person who had driven through the war years in their pre-war model, wanted a new car--AND RIGHT AWAY! Today, even some of those cars are gone.

Remember when owning a new Nash was an experience? And Nash's Metropolitan, a very small two seater? And the first Ramblers with their roll back canvas roofs and solid sides? If you went to Loras Academy in the very late '40s, you'll recall John O'Connell's 1950 upside-down bathtub, or was that a new Nash?

The Desoto which was in the price range between Chrysler and
Dodge and made by the Chrysler Corporation, is long gone.
Studebaker, that revolutionized the profile of automobiles in 1947
with its new styling, is gone. The class-act car Packard is nothing
more than a memory. (I always wanted one.) The Willys? Or did
those sedans go before WWII? They made Jeeps for a long time.
Then the new cars for the future--the brand new companies that
surfaced after WWII came along. The Kaisers and Frazers, made
by the same firm, that produced Liberty ships practically in hours
during WWII, had startling new innovations and, although they
didn't call their first lift trunk that opened up and down, a
hatchback, they introduced the idea in 1947 or '48. They also
created the "hardtop" as we know it today as well as the fabric
covered roof.

Of course the biggest innovator of all was Preston Tucker and his
1948 Tucker. Although his car didn't get off the parking lot so to
speak, he came up with the idea of the "pop-out" windshield, seat
belts and the concept of a workable rear mounted engine. Waiting
to still be adapted are his Cyclops headlight that turned when the
front wheels turned, quickly-replaced engines (15 minutes, he
claimed) and doors that opened into the roof to make entering a car
not quite such an undignified move. It was a great looking car and
only 51 (49 still exist) were ever made, and those were hand built.
But Detroit and the Federal Government in all their wisdom,
decided Preston was a crook and shut him down. A loss, surely.

While bicycles are pieces of work today and can do wonderful
things, back in the '30s and '40s, the epitome of bicycle ownership
had to be a Schwinn-built bike with streamlined tank,
"knee-action" shock absorbers on the front wheel, built-in horn,
headlight molded into the front fender, white-wall tires and gosh,
they were nice. I had the pleasure and privilege of owning one.
Second hand though it may have been, I loved that bike.
Three-tone beige, smooth riding, and anyone who rode it felt like
for the moment he or she was king of the road. Schwinn built those
bikes in both girls and boys' models. New Departure or Morrow
brakes were available on the rear wheel. One speed only--how ever
much leg power the rider could muster. No fancy gears. No clasp
brakes on the wheels. Just one helluva bike. The style lasted until

the 1950s and has been recently revived. One sold in February of this year for $2,500. That's inflation for you.

If a person was in a hurry or didn't have much wind or leg stamina, but did own a bike, for $99.95 back in the '30s and until late '40s, that proud bike owner could buy a Whizzer. Remember those? The engine fit within the framework and was started by simply pedaling the bike. The ad in most magazines bragged about the fact that the Whizzer would travel some unbelievable distance on one gallon of gas. I suppose it could, considering the size of the bike, the weight including the rider and small tires. For some reason, 100 miles to the gallon sticks in my memory.

Remember when about this time of year, your grade school class would start talking about a picnic? I can remember going on several such jaunts. Sometimes, if the teacher or nun were old, someplace on the playground would have to suffice. If it rained the day of, the picnic was held indoors. It must have been about fifth or sixth grade when such an outing was mentioned and I pictured the perfect spot in my imagination--along Highway 52, beyond the Little Maquoketa bridge at Sageville. There was a spot on the south side of the road that was wide enough to set up "camp," and eat our food and play games. How were we supposed to get there never once entered my mind. Walk? But we did have the picnic nevertheless, settling for a spot up behind Holy Ghost School or Church, since there weren't many homes up there at the time. It seemed like wilderness to us and from that vantage, the class could see clear across Couler Valley, although we didn't know the name of it then, to the hill on the other side.

The opposite hill was where we flew kites in the spring. Great activity, kite flying. Remember when oranges came wrapped in orange, red or some other color tissue? Those made great little devices to send up to the kite by inserting the string through a hole and letting the wind take over. They'd spin and whip in the wind, winding their way to where no man could go--to the kite. One of the more inventive kids made weighted parachutes out of the wrappers and they'd go flying upward along the string, held in place by a small wire hook. When the wind blew just right, the parachute would jump off the string and float back to earth. Flying a kite from the east to the opposite hill across Couler Valley, above

Pinard, Elm, Washington Streets, Jackson Boulevard, White Street and Central Avenue was almost a common thing, if the flyer had enough string.

There were a lot of outdoor activities from April to November. But in the month that began with April Fool's Day, boys and girls roller skated--on the sidewalks. Steel wheels on concrete had its own grating sound. Some families during the '30s and war years of the '40s, were stuck with one pair of skates and more than one kid. The solution was for one child to use one skate and another the other. They'd pump with their unskated foot and rest that pusher on the skated foot and coast, as though riding a scooter. Or one skate taken apart, served as the front and aft wheels for an orange crate scooter. Softball games were put together by the boys, and girls jumped rope and played hopscotch on the sidewalk or "jacks." Remember jacks? And girls got out their dolls and "baby" carriages and went strolling. There was so much to do and so little time to do it all.

Remember when Joe Baule's Variety Store had a talking parrot? My sister, who was the Phyllis Bob Gribben said hello to in last month's chapter, called and reminded me of that bird. She'd try to make it talk and when it did, she'd try to carry on a conversation with it. I'm sure there were other parrots around town at the time and could be even today. But the one I remember best lived at the Hein/Robey residence on McCormack. My folks would visit them once or twice a year and they would do the same in turn. Christmas was a special visit both ways. But that darn parrot. I didn't take to animals who could talk like me. At least use the same words. I didn't think I sounded like a parrot.

It's always fun to hear from old schoolmates. I got a letter from Bob Waldbillig, with whom I went to Holy Ghost through sixth grade. Haven't heard a word from him since. Bob and I had been pretty good friends through those years and when he wasn't around in seventh grade, I felt alone, as if I'd lost a friend, which I had. We made our First Communion together and he reminded me in his letter, that he was the only one to wear a suit. He said in his letter, "I don't know what that was about."

Bob was a real character, sort of like a young version of Ben Roth, the character of the north end. I recall one time Bob and I were in Al Trumn's grocery store, buying candy (what else?) and talking about World War II. That was probably about 1943 and we both decided that when we got out of school, we'd become generals (just like that) and singlehandedly win the war. Why sure! Of course! And when we finished that, we'd go to the State Theater's matinee on Saturday afternoon.

What happened to Bob in the seventh grade? He and his family moved to St. Anthony's parish. You'd think the least his parents could have done was consult me.

Remember When...?

AND LIFE GOES ON

The above title was used by John P. Mulgrew for 15 years *The Rockford Observer*, and the national (and later international) *Catholic Weekly*. Who, you might ask, was John P. Mulgrew? Does Jazbo of Old Dubuque ring any bells? Jazbo, a pen name Mulgrew used and borrowed from his pet bulldog, wrote verse and used that name whenever he contributed to Arch Ward's *Chicago Tribune* column, "Wake of the News." His verse and poems, quick little anecdotes and a few deep, penetrating thoughts from his columns were gathered each year, beginning in 1935 and continuing until 1949 (the year of his death), and published in booklet form.

Now the above is what anyone who recalls Jazbo usually knows about this shy and unassuming bachelor. But there was so much more to him that a book could probably be done on him and material would be left for a few articles.

Born in 1886 in Dubuque, Jazbo attended St. Raphael's grade school, Dubuque High School, and Saint Joseph's College (Loras), graduating in 1907 at age 21. Not unlike most writers, he had some newspaper background and wrote a column, "The Way The Wind Blows," for the *Telegraph Herald* for several years.

By the age of 25, he had a play on New York City's Broadway. "Sonny," the first of ten stage plays, had a respectable run and drew the attention of Thomas F. Swift, noted playwright of the time. Together, Jazbo and Swift penned "Bringing Up Father." The play, based on George McManus' comic strip of the same name, enjoyed a two year run. One of the road show companies appeared in Dubuque at the Majestic (Orpheum) Theater.

Over the next five years, Jazbo wrote another eight plays, one of which was based on another comic strip, Rudolph Dirks' "The Katzenjammer Kids."

This is sheer speculation on my part concerning Jazbo's first play and a little known fact about McManus' comic strip. While Maggie and Jiggs had a beautiful daughter named Nora, not too many people recall the fact that this couple also had a son, and the son's name was Sonny. Coincidence or a way of one professional paying homage to another? I have no idea. But it certainly is an interesting conjecture.

During his stay in New York City, Jazbo wrote stage material for several performers--a new breed of actor called a "stand-up" comedian. Among his stable of clientele were a couple of guys who would go on to unbelievable stardom: Fred Allen and Jack Benny.

When, in the 1930s, vaudeville was terminally ill and all but dead, the Depression struck hard and Jazbo returned to Dubuque. Since when he was young' he had lived in a spartan room above his father's bakery on the corner of Third and Main, he returned to that same room when he came back to the Key City.

While in college Jazbo had had classmates such as Urban "Red" Faber, who would go on to baseballs' Hall of Fame in Cooperstown, N.Y., and one Fred Kriebs, who would go on to become a priest.

Father Kriebs managed the struggling Witness and asked Jazbo to write a column. That column, "And Life Goes On," was a hit from the start and the decision to produce the famous (and today rare) booklets was made.

Nothing was beyond Jazbo's witty pen. In the '30s, there were two Thanksgiving holidays--Iowa celebrated one and Illinois the other. In his 1939 booklet, Jazbo wrote: "And now that FDR has taken to juggling holidays around, Min Callaghan rises to remark that now if he had only had the presence of mind to issue a proclamation setting back all birthdays, say a year or so he'll have the votes of all the women in the country practically in the bag."

In the same booklet, a poem that appeared originally in the *Chicago Tribune* was reprinted and strikes home even today.

"Old Folks"

Old folks facing the western sun
Must smile in a knowing way
When they hear the young folks elaborate
For sidling them out of the way;
They musingly shake their tired old heads
And apparently quite agree,
As Gus or Aggie explains to them
That a "Home" is where they should be.

"There'll be people your age to talk to
And visit with each day.
You won't be tied down --you can come and go
And have things your very own way;
Jim's so crowded, I have to work,
And Ella, you know, isn't strong,
So we've all agreed that a 'Home' is just
The place where you both belong."

Old folks facing the setting sun
Must smile in a gentle way,
They know just what's back of all this talk
And this manner a little too gay;
"Two can make a home for ten"
(A saw of a bygone day).
But ten can't make a home for two-
"So, we're ready whenever you say!"

Letters poured into Arch Ward's office praising the poem. Plaudits such as "...in three eight-line stanzas, he (Jazbo) created as heart searching an impression as Will Carleton had to take three times as many stanzas are true feeling and true native art.

"Restraint is wonderful." That phrase sort of sums up Jazbo of Old Dubuque. He could be succint in his verse and yet communicate volumes.

During World War II, Jazbo's writings appeared in the London edition of *Stars and Stripes* and were read over the British Broadcasting Company (BBC) on a serviceman's program by Pfc. John Vrotsos of Dubuque. Jazbo's words raised many serviceman's spirits during the war and brought home a little closer.

The "Desk Drawer Anthology of Poems for American People," which was compiled by Alice Roosevelt Longworth and Theodore Roosevelt was published in 1937 contained this Jazbo poem in a prominent position in the book:

> I'd like to write the sort of things
> Folks read and then cut out
> To tuck away and read again
> When there's no one else about.
> I really wouldn't care a lot
> For an ode on a marble tomb.
> But I'd love a place in a scrapbook
> Folks keep in the sittin' room.

Friends of Jazbo always said one could set a watch by him. He lived by the clock and anyone who knew his habits would know where to find him during any given time of day. He picked up his mail at a certain time of day, dropped in Mrs. Grady's at Third and Main for coffee every morning, visited the book department at Roshek's Department Store at 9:30 a.m. and, after a day's writing, made his 4:00 p.m. daily visit to St. Raphael's Cathedral for private prayer.

For the last nine months of his life, Jazbo lived at Mercy-Hospital although he was not particularly ill. His last poem was written there:

"Going Home"

   They're coming down the hospital steps,
     She carries the priceless armful
    With all the tender care in the world
    To be certain that nothing harmful
      Befalls this precious cargo.
     He flutters and hovers before,
   "Careful now, hon. watch your step
   While I skip 'round and open the door."

    And ever so gently they ease away
    From the curb in their spic little car
   For this is the journey they've waited for,
    And nothing must maim it or mar;
No one world tour could give them this ecstasy
     Wherever its course might roam
  As they head down the highway to happiness,
     They're taking the baby home!

The poem was found in the typewriter and had been written shortly before Jazbo departed on a journey of his own.

In place of Jazbo's usual light and cheery greeting at the beginning of the 1949 yearbook "Jazbo of Old Dubuque," Arch Ward, father of the All-Star baseball game and defunct All-Star football game and also a graduate of Loras College, wrote: "One feels a sense of futility in struggling to find words to preface the work of one who used language as a skilled craftsman. Actually, no foreword is needed for Jazbo's Yearbook. Jazbo left his own monuments in the works of homespun philosophy, humor and tender verse that we who were associated with him cherish most dearly now that he is gone.

"From the midwest has stemmed a vigorous literature that is distinctly American. It has been typified by such writers as Mark Twain, James Whitcomb Riley, George Ade, Booth Tarkington, and Ring Lardner. Jazbo of Old Dubuque carried on in tradition that which we midwesterners regard as a precious heritage."

Jazbo once said, "The big mistake with most of us, is: We look on life as a gift, whereas it's really only a loan." Jazbo made a loan of 63 years and probably never once missed an interest payment.

MAY

Remember when there was no Ninth Street between Bluff Street and that awful beginning driver's nightmare of an intersection a block or so up the hill? If a person wanted to go up University Avenue, he or she started up Eighth Street and veered off to the right. And do you remember the "flat-iron-shaped" building that nestled into the point of the "V" made by Eighth Street and University Avenue?

Remember when Interstate Power Company operated the buses in town and the fare was a whole nickel? A passenger could even get a transfer for that price and ride to the farthest point on the system. High school students and grade schoolers could ride for half that price during the school year by purchasing a roll of tokens.

Remember when a kid could go to the State Theater and see a double feature the current chapter in a serial, a couple of cartoons and a short subject film for the horrendous price of 10 cents? Popcorn was another dime, and a nickel got either a candy bar or a cup of pop. Where else could a girl or boy escape the harsh realities of the world for a quarter?

Remember when the thing to do after an evening movie downtown was to go to one of the restaurants or cafes on Main Street for a cola or malted milk? There was the Hollywood Grill, with its horseshoe-shaped booth in one front window. The grill was in the other. The Triangle Cafe stayed open later than Diamond's Cafeteria and presented some of the hardest booth seats in the city. There was Kerrigan's at Fourth and Central, which (wonder of wonders) is still there today.

On Eighth Street, Matt's Restaurant did business right across from the Grand Theater. Matt's place went through a series of growing experiences after starting out as a Maid-Rite sandwich shop. Then it became Matt's Restaurant and Grill and finally, Matt's Lounge and Restaurant. The last bit of action there was: "LOOK OUT! HERE COMES THE WRECKING BALL!" Make way for progress and a parking ramp.

The month of May is the beginning of a lot of things among which are the first truly warm days, and the first warm weather holiday, Memorial Day. There are also endings. Graduation from college spells the end of a lot of students' academic days. Just around the corner, graduation faces many high school seniors as well, shortly after the first of June.

Remember when the hope of a family lay in the good weather providing enough warm days and showers to have the flowers that grew in the house yard blooming in time for Memorial Day? Peonies were cut, and so were the irises, both early bloomers. If the timing was right, and spring was late, there were tulips if conditions were absolutely perfect.

Remember when, during World War II, the speed limit on the open highways was 35 miles per hour? That was to conserve the rubber in tires. Gas was rationed to curtail extra and unnecessary driving, thus making the precious rubber last that much longer.

Remember when there were hoarders? They would have supplies of sugar and butter and coffee and meat stuffs, and gasoline--yes, even gasoline stored in underground tanks that had been sneakily concealed. Where they got the stuff I have no idea. Of course--on the black market--but where was that "store"?

Remember the little flags that hung in windows, depicting that there was a serviceman or service woman from that house, serving his or her country. They were about 12x7 inches and had a wide, red border. The center was white and a blue star was centered in the white field. If there were more than one from that household, say two or three, there would be two or three blue stars. When a G.I. was wounded, the family was able to obtain a silver star to fit over the blue. In the event of a G.I. being killed in action, the star was a gold one. How difficult it must have been for a parent to take out that flag, change the star to one of gold and hang the flag back in the window. No one said they had to do it but they wanted the world to know they were proud of that son or daughter who had given his or her life in the cause of freedom, liberty and peace.

Remember when there were other things that appeared in the front windows of homes back in the '30s or '40s as well as service personnel flags? Cards. Vendor cards. Remember those? Let's say the lady of the house needed some ice for her ice box. If she had a Mulgrew Ice Company card, she merely placed it in the front window. When the truck drove down the street (very slowly), the driver scanned the front window of each house. When he saw one of those cards (they were about 10" by 10" or 12" by 12"), he would pull over to the side. He'd get out, chip off the amount of ice the housewife needed and take it to the kitchen door. But how did he know how much she needed? Simple. There were numbers on each edge of the card, 25, 50, 75 and 100. Whichever side was up, let's say 50, that meant the housewife wanted 50 pounds of ice. Really slick.

Remember when Humke's little panel truck made the rounds in neighborhoods? Humke's sent out their truck, loaded with breads and pastries. Their card had a big "H" printed in blue or black. The driver would blow the horn when he saw a card in a window, or should I say play the truck's horn, since it was a musical one, to attract the attention of the housewives. This was one call the kids of the house wanted to answer as well. Perhaps they could influence their mother to buy something super-tasty for dessert that night. Their cream puffs were out of this world as were their breakfast rolls and doughnuts. The bread was delicious--all varieties. Dum--dee-dah--dee! I can still hear it. I can also hear the words that kids all over the city sang whenever they heard the truck's musical announcement. "Humke's stale bread!" Of course it wasn't, but you know kids. You should, since you probably sang it yourself.

Remember in March's chapter when we talked about the large policeman who patrolled Eighth and Main for years, before Officer Jim Corbett took over? He was Officer Frank Williams. I remember him as having a face that had quite a few battle lines on it but he had a heart of solid gold and would help anyone who needed assistance.

Remember when during World War II, there were such things as Air Raid Wardens? Right here in good ol' Dubuque? Yessir. Air Raid Wardens volunteered to arouse their neighbors, to tell them to turn out their lights, in the event the G--d----- Nazis or yellow-belly Japs (they were the enemy and we had been brainwashed through movies, newspapers and radios to think of them that way) decided to strike at the heart of the nation, Dubuque, during the night.

My dad was an Air Raid Warden. I was proud of him. He kept his white helmet, with the appropriate C.D. (Civil Defense) sticker on the front, in a closet on the first floor of our home. Proud? I mean, proud. It was my dad's duty to "save" the neighborhood in the event this striking horde from hell, managed somehow, to get through all the defenses of the coasts, fly over a thousand miles from the east coast and well over 2,000 from the west, to bomb Dubuque.

I know the Civil Defense thing was to make the entire country aware of the war and to be prepared, but really. That's the attitude today! Back then, in 1942, '43, and until the end of the war, Dubuque held I believe one practice air raid and one "brown-out." During the "brown-out" lights were kept on but no light was allowed to escape to the outside, while downtown lights were merely dimmed.

Being an attentive and loving son, I "volunteered" to help my dear, too old-for-the-draft dad in his duties. He promptly refused. I couldn't understand then but I do now in retrospect. He knew me. Boy, did he know me.

I guess I was about 10, maybe going on 11, when the practice air raid took place. The sirens sounded and, having excellent hearing, I heard the alarm first in our house. My sister, Phyl, heard it second and Dad and Mother last. Maybe two, three seconds elapsed maximum . Before he could put his paper down , I was to the door. By the time my dad got his helmet and flashlight, I was half-way down the block, yelling at the top of my ten-year-old voice, "The Nazis are coming! Turn out your lights! The Japs are coming! Turn out your lights!" Those that didn't hear my squeaky voice, were further aroused with a run up onto the porch and a pounding on the front door, added to the verbal warning. It was going on nine o'clock, and some were already in bed.

The block we lived on, had houses on one side of the street and only four on the other. It took no time at all to cover Dad's route. By the time I finished he was aiming the beam of his flashlight onto the house next to us. When I told him "we" were finished and the bombers would fly right over us without noticing Dubuque, he "ordered" me home. Being a good Junior Air Raid Warden, I obeyed. Later, when he got home after making the "official" round, I was given a good, stern talking to and was made to promise not to do something like that again. If I was to man the "home office," I could do it. I could follow orders. After all, it was war time.

Remember when before, during and after World War II, the American Legion Drum & Bugle Corp did their thing in just about every parade that was presented in Dubuque? The thing I remember most about them, if not the music and terrific drumming they did, was their highly polished helmets. If the sunlight was reflected on those suckers, it could blind a person. I wonder what happened to them? Maybe they were painted and used by Air Raid Wardens during the war. Who knows? I don't.

Remember when you could get two scoops of ice cream side by side on a cone? And for a nickel? If there was one diversion that helped many families through the tough times of the '30s and World War II, it was going for an ice cream cone on a Sunday afternoon or a warm evening. If there were four in a family--mother, father, two children-- A treat, a family outing, entertainment and some all important "togetherness" was had for 20 cents. The "togetherness" was important and still is today but how many families partake?

Remember when the choices for those ice cream cones were many? There was Kruse's in the 24th block on Central, where a sandwich shop operates today. People would line up for a long time to be waited on by the six or seven people who were scooping. Down the street, in the 1000 block, the Co-op Dairy sold the best White House and chocolate money could buy. Up on the hill at the Hillside Confectionary, the darnedest cones of ice cream were sold. The ice cream was shaped like a cone and after being unwrapped, simply dropped into the sugar cone. The peculiar shape alone, made the ice cream taste that much better. Finally out in Key West, the Oakland Dairy sold scrumptious ice cream that always pleased the palate. There were others but I'm too full and can't continue this particular sojourn through Dubuque's flavorful past. We'll do more later.

Remember when during the summer months, radio's stars, such as Jack Benny, Fibber McGee and Molly, Fred Allen, Edgar Bergan and Charley McCarthy, and most of the dramatic shows such as "Inner Sanctum," "Lights Out" and all of the "serious" programs had substitutes for those three months or so. There were no such things as reruns. Now, that alone, makes the memories of such things, beautiful and good.

And there were other things that, when dredged from the memory banks of someone, immediately flash a warmth through the recollector as well as anyone he or she might be talking with at the moment.

How about a ride in the country on a Sunday afternoon? All right. Not during World War II because of gas rationing and the shortage of tires. But in the '30s and following World War II, when such restrictions were non-existent, such an afternoon was relaxing. Can you imagine going for a ride, just for the pleasure of it, today? On today's highways and byways? People drive like there is no tomorrow. If the speed limit is 50, the vast majority of drivers sail along at 55 or 60. If it's 65, the way it is on interstate highways, look out. Seventy and even higher in most instances, is more the rule than the exception. If you want to try an experiment, drive the speed limit on any highway and keep track of how many cars pass you and how many you pass. It's a real eye opener.

I feel we've lost most of the good ways to relax. Oh, sure, you can have a drink and "relax," and I've done that, the way any of you readers probably have done at one time or another. But, to simply relax without any kind of help, other than to do something that is completely unimportant, uneccary and in most cases, unwanted by anyone today, is almost a thing of the past.

Society is too hyper and when I conjure up memories of bygone eras and, if for only a moment or two, help someone relive the past when prices were low and grass for example was something that needed to be cut and nothing else--when a good time might be a conversation, then Remember when...? will have served its function.

Remember when a person could go to Trenkle's Market at 1225 Central and get a supply of sausage and "exotic" meats for the week. By exotic I mean spiced beef loaf or corned beef or landjaeger. My late brother-in-law, Ben Roth, worked there and with his discount, purchased for the week of May 2, 1972 (see, one doesn't have to go back to the '30s at all) the following: 10 brats; 10 slices minced ham; 7 pressed ham ; 14 braunschweiger; 3 corned beef; 6 olive loaf; 9 meat loaf; 4 cooked salami; 2 soft salami; 8 pickle & pimento loaf. All of that cost $3.79. If that isn't a good memory, I don't know what is. Go price the same stuff today and you'll see what I mean. Ah, inflation. And Ben had seven kids.

Remember when the Wage and Price Control Board came into power in 1942? If that isn't a sweet memory, then how about the 9¢ loaf of bread they ordered? How about a pound of bacon for 39¢? Or a dozen eggs for 48¢. Coffee, 56¢ a pound and sugar, 34¢ a pound. Wouldn't it be wonderful to have those food prices with today's wages and incomes? Yeah!

Remember when slogans would come along every now and then and be all the rage? Twenty three skiddoo! Oh, you kid. Hubba, hubba, hubba! During World War II, we had slogans such as: "Keep 'em Rolling!" "Keep 'em Flying!" "A slip of the lip can sink a ship." "Buy Bonds ' til it hurts!" Whatever happened to slogans? They went by the wayside when someone came up with: "Have a Good Day." I miss slogans.

Remember when during World War II, the government encouraged people to plant gardens? What seemed like overnight, almost 6,000,000 victory gardens sprang up and people who had various colored thumbs from green to dirt black, were suddenly farmers and what have you. Not that there weren't legitimate truck famers and so on before then. But people dug up their lawns and planted vegetables. It was an effort that carried its own reward.

And speaking of rewards, War Bonds were sold like crazy. There were War Stamps and War Bonds. Save $18.75 worth of stamps and you could trade it in for a $25.00 War Bond that cost $18.75. A $50.00 bond cost $37.50 and a $100.00 bond, 75 dollars. In ten years, the bond was worth its face value, and you were helping fight the Axis. Believe it or not, $49,000,000,000 worth of bonds were sold (or bought) during the war. Kate Smith, the Song Bird of the South, sold $40,000,000 worth in 16 hours.

Remember when scrap drives during the war were conducted? How many toys, pots, pans and other pieces of metal wound up on scrap heaps. At first, it was possible to gather 4,000,000 tons in two months but once the message became clear that doing things like that would help, 5,000,000 tons were collected in three weeks.

Remember when leg make-up took the place of silk stockings? Silk was vital to the war effort and enterprising cosmetic companies quickly came out with leg make-up to look as if the lady in question was actually wearing stockings. The make-up even came with a liner pencil to put on the seam in back. I was only 11 or 12 but, wow, that was really something, even for a kid to see--women without stockings and wearing leg make-up. At least there weren't any runs.

Remember when the miracle of production began taking place in 1942? FDR called for the production of 60,000 planes; 45,000 tanks; 8,000,000 tons of new ships. Joseph Goebbles, Hitler's Minister of Propaganda, called it: "Loud mouthed American bluff and bluster." Little did he realize... Liberty ships were built in 14 days; 300,000 planes were constructed; 100,000 tanks; 70,000 warships; 20,000,000 rifles and 41,000,000,000 bullets were sent to do away with the evil forces of the Axis. In fact, war production accounted for 41% of the GNP.

Remember when in May, high school students' thoughts turned to Spring Proms and who was going to take whom and who was going to wear what and on and on and on? A carnation corsage would cost about $3.00 or so. A for-real orchid could be had for around $6.00 to seven dollars. The rental on the tux for a guy if he wanted to wear a "monkey suit" was darned reasonable, and the guys started begging, promising and doing unasked for work around the house weeks in advance, to get the family bus for the night. And look at today. You don't want to, but I heard that in some communities, kids spend lotsa dollars for chauffeured limousines, dinners in posh clubs, while girls spend *mucho dinero* on dresses and well, things have changed, haven't they.

Remember when Memorial Day was actually celebrated on Memorial Day or Decoration Day? May 30th? Today, we celebrate it or observe it, whichever you prefer, on the Monday prior to the 30th of May. I wonder if someone will think to move any of the other holidays such as Christmas or the Fourth of July? I hope not.

The picture in this chapter of the Ice Harbor from the roof of the Julien Motor Inn or as they called it way back then, the Julien Hotel, shows the boat houses that once lined the shore. It's a darned interesting picture. The flood wall and gates aren't there and the Illinois Central Railroad Station is. The Illinois Central freight has come from the west and is heading toward Chicago. By the way, the photographer who took the picture, Claude Wyrick, was from Cascade and took a lot of photographs of the area.

Remember when commercial fishermen plied the Mississippi? I asked Ray Richey if he ever kept his commercial fishing boat in one of the boat houses lining the Ice Harbor and Ray said, "Commercial fishermen weren't allowed in the Ice Harbor." He and his tiny wife, Marcy, fished the waters of the Mississippi for many years. There were, back in the 1970s about a half dozen commercial fishermen who made their livelihoods by catching fish in wooden traps and hoop nets, pulling them in, every 48 hours during "nice" weather. In the winter, they checked their traps only every 96 hours, weather permitting.

Commercial fishermen dressed, that is skinned, cut off the head and gutted each fish. A trucker from Fulton, Illinois came to Dubuque three times a week and picked up the catch and took it into Chicago. Today, there are few if any commercial fishermen working the waters of the Mississippi. But those who do recall the days of commercial fishing, should also remember when the Lincoln Fish Market operated by Fred Duesing at 916 Lincoln Avenue was in full swing. Remember the yellow-with-black-letters-lighted sign in front? About the only competition in Dubuque was the Dubuque Fish

Market that was run by Noah Faust at 688 Central Avenue. It would be a lot more appropriate if one of their first names had been Jonah but what the heck, I guess Noah is as close as we can come.

A few memories to tickle your recollections. Remember when Kresge's 5¢ to a Dollar Store on the corner of Eighth Avenue and Main served a mean hot fudge sundae?

Remember when if you were in the market for a thick, and I mean thick malted milk, you didn't have to worry about where to go. You'd head for Diamond's Cafeteria on the corner of Ninth and Main. The best french fries downtown? At the Hollywood Grill, corner of Fifth and Main. How about the mouth watering aromas that floated across Neisner's 5¢ to a Dollar Store on the corner of Seventh and Main. They served hot food and some great sandwiches--most notably their tuna salad. And while F.W. Woolworth Company at 735 Main Street didn't have a lunch counter, they did have a great candy counter, as did all the rest. There was something about Woolworth's store--the smell of merchandise that none of the other stores had. I don't know what it was. Poor air circulation possibly, but a person could be led there blindfolded and the location would be instantly identified just by the smell of the place. It wasn't a bad smell but one that smelled of merchandise--the only way I can describe it. They had a superb toy counter, too.

Remember when the 600 block of Iowa Street could have been called Auto Dealers' Row? Bird Chevrolet was at 600 Iowa. Tad Schrup operated a car lot at 645 and Conlon Hudson Company sold their automobiles at 650 Iowa. To top matters off, Bill Malley managed the L.L. Coryell filling station, the way service stations were called back then. Lee Henkel operated the ignition service and Special Radiator Service at the same address, 698 Iowa.

Well, with robins singing their "birdie, birdie, birdie," song early every morning and late every evening, and being on daylight savings time since April, what else can it mean but summer will soon be here?

Remember when Main Street had two way traffic, and a pound of bacon cost maybe 25¢ up to 40¢ per pound. Those were good times but one didn't make near the money people do today.

Remember when an evening's entertainment was perhaps a walk around the block? By the time the walkers stopped and visited for a minute or two with everyone the walker or walkers might know, and that usually meant everyone who was out sitting on the front porch or working in the garden or cutting the grass, a couple of hours passed. All the latest news (not gossip because people didn't gossip in those days--HA!) was gathered and taken home to chew over by the walkers.

Back then, everyone knew the neighbors and were friendly toward one another. Everyone for the most part was truly concerned about each family's children and if one youngster stepped out of line, the parents of said offender were aware of it before the poor kid got home. And that was good. Nothing new in the idea of "A village to raise a child." We did it by the block back then and it worked a lot better because it wasn't spelled out for anyone. It just sort of happened and anyone knows that things that happen spontaneously, such as that, are generally good.

It was along about this time o' year that local baseball teams would start stretching and showing off their prowess with bat, ball and glove. While none of them ever made the majors, their intent was to play baseball and enjoy the game.

Guys like Danny Beck and Ray Braun, who I saw at Mass at St. Mary's one morning. I hung around for a while, but missed which exit he took. Tommy Breitbach and Tom Byrne. Bob Hoerner (and I have a story I'll spin later about Bob when he challenged Satchel Paige), Jim Kieffer and Merle Mathis. Merle had the same ball-player-sloped shoulders that Doc Hipschen had, only Merle wasn't quite as big.

Then there was the one and only Cuz Ottavi. Now there was a competitive guy. He played baseball, basketball, football, and was a dash man in track. He coached on the high school level, and passed his competitiveness on to his players. Finally, Ed Schiltz and Bob Schlueter. Don't forget Rod Eberhardt.

The Dubuque White Sox sponsored themselves, believe it or not. Each one put up so much money at the beginning of the season, bought their own uniforms and paid their own expenses to and from out-of-town games, where they got no part of the gate. Now that is determination, dedication and love for a game.

The story about Bob Hoerner and Paige came about when Leroy
"Satchel" Paige and his All Stars played in Dubuque down at the
Fourth Street field. I don't think it was yet called Petrakis Park. Bob
Hoerner was playing center field and made a shoe-string catch off a
fly ball driven by Paige. When Bob and Satchel passed each other,
Bob was going in to bat and Satchel to the mound to pitch. Without
stopping, Paige said, "Man if you caught that ball, I'll strike you out
in three." Bob was up to bat in that particular inning and drove the
ball out of the park. I'd like to say on the first pitch but that I don't
remember. What a guy! I remember that game as if it had been
played within the last few days. I also watched Bob play for the
Sioux Falls Canaries, whenever I was there visiting relatives.

HE WAS ONLY NINETEEN

Whatever his motivation, he was underage when he did it. He'd been too young to sign up in 1916, when Captain Clyde L. Ellsworth, Captain of the Govonor's Greys (of the Dubuque National Guard) put out a call for volunteers to serve the Federal Government on the Mexican/United States border.

But when another call went out from Ellsworth, seven months after the Governor's Greys returned from the southwest, he went to the armory on Ninth and Iowa and signed up, lying about his age. When the National Guard unit left for Camp Dodge and their assignments in World War I on a Chicago Great Western troop train, he was with them.

The train left Dubuque at 1:45 p.m., a Wednesday afternoon, August 15, 1917. There had been a parade feting the Dubuque unit and there seemed to be an almost party-like atmosphere in the air. Stores had closed and people lined the streets, cheering. The last private in the parade carried the company's mascot, a dog.

When they arrived at Camp Dodge, near Des Moines, 74 of Captain Ellsworth's men were transferred to Company A in the 168th Regiment of the 42nd Division-the famous Rainbow Division. He had been promoted to sergeant and was one of the 74 transferees.

He had no idea that while marching along in that Dubuque parade, he was enjoying his last view of home. He was only 19. He was in love with life, and he was going to serve his country. He'd help end the war, and come back to Dubuque, and spend his future here with family and friends.

By June, 1918, the Rainbow Division was shipped overseas and the Governor's Greys, while no longer a military unit as such, had had its men transferred to other companies within the 42nd Division.

He must have felt like a stranger in a strange land when they landed in Europe. Without fanfare, the 42nd moved to the front. The fighting was fierce when his platoon advanced toward Chateau Thierry, outside of Paris.

He was a good soldier--a good sergeant, and because the platoon commander fell ill, the mantle of leadership settled on the young man's shoulders.

The order came to charge from the trenches toward the Huns--across the "no man's land" that separated the opposing force. Leaping out of the ditch that had protected his platoon, Sergeant Matt Spautz led the way. The enemy's fire increased when the doughboys charged.

Bullets, howitzer shells and mortar fire sent missiles of death whining at the Americans, who returned as much fire as they could while they advanced. One of the pieces of lead slammed into Spautz and he went down, only to scramble back to his feet and continue leading his men. Another slug tore into his body, and he went down a second time. Apparently realizing his wounds weren't that serious, he again got back to his feet and stumbled forward, firing his Springfield .03 rifle.

When they drew closer to the enemy lines, a third bullet pierced Spautz. Reeling, he fell, seriously wounded this time. Red Cross volunteers followed the advancing Americans at a distance, rendering aid to those doughboys who had fallen. When they came to Matt Spautz, he waved them off, giving orders to get his wounded men off the battlefield first. The last man taken from the field, Sergeant Matthew Spautz, died enroute to the hospital.

He was buried in France and 53 days later, John J. "Black Jack" Pershing, Conmander-in-Chief of the Allied Forces in Europe, signed the certificate, which awarded Sergeant Matthew Spautz, the Distinguished Service Cross.

Two years later, his body was exhumed and brought back to Dubuque, where he was reinterred at Mount Calvary Cemetery.

He was a good soldier. He was a good sergeant. He was only 19 when he died for his country.

One of 32 farm sales cried by auctioneers J.G. Tigges and
A.M. Hendricks in February, 1936. (Author's collection)

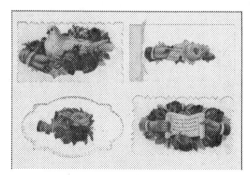

Calling cards
of the 1890s.
Madonna J.Heiberger card
is from 1921.
(Author's collection

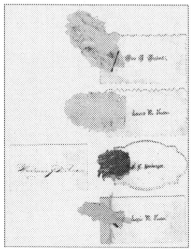

JUNE

I once received a telephone call from Sam Young. Sam admitted to having been born in 1911, which made him just about 80 at the time of our talk. Sam was trimly built and in excellent condition. When Sam began playing ball in the late '20s, George Gau was still active in baseball and he and Sam were teammates.

Sam played from 1928 until 1933 and had many fond memories of ball games played in Dubuque. As the team's catcher, he caught for quite a few pitchers, including John Matous, who, according to Sam, "threw bullets."

Sam pointed out that when they played softball, the players didn't use gloves. In those days, players were players.

Remember when there were baseball players who played in Dubuque and had names such as "Iron Man" McGinnity? "Pants" Rowland? "Old Hoss" Radbourne? "Chief" Meyer? All played professional baseball at one time or another in the "Key City." "Iron Man" McGinnity, at the age of 52, pitched 206 innings, won 15 games and managed the ball club to lead the Dubuque team to the Mississippi Valley Championship. "Iron Man" is in the Hall of Fame at Cooperstown in New York because of his 247 victories in 10 seasons while pitching for Baltimore, Brooklyn and the New York

Giants. By the way, Leo "Chief" Meyer of Dubuque caught for him when he played here.

Remember when there was nothing more relaxing than going to the ballpark and maybe watching a double header. Remember the words of the song that included: Buy me some peanuts and crackerjacks...

Remember when there was plenty of baseball and softball to watch? There still is, but today's games are played on well manicured fields and have all the conveniences needed to play the game. Remember when ball was played at Rafferty's Field? Where? You know. Where the new Eagle's Super Market is located on South Locust. Comiskey Field on the north end of town was the site of a lot of good games as well.

Remember when there was a place called Petrakis Park down on the Fourth Street Extension? It's gone today but that park at one time, was the home of the Dubuque Packers. The Packers was a farm club of the Chicago White Sox. Dubuque ball teams have had many connections with the White Sox over the years all because of the fact Charlie Comiskey began his baseball career right here in Dubuque as a 19-year-old pitcher/first baseman on the team that won the pennant his first year. That same team went on to play and defeat the Providence club and the Chicago Cubs, both of which were the top teams in the National League at the time. Dubuque claimed the world championship when it knocked off the Cubs, 1-0. Charlie Comisky went on to help start the American League and the White Sox, which he owned. By the way, do you remember what Petrakis Park was called prior to that name? It was the Dubuque Athletic Field.

Remember when the movie *Field of Dreams* was produced in the area? You should be aware of the name, "Shoeless Joe" Jackson. Am I right? Did you know that "Shoeless Joe," following his banishment from professional baseball forever, is thought to have played on the Dubuque team, which won the 1923 Mississippi Valley League Championship, using the name, Fred Spurgeon. Without going into the entire account of his being banned, let it be said that it was a pretty sorry state of affairs when the man who is considered to have been the greatest baseball player who ever lived is not in the Baseball Hall of Fame. Consider this: of the eight White Sox players accused of throwing the 1919 World Series, all had atrocious batting averages and fielding and pitching records. All, that is, except "Shoeless Joe," who played errorless ball, batted .375 and drove in six runs. He certainly had a strange way of throwing games. Well, maybe someday.

Remember when southenders went swimming in Rafferty's Slough? That little pond of back water is still there and probably has memories such as never experienced by the "Mighty Miss" that flows nearby. The Central Pacific Railroad tracks separate these two bodies of water and, when those tracks were owned by the Illinois Central and the I.C.'s coaling facilities were still in existence, that's when the swimmers did their thing.

It was considerably wetter around Maus Park and vicinity before and yes, even after the dams were built. Moore's Mill or the remains of it, I should say, hugged the foot of the hilly bluffs, its chimney giving a one-fingered salute to the world as it pointed heavenward. During the early '30s, once the depression really hit the Key City, Dubuque's very own "Hooverville" suddenly appeared. The unemployed who had been evicted from their homes--people traveling from one place to another, searching for that all-elusive job--put together their own community of shacks, shanties and cardboard box houses along the shores of this little bit of back water.

But before and after "Hooverville," the residents of "Little Dublin" found relaxation and enjoyment around the "ol' swimmin' hole." While the water was neither clean nor sanitary, people still swam in it in the summer and skated on it in the winter. Soot from the trains had to be swept off before any serious skating could be done. Bonfires would be built along the shores and cold hands, feet and other parts of the human anatomy could be warmed.

Remember when one of the worst jobs around the kitchen was applying blacking to the old cast iron stoves that graced many kitchens in the past? With their reservoirs for warm water, and hot spots and not-quite-so-hot spots on which to cook and warm different dishes, those monsters of the cooking-way were miracles unto themselves. Polishing the chrome and blacking the rest of it was a mess and a pain in the neck. But, there were pies and cakes and roasts and chickens and homemade bread and rolls that, when compared to today's output of -pop- it in- the-oven-and-it'll-be-ready-before-you-know-it fast foods--well, darn it, there just isn't any comparison.

Bread baking in an oven did something magical to the entire house, perfuming it with a mouth-watering scent. I remember my grandmother in South Dakota making chicken that had been browned on top of the stove--ambrosia! Her pies had flaky crusts and the best darned fillings that were fresh--not frozen or poured from a can.

Remember when most families had a garden of some sort--vegetables, grown in their own backyard--turning the earth over each spring and smelling that divine, fresh aroma--planting their seeds for whichever vegetables they intended to grow, in rows or a bed for lettuce? Was there ever anything so tasty or tempting than a fresh lettuce salad, right from the garden, with fresh tomatoes and onions cut up and mixed with hot bacon grease and vinegar and the bits of bacon throughout?

Remember when a person could tune in the floor model Stewart Warner radio or whatever brand, and hear sometime around 9:00 p.m. or later: "From the Ritz-Carlton Hotel in the city of Boston, overlooking the beautiful Boston Commons..."? Or maybe you Remember: "From the Glen Island Casino in New Rochelle, New York..."? How about: "From the Aragon Ballroom..."? No matter where the Big Bands went in the '30s and early '40s, anyone listening in felt as if he or she were right there.

Remember when movie houses held "dish" night? Theaters attracted patrons by giving away a different dish each week to eventually make up a set. Long-range plans, indeed. Imagine a place setting for 12 people--dinner plate, salad plate, soup bowl. Why, the management had a customer for 36 weeks. Then there were the meat platters and the bowls, etc.

Remember when the circus came to town? Now, if you were a kid, say maybe nine or ten and knew the circus was coming to town, where would you go on the day it was supposed to arrive? Why to the train yard, of course. That's how the circus came to town prior to the 1960s. Now, why did I use such a late date? Because the last really big circus to hit Dubuque, as I recall, came in on the train and had rail flat cars parked along Third Street, east of Central Avenue and the seven tracks between Central and the spurs that serviced the Dubuque Boat and Boiler Works, The Chicago, Burlington, and Quincy Railroad freight house, known better today as the Fred Woodward River Museum, and quite a few other industries along the river.

But, WOW! the circus was in town. It was sheer magic watching elephants used as tractors and bulldozers, pushing the multi-ton wagons off the flat cars. And, if the weather was just right, in other words, not snowing, some of the performers, if not all, would give bits and pieces of their acts on the way to the circus grounds, north of town, near the Melody Mill Dance Hall.

I couldn't have been more than three, maybe four years of age, the first time I sat on my grandparents front porch on Central Avenue, waiting for THE PARADE! Gosh, and when it came, it was like storybook time, fantasy land, and your favorite radio program come to life all wrapped up in one beautiful, glowing package. The wait was endless. My sister, Phyllis and I got to my grandmother's home about eight o'clock in the morning. The train was due to arrive about ten and by the time the parade started, it would be close to noon. When the lead ponies of the parade arrived in front of my grandmother's house in the 3000 block on Central, believe me, the anticipation had grown to monumental proportions. But it was worth every hour, every minute, every second's worth of wait. To a four-year-old, a forty-year-old, or a one-hundred-and-four-year-old, the wait was nothing. The circus was in town.

Ye-a-a-h-h-h! Of such memories are lives built on and recalled with as much gusto and excitement as the day it happened.

Remember when carnivals came to town? A totally different setup but still there builds within certain ones of us, nostalgia galore even for those types of attractions. Those collections of side shows featuring freaks or so-called freaks of nature, out-and-out chicanery, games of questionable chance that lined the midway and rides that would be rough enough to make one want to get rid of the junk food one'd eaten along the midway such as ice cream, cotton candy, hot dogs, hamburgers and any other sort of exotic food "treat" being offered, were at the best, a collection of gimmicks to make one forget one's troubles during the heavy years of the depression. Of course, one lost nickels and dimes, too. Sometimes it cost to get into the show and sometimes it didn't.

But they were fun, especially if those golden years known as the teens were upon the shoulders and mantel of the attendee. Take a date? Why not? After all, she knew the guy wanted to take her on the rides just to scare her. Scared, she'd have to seek out his muscular, male, muddle-headed heroism and feel safe in his arms. Honest to Pete! The games we played, and I don't mean on the midway. Maybe it's good that the only carnival that currently comes to town is at the County Fair.

At one time I asked for the locations of horse troughs around town. Among the callers who volunteered to help with that world-saving task, was Bill Oglesby, 91 years young and as sharp as a horseshoe nail. Bill mentioned the longest list of anyone who called or wrote to me. The list he gave me follows: 26th & White Street; 18th & Central; 6th & Iowa; Flat Iron Park; Asbury Street and Clarke Drive and Southern Avenue. Another caller mentioned the one at Dodge and Bluff and one at five points near Finley Hospital, while still another recalled troughs on either side of the Court House. While no one mentioned the fact, I personally feel there should have been one or more horse troughs around City Hall since the Farmer's Market was a gigantic operation in terms of produce, vendors AND horse-drawn farm wagons. Pictures I've seen showed just about a team of two to every wagon with the single horse drawn buggies and buckboards in evidence as well. Certainly, those animals needed water for that long trek home. If there weren't any troughs there for them, then by jinks (or is that high jinks) there should have been.

Rack your brains and try to recall the Autocar Truck.

Remember when I mentioned in the April chapter about the ballroom in Center Grove? The Crystal Ballroom? Well, Carol Loetscher called me and we reminisced about it for a while. I enjoyed every minute of our talk. Carol's paternal grandfather, Ed Bartels, owned the ballroom as well as Bartel's Cabin Court on old Highway 20. Remember that? The court was on the left hand side of the road, when heading west a few blocks beyond the viaduct that crossed the Illinois Central Railroad tracks at Center Grove.

Dances were held at the ballroom, every Wednesday and Sunday night and was the scene of many wedding dances. Mr. and Mrs.

Peter (Maylo) Riniker were married and had their wedding dance in the Crystal Ballroom 50 years ago. Ken Mozena and his bride did the same and Ken likes to tell how his and his wife's wedding at the Crystal Ballroom took the largest share of the door receipts up to that time--$184.00.

Remember when Cosley bottled sodas were sold at the ballroom? Orange? Strawberry? Cream? Root beer? Lemon? Grape? There wasn't any of the hard stuff sold on the premises, although there were those few adventurous souls who were willing to take the chance of crossing paths with Walter Hoerner, the bouncer. If discovered, the errant dancer was asked politely by Walt, to "take that stuff outta here," and then come back to the dance. Walt didn't catch all of them but he got more than his fair share.

Western band, "Sheriff" Tom Owens and his Cowboys, were a big draw back in the '30s and '40s. Tom and his men whipped up favorite cowboy ballads and western tunes as well as hits of the day, such as "Beer Barrel Polka."

Oh, there were other bands that, if you were there, you will remember just at the mention of a name. Bennett Gretten in the '30s. "Tiny" Hill whose signature song was "Skirts," was a frequent attraction at the Crystal Ballroom. And there was Skippy Anderson's band and Luke Ritz's band. Luke Ritz's real name was Charles "Chuck" Luckritz. And there were local bands that played there as well. Irv Behr and his band, Clarence Zahina and his outfit showed up quite regularly, as did Joe Costa and Joey Paradiso. Ray Alderson was another popular local bandleader.

Of the road orchestras or bands, Leo Pieper was my favorite. Leo played accordion and had a highly talented bunch of musicians in his group, following World War II. Not that the other bands, local or imports, didn't have good musicians, because they did. But Leo's group featured a great drummer in Billy Hauck and an exceptional brass section. The Veronica Lake look-a-like singer, Ronnie Decker, didn't hurt the scenery at the ballroom either.

A peculiar aspect of the Crystal Ballroom was the wooden windows that opened outward on the west side of the building to let in fresh air. It was the days before air conditioning and such, and a breeze from the west after stompin' to some fast tune or other, helped cool off the dancers as fast as a bottle of Cosley "pop."

Remember when, during WWII, Coca Cola was scarce? That was one reason Cosley was so popular at the ballroom. Then, too, liquor by the drink was illegal and naturally there were never any containers of such liquid near any of the ballrooms in the area. The last statement was made with my tongue completely in my cheek.

Remember when Leo Greco played with his band at Pape's Ballroom in Lower Balltown? Now, there was a place to go to watch the Saturday night fights. What a place. Memories of precious quality to those who have them. To those who don't, my regrets because you really missed something in the ballrooms that used to dot the country and in large cities and small, as well.

Remember when your date would "throw you over" for a dance with "Dreams" Harty? There wasn't a woman dancer of the times who wasn't willing to stand in line for an hour just to have an opportunity of gliding across the floor with Dreams. A bit on the "pear-shaped" side, Dreams normally dressed impeccably like George Raft in any of his flicks, when he played the roll of a suave dancer. Dreams wore sideburns on occasion and a little moustache that helped charm the ladies who wanted "just once around the floor" with him. It must have been worth it. He was seldom idle on the sidelines of the Crystal Ballroom or Melody Mill Ballroom. And he was smooth on the floor despite his weight and build.

One final memory about the Crystal Ballroom. Ed Bartels ran a form ad in *The Telegraph Herald* for many years. It appeared on the page with ads for the movie theaters. The heavy border of the advertisement, surrounded the wording, which read across the top: "Come Early--Stay Late." Across the bottom of the ad, the advice that there was: "Free Taxi--Eighth and Bluff," was plainly visible. In between, the name of the dance band and date of the engagement, was printed in large letters.

One particular year, when Christmas fell on either a Wednesday or Sunday, the two nights the ballroom was opened each week, the date, December 25, was given and right below it, the following advice: NO DANCE.

I often wondered how many people went to Eighth and Bluff for that free taxi service that night.

Remember when soap operas ruled the daytime hours of network radio? People think there are a lot of them today. Today's numbers are pretty small compared to those of yesteryear. Granted TV's offerings are longer but sheer numbers of the 15 minute radio soap totally overwhelm. On radio one had the choice of: "Big Sister," "Ma Perkins," "Young Doctor Malone," and "The Guiding Light." That's an hour's worth right there. "Today's Children," "Life Can Be Beautiful," "Right To Happiness," and "Backstage Wife" made up another hour's worth of misery and mayhem. "Stella Dallas," "Lorenzo Jones," "Widder Brown", and "Painted Drees" made more worries, troubles and occasions to weep a little for the housewife of the '30s and '40s. "Bachelor's Children" was a morning soaper as was "Our Gal Sunday" and "The Romance of Helen Trent." The one thing that always struck me as being hilariously funny, was the fact that whenever Helen and her fiance of long standing (years and years), Gil Whitney addressed each other, they would usually use their last names as well. How proper can a couple be?

On Sundays if you liked railing preachers there were quite a few riding the air waves. Billy Sunday and Father Coglan were just two.

And newscasters from the '30s and '40s were legends in their own time. H. V. Kaltenborn; Lowell Thomas, who lived to be 3,000 years old it seemed; Floyd Gibbons; Walter Winchell (Good evening Mr. and Mrs. America and all the ships at sea! Flash!); Fulton Lewis and later on, on television, his son, Fulton Lewis Jr.; Edward R. Murrow, the dean of all newscasters in most people's books and Gabriel Heatter (Good evening. Ah, yes, there's good news tonight.) Remember 'em?

And the kids had their favorite programs, too. High adventure rode the radio waves of America shortly after school was out. Around Dubuque, a kid could come home from school and start a half dozen adventure programs that began with "Hop Harrigan" at 4:45 p.m. ("CX-4 calling control tower." "Control tower calling CX-40. Wind, southeast. Ceiling 1,500 feet. All clear." "Okay! This is Hop Harrigan coming in for a landing.") Hop's adventures with his mechanic, Tank Tinker were always exciting. Then at 5:00 p.m. Milton Caniff's "Terry and the Pirates" came on, followed by: "Faster than a speeding bullet!" [SdFX gunshot] "More powerful than a locomotive!" [SdFX roaring steam locomotive] " Able to leap tall buildings with a single bound!" [SdFX rush of wind] "Look! Up in the sky! It's a bird! It's a plane! It's Superman." At 5:30 p.m. "Jack Armstrong, the All-American Boy" came on, along with Billy and Betty Fairfield. Why, without those three, Jack especially, we'd have lost WWII.

Then at 5:45, "Tom Mix" rode into your home with Sheriff Mike Shaw (who was played by Harold Peary better known as the Great Gildersleeve). Tom rode Tony, the Wonder Horse and worked with Archer Essex, his FBI agent pal. 6:00 p.m. found "I Love A Mystery" (later "I Love Adventure" on was it the other way around?) with Doc, Jack and Reggie. Reggie was played by Tony Randall.

There were other adventure programs for kids that some adults found interesting as well. "Little Orphan Annie," "Renfrew of the Mounted Police," "Red Ryder," "The Lone Ranger" And "The Green Hornet." The last two were an interesting pair since the Lone Ranger, whose real family name was Reid helped raise his nephew, Dan Reid, whose son grew up to be owner of a newspaper and hired Kato to drive him around when he was the Green Hornet. Now, isn't that interesting? Both programs originated out of WXYZ in Detroit, which also spawned "Sergeant Preston of the Yukon."

Remember when your skin crawled to "Inner Sanctum," "Suspense,"Lights Out," and "The Hermit's Cave" to name only a few.

Remember when trolley cars and buses were a nickel a ride? School kids could buy a roll of bus tokens for a buck and ride the bus 40 times. I point this out only because while walking past a Keyline bus the other day, I noticed that adults can ride for $.80 now. I guess that's what's called inflation. With that school token, which was good only during the school year, the rider could get a transfer and ride up to Senior High or Loras Academy, Visitation, Immaculate Conception or Saint Joseph's if the bus from your home didn't go past those schools.

Remember when the trolley went up Shiras Avenue and angled off to take a more gradual grade up to the turn-around where the big eagle hovers today? The grade is still there, but I've never tried walking it. Lousy legs, you know.

Remember when I mentioned fish markets a while back? Remember Logan's Fish Market at 2200 Rhomberg Avenue?

Remember when the quarry below Eagle Point Park was in operation? The conveyor belt went right over the road that led up to the toll house and the Wisconsin-Iowa Bridge. Ore cars lined the tracks and were loaded with gravel and rock to go only where God and the Milwaukee Railroad knew.

Remember when Zehentner's had a grocery store where the King of Clubs has been for a long time? 1902 Central Avenue. I remember the store well. It had a real "foodsy" smell to it, and they used to sprinkle water over their fresh produce to keep it crisp and fresh. They still do the same thing today, but it's not a new idea.

Remember when you could buy a suit of 30 or 40 bucks with alterations free? Some of those suits had two pair of pants and included a vest.

Remember when Peru Road was made up mostly of truck farms and produce was brought to the Farmer's Market by horse drawn wagons?

Remember when a young man's dreams and desires for transportation involved not an automobile but a horse and buggy? Take a note of the dapper guy sitting in the two seater in the picture. Now, I ask you, what woman wouldn't swoon at the idea of a ride through the countryside with him? Note the sailor straw hat he's wearing, the gloved right hand for handling the reins. Topper, his horse, complete with "fly netting" to keep the pesky things from biting him, must have handled easily, if my dad needed only one glove for the reins. Yeah. That's my pop, John G. Tigges, sitting there in all his glory. He was about 22 years old when the picture was taken and prouder than a peacock of Topper and his buggy. And yes, Dad told me on occasion, when two rigs met up on a country road, they'd race. Why didn't he have a car, you might ask? After all it was only 1912, and cars weren't nearly as dependable then as a good horse and buggy. Dad, being conservative, waited until they were more proven. I believe his first automobile was a Dodge Touring car.

'Nough 'bout Dad. Oh, by the way, he became an auctioneer, farm implement salesman for Farmers' Supply Company and then J.J.

Behr Implement Company before running for county supervisor. Of course, I'm proud of my dad. Everyone should be proud of his or her father. So, while Dad has been gone for quite a few years, I'll always wish him a Happy Father's Day.

I'll wind up this portion with a Burma Shave sign: His face was smooth/ And cool as ice/ And oh, Louise/He smelled so nice/Burma Shave.

Remember WPA, PWA, NRA, CCC and other alphabet agencies put together by FDR (why not?) during the depression? A couple more I'd like to mention were the PWAP and the TRAP. The first, Public Works of Art Projects and the Treasury Relief Art Project were established to benefit out-of-work artists and different communities across the nation, by having artists paint murals in public buildings. In Iowa and naturally most specifically here in Dubuque, the most important legacy of the New Deal Arts Programs remains today in the murals that are in the Post Office and the one in Dubuque Senior High School's auditorium. There were some 50 federally funded such murals completed from around 1934 or 1935, until the beginning of the Second World War. The majority of the Iowa paintings were from the Treasury Relief Art Project. That particular program enjoyed a guarantee of 100% of the cost of each new federal building erected during that period of time, and if it included provisions for a mural, it, too, was funded to the amount of $500 to $1,000 or more to the artist whose proposal was chosen in competition with other artists.

Not too surprising, the murals generally depicted farm scenes and themes. The three in Dubuque, which represented six percent of the 50 painted in the Corn State, presented historical or river scenes. Wasn't that appropos? The Senior High School mural depicts a steam boat turning toward shore where a group of people, who appear to be dressed in costume from the 1870s to the 1890s time period, are waiting. The painting is on the left-hand side of the proscenium above eye level.

I remember the first time I saw it, sometime around 1942 or '43. My dad took me there to see "Bring 'Em Back Alive" Frank Buck, the big game hunter and trapper. He dazzled the audience with his believable - staggering stories.

The other two Dubuque murals are in the Post Office. I'm willing to bet that thousands of people have walked by them and never once noticed them. They're in the entrance on the north side of the building that faces the park. Entering or leaving, just stop and look above the grill work that lines the west side. There it is. On the opposite side, the searcher will find the other mural. One depicts the Julien Dubuque limestone grave marker in the background, standing on the promontory overlooking the river. A "high" bridge and the shot tower stand a little closer, while in the foreground, the main subject of the painting, a covered wagon wth a few pioneers standing nearby, are apparently moving into the territory. Opposite of the mural is one of a riverboat plying the Mighty Miss, a family of three watching it.

Grant Wood supervised the Public Works of Art Project in Iowa. Some had hilarious themes of which I will mention only one. Mount Ayr artist Orr Fisher, painted "Corn Parade" for the Post Office located there in 1941. While the background setting of the Post Office is real enough, the parade itself is pure humor. Complete with a beer-bellied clown with legs that most cheerleaders would kill to have, an ear of corn approximately twice the size of a railroad tank car on top of which is a band with none other than E.C. Segar's Popeye playing bass drum; a horse rearng on one hind leg; a weird appearing tractor that's pulling the huge ear of corn float; a pig following said float and Shirley Temple watching the parade has to tell you about the artist's and the community's sense of humor.

A quicky: If necking on the highway/ Is your sport/ Trade in your car/ For a davenport/ Burma Shave.

THOSE WERE THE DAYS, MY FRIEND

That time of year is upon us again and most people will be looking forward to a "restful" vacation of a couple of weeks someplace other than at home. Ah, think of what could be done this year...

How about a few thousand mile automobile trip to Yellowstone National Park or one of the other many beautiful areas set aside by the government for hearty vacationers? Or, maybe people who have the blood of a frontiersman flowing through their veins and are a courageous camper who can "rough it" for their entire holiday. If someone is a "river rat" and owns a boat of some sort or other, that person will probably spend leisure time on the Father of Waters getting tanned and ridiculously healthy looking. Perhaps a series of mini vacations, visiting different places that are within a day or two driving time, might be to someone's liking.

The choices are manifold and getting more and more difficult to make while new ways to spend our leisure time are thought up and thrust upon us. A family doesn't only spend time but a great deal of money, seeking that bluebird of happiness.

It has not always been thus...

Tourism has become big business since World War II, when a whole new way of life came our way. Has the reader ever asked what people did for vacation and recreation and leisure before December 7, 1941?

First of all, there were no paid vacations as such; time off was available but at one's own expense. The unions were beginning to materialize and make inroads toward such fringe benefits as paid vacation, health insurance and so forth, but for all practicality there was painfully little about which to shout.

The automobile was not the convenience then, that it is today. It was a luxury. If a family had a car and could afford a few days or a week off work without pay, where would they go? Yellowstone Park? The Black Hills? Lake Okoboji? Notice the destinations are getting closer to Dubuque? Why? Because the roads were fit more for horse and buggy travel than a Chevy, Ford, Duesenberg or Willys Overland.

By 1928, for example, Primary Road number 20 extended only 50 miles to the west of Dubuque. Highway 151, which began life as 161, was not begun until the end of the 1920s. If one wanted to go to Okoboji by car the plan would be two days going and two days returning. A family would also have to impose on some good-natured farmer with whom to spend the night since motels were scarce as paved highways.

If one wanted to go someplace in a hurry, it would have been smart to turn to the rails and the comfortable passenger trains of the day. Package deals were available to go just about anyplace in the country by train, much the way it can be done by auto today. In 1926, a trip to Yellowstone, assuming a person could afford the time off and had the dollars for such a trip, could travel via the Chicago Great Western Railway and another road for $66.90 which included a double berth, round trip. But considering an average working man might be making $20.00 to $30.00 a week, six days a week, 12 hours a day, more than likely such a journey would be a once in a lifetime proposition at best and not a yearly junket.

Air travel did not become popular until after World War II. But if people had the intestinal fortitude, flying was available in the 1930s during the daylight hours. When the plane, usually a Ford Trimotor, landed because of approaching darkness, the passengers would be whisked away to the railroad station, leave town in a Pullman and sleep to the clickety-clack of steel wheels on steel rails all night. The next morning the procedure was reversed in another setting and the passengers flew off into the sky, thus making their way across the country in grand style. The Ford Trimotor was travel luxury at its epitome-wicker seats for 11 people in a cabin five feet in width. Wow!

So, if ordinary people did not have a paid vacation, were not making the money necessary to travel by rail or air and could not take an automobile, assuming they had one, more than a few miles from Dubuque comfortably, what did they do for leisure time?

Before July 9, 1919, one of the most popular spots in the area was Union Park. Nestling into the hills north and west of the city, this mecca for good-time-seeking people, offered just about everything available in the form of recreation known at the time. A roller coaster offered thrills and chills but never spills; a merry-go-round titillated the more staid patrons; a wading pool for those whose tootsies were torrid; pavilions for picnic lunches; beautiful paths through the woods and hills crisscrossed a stream 11 times with foot bridges and made the perfect background for the wooing of young maidens. The only way people could get there was by trolley car and thousands of people went there every summer. Tragically, that little touch of Eden was destroyed by a flash flood.

Not all was lost when Union Park died its watery death. A large dance hall, appropriately named Danceland was salvaged and rebuilt north of Dubuque and east of what is now Highway 3-52. "Melody Mill" offered some of the biggest names in music and whenever some band such as Harry James, the Dorseys, Guy Lombardo or Lawrence Welk played, the place was jammed.

The Centergrove Ballroom was another social center for dancing in days gone by and certainly more than one toe was unceremoniously stepped on at the Julien Hotel's dance functions.

Union Park did, however, have a neighbor that died a somewhat more normal death--Nutwood Park. Nutwood, established across the road and serviced by not one but two street car lines, actually preceded Union Park and was in reality a racetrack. Before the turn of the century, as many as 8,000 fans would flock to the north of Dubuque and witness the races. To make certain the customers got their money's worth, boxing matches were held in the evening.

After 1900, attendance began slipping and the area eventually became the first airfield in the tri-state area. When Melody Mill was erected at the northern end of the field, the airport was moved to City Island. Today a lumber yard, a furniture store and several other businesses guard the memories and secrets of leisure time from the past.

Sports were another favorite pastime but for the most part the more simple things were sought out by leisure lovers of old. After putting in ten, 12, or 14 hours on the job, bowling, racquet ball, tennis or golf were not foremost in the mind of a working man. Instead, a quiet evening of conversation with family and friends on the front porch swing soothed his frayed nerves when work around the house such as weeding the vegetable garden and cleaning the chicken house (a lot of people had both) was caught up, a drive during the evening or Sunday afternoon in the family car through the countryside would culminate with an ice cream cone from the Old Mill or the Co-op or Kruse's.

But before the automobile gained popularity, the horse and buggy were the favorite mode. Most people living in Dubuque today can undoubtedly trace their heritage back to a young dandy sparking his girl in a buggy. A quiet night with a full moon lighting the way and nothing but the clip-clop of his horse's hooves intermingling with the flip-flop of his erratic heart beat, brought on by the nearness of the dainty, sweet smelling lady next to him, would provide hours of leisurely recollections in the days ahead.

Horses were a measure of the young man's worth. One place where many such measures could be viewed was the annual horse show which was presented each year at the Silver Acres Farm. Hackney ponies, Morgan horses, thoroughbred riding stock, and giant draft teams were put on display and through their respective paces. Ribbons were handed out by judges in the different events and competitions and everyone who attended would go home and relive various spectacles for the following six months. The rest of the year was spent in anticipation of the upcoming extravaganza the next August.

When the price of a radio kit could be gathered and the instructions followed precisely, a new form of entertainment was available. If a person was fortunate enough to have one of those huge boxes in the living room (or was it a parlor then?), miracles were for the having by the delicate twisting of three knobs. With precise manipulations, Harry Snodgrass, an inmate in the Joplin, Missouri prison could be heard playing the piano or organ. In a scene to be replayed 25 and 30 years later when television would be unique in a neighborhood, the owners of that wonderous invention invited friends and neighbors in to listen to the music.

So prior to World War II, all was not work and no play. There was swimming at the Eagle Point Beach before the first municipal pool was built; Spiegel's Swimming School was located at the Ice Harbor and, according to one who swam there, where a lesson was never given; trips to parks by street cars; dances; sports; horse races and shows and buggy rides; ice cream at the end of an auto ride when all you had at home was a leaky ice box; organ music all the way from Missouri; riding in a rumble seat to cool off before air conditioning; excursions by boat; excursions by rail to far off exotic Wahpeton or McGregor; all of those were escapes from tension brought on by long work hours.

It might be interesting to try some of them ourselves to see if they work better than some of the ways we use today, to unwind.

DOWN ON THE FARM

The time I spent vacationing on my grandfather's farm represents memories I shall never forget. My mother's relatives were excellent farmers and thrived, even during the Great Depression of the '30s.

By the time I was visiting that farm, my three uncles were doing the work and managing it. It had grown from a 160-acre farm to holdings of over 1,200 acres plus several other farms which were rented out on a share basis. It's interesting to note here, that in the 1930s, there were 222,000 farms in Iowa and that over half of them were owned by banks, corporations and land-holding companies.

But what are the memories I hold so dear today--memories that began 60 some years ago? One of the earliest dealt with a half barn door. I had a cousin from another city who came to the farm whenever my mother, sister and I visited. Even at this late date, some of our exploits are still discussed. Imagine--a legend in my own time--or should that be mind?

But that barn door, to Al, my cousin, and me represented a raft that could be floated in the mud hole in the pig pasture. Never mind the fact that between the two of us, we weighed less than 100 pounds while the door weighed about the same. The problem facing us was getting the door from the east side of the corn crib to the pigs' mud wallow about two and a half city blocks away. The only thing that kept us going was the image of two five-year-old pirates on that raft having the time of their lives.

We started our push-pull, drag-grunt operation right after an early breakfast around 7:00 a.m. and worked our five-year-old butts off until 12:00 noon. Our mothers called us in for dinner because our uncle Nick, was coming in from the field where he was cultivating corn. He took one look at our half day's work and with one hand, picked up the barn door and carried it back to where it belonged. Our days of piracy had ended before they had begun.

My farm family's car at the time was a Model "A" Ford of 1929 vintage--a two-door that sounded more like a sewing machine while it perked along the gravel roads of the area. Some of the roads were nothing more than two parallel dirt paths with weeds and tall grass separating them. As high off the ground as the Model "A" stood, those stiff weeds still managed to brush the bottom of the car and make quite a racket, or "Grandma's shivaree," which was what we kids quickly dubbed the sound.

In 1937, my uncle Greg and aunt Margaret were married. All of the cooking was done by neighboring farm wives and it was at that wedding meal, that I tasted the best--the very best cherry pie I had ever eaten to that point in my life. So, all right. How many had I had by age five? I have no idea but that one particular cherry pie was super memorable. And I'm happy to say it was surpassed by my wife's cherry pie about 12 years ago when a friend dropped off some cherries from trees in her backyard. I pitted them and Kathy made the pie--actually two of them. And were they good? I salivate at the thought.

After the wedding mass, during which Al and I explored the floor of the church and checked out some of the legs and feet sticking in our faces, everyone headed for the bride's home where the reception and dinner were to take place. There was a big ball game behind the barn, in the cow pasture, but I didn't care. I was still trying to con another piece of that cherry pie, which if I remember correctly, I got.

Life on the farm then, was not as complicated as it is today. Each farm was a self-sustaining unit. A garden furnished ample produce for the farm wife to can and preserve for use through the winter months. Pigs provided smoked hams and bacon, pork hocks and pork steaks, as well as head cheese, different sausages and lard. Cattle produced not only milk from which butter and cream were obtained but meat for the table. My grandfather and uncles raised Poland China pigs and Shorthorn cattle. The latter provided a rich milk and good meat. Cream was separated and sold after the family's supply was taken out.

Manure from the animals was used to fertilize the fields. Power was provided to do the field work by either horses or mules for many years and in 1938, they acquired a John Deere tractor, much to the chagrin of my father who sold Farmall tractors. To me one of the most lonesome sounds was that of a John Deere two cylinder tractor cultivating a field, crescendoing in sound when it reached the top of a rise and almost if not completely disappearing when it moved into a lower part of the field. That putt-putt sound will stay with me forever. Of course the tractor could do something that animals couldn't. It could power the threshing machine or thresher or separator. The last was its proper name but could be easily confused with the separator that separated the cream from milk. As a result most of the threshing machines were called just that. Before tractors with power take-off such as the power-driven pulley over which a long belt was placed and extended to the threshing machine, steam tractors furnished that power.

I'm old enough to recall seeing one or two of them in operation when I was young. The black smoke hanging in the sky. The chugging of the one-cylinder engine. The whistle to release steam pressure on occasion. Something was lost each time a new innovation came along. The steam tractor for the gas-powered tractor--the threshing crews and attendant equipment for the efficiency of a combine and so on.

One of the more unforgettable things about farming in the 1940s and before, at least for a kid from the "big city," had to be taking lunch to the men in the field around 2:30 or 3:00 in the afternoon. Baskets were made up that held cold chicken from the noon meal, home-made biscuits with raisins and the best smelling coffee in the world. Those field repasts were the best "picnic lunches" I ever had. Forget the fact that maybe the field they were working in was a barley field and that the shocks were being stood up to dry after reaping. The food made up for it all.

Why forget about that fact? I've shocked barley and it is the worst job encountered in the process of harvesting. Why? Well, when I did it, my uncle Larry, gave me one of his blue work shirts to wear and told me to roll down the sleeves and not to tuck it in my jeans. He wore his shirt over his bib overalls. The reason was to keep the heads of the barley from getting inside our clothes. Those long beards were some kind of misery inside a guy's shorts, believe me.

Before corn-picking machines arrived on the scene, corn was husked by hand. A small knife in the shape of a hook or comma, was strapped to the palm of the cutting hand. In one motion, the ear was grabbed with the free hand, cut off with the knife and then stripped before sailing it through the air toward the wagon outfitted with one high side that acted as a backboard. Seldom missing, the farmer could harvest quite a few acres of corn on a given day. In fact, contests were held and I believe still are to this day although, husking by hand is swiftly becoming a lost art.

With the advent of the one-row then two-row corn picker which was pulled by two and then three-horse teams, mechanization took over another aspect of farming. Today, large machines move through a field doing all the jobs in one pass. No more standing shocks of corn stalks to dry for animal fodder for the winter.

Farming has changed about as much as medicine has--from doctors who used to accept a chicken for a house call (and that could happen in town, as well) to the highly sophisticated specialists in every known field, we have today. Drive through the countryside and notice there are few barns left in use. Farms without animals since the farmer there raises nothing but field crops. Or one can find dairy or beef operations with nothing but cattle or, and this is the big controversy today, pig lots. All specialized for just one job.

I miss the farm of yesteryear. Farmers then, never went hungry. Today, it's a rare sight to see a vegetable garden on a farm, unless it happens to be a garden farm. Will the family farm ever come back? Not as it was in the past. Is that a shame? Of course it is. Farmers then were the most independent people on the face of the earth. On rare occasion, when the crops were bad (and when was the last time Iowa had a truly bad crop?) a trip to the bank was necessary, but not every year. The farmer of the past had a special relationship with the banker. And today's relationship is special, too, only more businesslike and on a much more frequent basis.

If nothing else, I guess it's progress.

HAPPY ANNIVERSARY
A Short Story

I guess I'd always wanted to kill my wife. Even before she was my wife, I had planned to be her widower. Why? She had money. It was that simple. I had nothing but my looks and ability as a lover while she had money and not much of anything else.

She was pudgy--no, make that fat. And short. She stood about five feet tall and weighed in the neighborhood of 180 pounds, which for a woman, is a ridiculous amount of weight to cram onto such a small frame.

But, she had money. And I wanted control of it--without her around to ask about this expense or that--why I had spent this and why I had spent that.

Velma also had contacts. Business contacts and social contacts that I found most interesting--especially the social contacts. Through Velma, I had met some of the moneyed people in the Chicago area and also, I might add, some of the more attractive women in the Windy City. In fact, Velma introduced me to Carol, who became my clandestine lover--my mistress.

I would have done anything for Carol and she knew it. The best thing about that situation was, she didn't take advantage of me in any way. But I wanted to do things for her. She came from a privileged and once-moneyed was that I wasn't rich--not even nouveau rich. I had access to money but it wasn't mine.

When I said before that I wanted control of Velma's money without Velma being around to question my use of it, I didn't mean she was tight. Quite the opposite, in fact. She was rather generous with it where I was concerned. She seldom asked for an accounting of my $1,500 a week allowance. The only problem was, I could have used five or six times that amount to take care of Carol and provide the lifestyle to which, she told me, she had once been accustomed.

So, now you see what my problem was. I had to get rid of Velma without getting rid of her money.

Of course, she had made me sign a prenuptial contract that had me agree to a set amount of money, in the event we divorced. Since she had no one to leave her millions to when she died, I was elected. She even said so in front of me in the attorney's office. That was where the seed of my idea was planted. And, the stupid lawyer just sat there and smiled, nodding his approval and understanding, failing to pick up on the opportunity for premeditated murder, Velma had so stupidly laid out for me.

When we had been married for almost three years, we signed a lease agreement for the top floor condo in a new high-rise building on the near-north side and close to Lake Michigan. It was there I formulated the plan. And, it was simplicity itself. I intended to throw her off the balcony and allow myself to become her rich widower.

No matter now.

I went to a pawn shop the day before our third anniversary and bought a used diamond and emerald brooch for a couple hundred bucks, accepting the broker's word that it was worth about eight grand, and had it gift wrapped. After all, if I were to play the part of the grieving husband, I had better have some pretty good background actions going for me to allay any suspicions from the authorities.

Just about everyone we knew, accepted the idea that we were happily married and that Velma had been most lucky not to have married a money-hungry fortune hunter. Hah! Was I good or what?

On the bright side, where my marriage was concerned, was Velma's low sex drive. Carol's on the other hand made up for any lack of homefront activity. Whenever I hinted at a "special" night to Velma, she always giggled and tittered and I would perform my husbandly duties to the fullest she would allow, which thankfully, wasn't much.

So, the stage was set for my ascension to wealth. The night of our third anniversary, she insisted we dress formally for dinner. I had told her I wanted a quiet evening for the two of us and she agreed, saying that would make her gift for me all the more surprising. Because I was so wrapped up in my own plans for her, I didn't give much thought to her gift for me.

We finished dinner and after the maid had cleared the dishes from the table, Velma and I strolled onto the balcony and looked out over Lake Michigan. It was a clear, June night and Velma chortled to herself about something. I didn't pay any attention.

She looked at her watch and mumbled, while I thought to myself that "now is the hour."

I put my arm around her shoulder and we both leaned forward on the balcony railing. When she was resting there, I dropped my arms and stooped quickly, grabbing her ankles, and upended her.

She sailed into the dark night to the chorus of, "Surprise! Happy Anniversary," coming from the guests standing behind me--the guests she'd invited to surprise me.

I'll never forget the shocked looks on their faces.

One of the many "gangs" that thrived in the '30s – only they were "good gangs." (Contributed)

Brown's popcorn had no equal. (Contributed)

"Bull of the Woods" showed life in a machine shop. The cartoon by J.R. Williams ran for many years. (Contributed)

JULY

Remember when there were six high schools in Dubuque? Today we have three big ones. Do you recall the names of those six schools from yesteryear? Loras , which was for Catholic boys and was a part of Loras College. Saint Columbkille's High School was a co-educational effort by Saint Columbkille's Catholic Church on Rush Street. The Immaculate Conception Academy, an all girls' school with boarders as well as day students, was operated by the Sisters of Saint Francis. Visitation Academy on Alta Vista was run by the Sisters of the Visitation and the students were young ladies from around the city. Saint Joseph's Academy for girls was managed and instructed by the Sisters of the Blessed Virgin Mary. Of course Dubuque Senior High School was the sixth high school in town way back in Remember When times. Of the six schools, the buildings are all pretty much intact with the exception of Saint Joseph's Academy. It was in the 1200 block on Main Street and was situated at the site of what is today a bank.

Remember when U.S. 20 entered Dubuque from the east on Fourth Street, turned north on Central Avenue, turned west on 14th Street and went up Loras Boulevard? Getting caught behind a semi-tractor trailer of the day was always a thrill, zooming up the hills at speeds ranging between four and maybe ten mph. When Loras intersected with

University Avenue, the federal highway headed in a sort of westerly direction on University, then wound its way over a couple of hills, headed south across the old viaduct above the Illinois Central Railroad tracks and eventually wormed its way westward. At one time, there was an alternate Highway 20 that went up West Locust and rejoined the other at Asbury and University.

Remember when budding young tennis stars could practice their serves and volleys on the tennis courts that were the lid of the Third Street water reservoir? No fence then such as there is today. What happened? World War II paranoia, that's what happened. Fifth columnists might get at Dubuque's water supply and foul it up in some way. The fence stopped forever the game of tennis in that neighborhood.

Remember when there was such a thing as a noon whistle? In fact, there were quite a few whistles when a person thinks about it. One at 7:00 a.m. that started the work day; one at noon; one at the end of the noon hour; and one at the end of the work day. If a person worked 10 hours a day (and most people did back then. After all, it was an improvement from the 12-hour day. Right?) and started at seven in the morning, he or she was finished at 5:30 or 6:00 p.m. depending on the length of the lunch period. A good hourly wage back in those days would have been somewhere between maybe 20¢ and 45¢ an hour. Oh, yeah! Those were the good old days. But read on.

Remember when a person could go to a grocery store and purchase a large box of Post Toasties for 10¢; two rolls of toilet tissue for 9¢; a dozen oranges for 12¢; a loaf of Sweetheart bread for a dime and a gallon of vinegar for 19¢? A total of 60¢. Now, if we could somehow manage to bring that aspect of the past back along with today's standard of income--wow! Then, *these* would be the good new days!

Remember when the subject of "dish night" at the movies was mentioned? Well, if you remember that, then you surely remember "Cash night." Right? "Cash night" was another gimmick thought up by some enterprising theater owner someplace in this great nation of ours, to bring in customers to view the current movie. It doesn't matter as to who originated the idea, it's just important to know about this piece of lost imagination and Americana. Games that resembled bingo and any of its variants, were played by the movie audience before, between or after the double feature. Prizes as large as $100.00 were offered at various times. And that, my friend, was a ton of money back in the '30s and '40s.

Speaking of money back in the '30s and '40s, do you remember when going grocery shopping was more of a bargain hunting journey than grocery shopping? Anything to make the dollar stretch. What treasures by today's standards. Most meat cost between 20 and 30¢ a pound. Butter was about 28¢ a pound and for 29¢ a dozen eggs could be yours. A quarter could buy a pound of cheese and 2¢ got you a pound of potatoes. Imagine, 100 pounds of potatoes for around two dollars.

But prices weren't only low in the food department. Furniture was the same situation. Forty five dollars for an eight-piece dining room set. Fifty dollars for a three-piece bedroom set, while a double spring and mattress went for around twenty-five dollars. A wool blanket to pull up around your ears on cold winter nights when the fire in the furnace died down, would go for one dollar. A 9x12 foot wool rug set the buyer back six bucks.

And it wasn't just food stuffs and furniture. Appliances were priced ala bargain-basement prices as well. Two bucks for an electric iron. Nine times that amount, or $18.00 for a vacuum cleaner. Washing machines (throw out that washboard *NOW!*) went for as little as forty-six dollars. Twenty-nine dollars would buy the best gas stove available.

And clothing wasn't exempt either. By today's values, low, low prices galore were everywhere. Think of it. A woman's cloth coat for $6.98--a wool dress to put under the coat for as little as one dollar ninety-five cents. Her legs could be adorned with real silk stockings for $.69 a pair and on Madame's feet? A pair of leather shoes for one dollar seventy-nine cents. Can you believe it? Completely outfitted for $11.41 not including m'lady's unmentionables.

And the men could do the same. Eleven dollars bought a man's overcoat or a wool suit. Have you priced a silk tie or white shirt lately? Back then, either one for half a buck. A good pair of shoes ran about $3.95 a pair.

And the kids made out like bandits as far as toys were concerned. A doll buggy cost four dollars ninety eight cents. A tricycle--three dollars ninety eight cents. A BB gun? Just seventy nine cents. Dolls were $.50 to a buck and a boy could get an electric train for as little as $1.98 (Marx) or $6.00 (Lionel). I know that the last price is as exact as it could ever be. My Mom and Dad managed somehow to work that $6.00 for a train into their budget. And as the saying goes, the rest is history when one looks in my train room and sees all those trains.

Of course, if a person earned $10.00 a week in a store clerking or in an office, they weren't too bad off, were they? Factory workers earning $.45 an hour would take home something less than $22.50 after taxes. I guess all things are relative after all.

Remember when the south end of Dubuque was called "Little Dublin"? Of course you do. What was the north end of Dubuque called? You got it. "Germany." And how about the "no-man's land" in between? It, too, had a name. Remember? It was called "Babel."

Remember when during World War II, Kelloggs Pep offered wood cut-out airplane silhouettes, of WWII fighter planes such as the P-47 Thunderbolt, P-40 Kittyhawk or Tomahawk, F4F Wildcat, F6F Hellcat and P-51 Mustang? Those models first came printed on fairly decent balsa wood and were not that difficult to cut out and assemble. But, then while the war continued and balsa became unavailable, the printing was done on bass wood. I can fully appreciate the use of bass wood today but then, as a nine or ten year old kid, without much patience and a single-edge or double-edge razor blade as a tool, the neat models suddenly turned into caricatures of the planes with nicks out of them here and there where there shouldn't have been any nicks or notches. And the middle finger of the modeler's cutting hand, in my case the right, was sliced up like a fancy carrot for a fancy salad. Not deep, bloody gashes but just the outer layer was sliced up. A mark of flying adventure, ingenuity and knowledge gained from our simple breakfast food to be prepared in case we were attacked. At least, we would be able to tell our planes from those of the enemy.

Another airplane gimmick of the Second World War came to the youth of America from Wheaties, Breakfast of Champions. They offered three-dimensional aircraft that could be had for one or two box tops from Wheaties and ten cents. I don't recall right off how many planes were available or how many one received for that dime, but I do recall they were fun to build. Some of the planes I recall were the P-40 Flying Tiger with the shark's mouth painted around the air intake below the prop, the Japenese Zero and if memory serves correctly, one of the Grumman planes, either the Hellcat or the Wildcat. When cutting out and building those models, it was advised to glue a coin, a nickel or a penny in the nose and with that balancing bit of metal, the model would glide-like a brick. I followed instructions but the darn things looked better hanging from a thread in my bedroom than they did airborne in free flight.

Remember when I mentioned the Autocar? Well, someplace close by, there is a picture of one I ran across in an old issue of LIFE magazine.

Now, do you remember the Autocar truck? I'm not certain if there was a dealer in Dubuque.

Remember when dancing around a Maypole was a sure sign of approaching summer? The facts as presented by Linda Digman, rang a bell in the back of my head (don't you have one there, too?) and I recalled having seen at one time, a picture of some school children dancing around a Maypole. I called my good friend, Bob Klein, at Loras College's Wahlert Memorial Library about it. He, too, recalled such a photo and had his people go to work. They found it.

The Maypole dance and celebration of spring was an important function at the University of Dubuque and other colleges as well, at one time. There were dances by "The Gardener," who, after relieving his feelings with a dance, summoned his helpers, "The Sunbonnet Girls" and "The Overall Boys." They would appear with sprinkling cans, hoes, spades and other garden tools. After miming their way through flower-bed tending, they ran off and other characters came "on stage." The entire production was held outdoors, weather permitting, of course. "The Goddess of Sleep" and "The Dream Fairy" made their appearances, sending the Gardener to dreamland and even "The Scarecrow" got into the act. A Queen and her court, chosen from among the student body, were on hand and the Queen's coronation concluded the festivities.

Even grade school children had their own dance around the Maypole. A simple celebration for the arrival of spring. Something lost. Something perhaps that should not have been lost at all.

Since we're going back to things lost, how about remembering when the Dubuque Girls' Band and the Dubuque Girls' Novelty Orchestra were in existence? The last one mentioned played for dances and special events in and around Dubuque during the '20s. The musicians from the Novelty Orchestra, were also members of the Dubuque Girls' Band, which had 32 members. Sam Dovi directed the musical ensemble. Aurelia Scott, Ruth Bowden, Madeline Eitel, Marie Wachter, Thelma Lillig, Luetta Zaph and Ruth Crawford were the merry music makers. This dance band even boasted of its own custom-built bus. Jack Lillig, Thelma's father, had a bus-like top built for a truck bed and--presto--chango!--the orchestra had its own bus.

Ruth Bowden became Ruth Dukes while Thelma Lillig changed her name to Thelma Geisheker and earned a local reputation as a cellist. Ruth Crawford's married name was Ruth Olson.

Remember when stores weren't open on Sundays and movie theaters and restaurants were? Then, most people went to church and came home to leisurely read the Sunday papers. Remember the full-size comic pages? At one point, The Telegraph Herald had a loaded tabloid section, just like it does now. It featured Alley Oop, Freckles and his Friends, the Willets, Our Boarding House or Major Hoople and Captain Easy and his buddy, Wash Tubbs, among others. In time, the tabloid became a full-size section and then resumed the tabloid size.

Once breakfast was eaten, the lady of the house, "Mother," would begin preparing Sunday dinner, which would be eaten around noontime. Following a meal of, let's say, roast beef, potatoes, carrots and onions, coleslaw, homemade bread and dessert such as apple pie, the lazy part of the day began. Maybe a swing or a lounge on the front porch would be visited for a catnap. Perhaps a ride in the country, capped off with an ice cream cone before going home for a light supper, followed by the evening's radio entertainment.

Remember when the only way to get cool during hot, summer days was with a glass of lemonade and a bamboo/straw fan or maybe a cardboard one with a company's advertisement? That was before electric fans were plentiful. Beautiful hot days bring those hand-held fans to mind. Quite a current of air could be sent toward a person's face to cool a sweaty brow. And lemonade will cool the hottest person--even if it's at room temperature. Naturally lemonade was all that much better if there was a hunk of ice or two in the glass.

Remember when you were a kid and a big evening's entertainment was catching fireflies in a quart jar your mother gave you? Those little flashing "neon bugs" hovered over the family's garden or front yard, just waiting for "big game" hunters to come by. Once some were caught, a kid would sit and stare at the blinking display going on inside his glass cage for hours.

Remember when one or more predominant sounds of the good ol' summertime was the whirring of a reel-type lawn mover? Today, we get the roar of a one-cylinder push-type power mower or the double or triple-loud sounds of a riding mower. But the reel-type mower had a certain charm to it. It required muscle power and without looking, a neighbor could tell how energetic the pusher might be. The occasional burst of energy to trim around a peony bush or tree, gave a high pitch whine while the pusher stood still and push forward mightily. If you've done it, you know what I mean.

Remember when your mom and dad would sit on the front porch or back porch after working in the family's garden and cool off? When the temperature was high enough, pretty much like it tends to get around here, a decision would have to be made? Once the moon rose and appeared to be almost twice as big because of the thick, hot air, and it was bedtime, your mom would look at your dad. If you lived in a two-story house and didn't have but one electric fan or maybe even none, they would decide to sleep on the first floor. Couches were commandeered by the parents and the kids got to "camp out" on the floor. Lying there waiting for an errant breeze to enter through one of the open windows seemed to be the only entertainment, while hoping the sandman would come 'round.

Remember when, while lying there in the dark, either in your bed or on the floor down stairs, the sound of a far-off steam engine's whistle carried through the night? What a lonesome, intriguing sound. Where was it going? Was it a freight train or a passenger train? Was it roaring through the night or fighting uphill along some grade?

And at the same time, remember when there were nothing but river boats, powered by steam? Their whistle could be heard for miles, too. The side wheelers and the stern wheelers would ply the waters of the "Mighty Miss," pushing their loaded barges and log rafts up and down the greatest river in the world. On occasion, excursion boats would come to town and couples, both married and those just dating, would go aboard for a moon-light cruise of several hours.

Normally, boats such as *The President* and *The Avalon* would dock sometime in the morning and there would be an afternoon cruise that mothers and kids would flock to by the dozen. The lovers and dancers got on board for the seven-to-eleven moonlight excursion. There might be one or two dance bands on board and dancing and sparking and lots of hand-holding went on during those four hours. And wasn't that nice and innocent and wouldn't it be nice if, even for just one evening, that innocence could be recaptured?

Remember when every car had an "A," "B," "C," or "D" sticker on their windshields, which informed the gas station attendants how many gallons of gas the motorist was entitled to during World War II? "A" cards got three gallons. How many did "B," "C," and "D" get? Do you remember?

Remember the O.P.A. during World War II? The good old Office of Price Administration. Wise men, much wiser than anyone I knew at the time, I guess, fixed the price of this and that and the other thing, just so there would be no unfair profiteering from the war. Of course, even if a person had the price of a this, a that or the other thing, finding a this, a that or the other thing was practically out of the question anyway, so what difference? Just more governmental control.

And speaking of World War II, you naturally would recall 1942. What songs were popular at the time? Remember "Jingle, Jangle, Jingle"? That was a reference to the noise spurs made. "I've got spurs that Jingle, Jangle, Jingle, as I..." Another song with western roots was "Deep in the Heart of Texas." "The stars at night are big and bright [clap, clap, clap, clap] Deep in the Heart of Texas..." and what was to become a Christmas classic, ranking right up there with almost all of the ancient songs sung for hundreds of years, "White Christmas," which was introduced by Bing Crosby and written by Irving Berlin.

Aside from songs that were released in 1942, remember when Colonel Jimmy Doolittle led a flight of B-25 Bombers from the deck of *The Hornet* aircraft carrier? The North American B-25 Bomber was unique because of one factor. Do you recall what was so different about the B-25 from every other plane that flew during World War II for the United States? The answer comes later.

Let's go local. Remember when Becker Hazelton operated between 2nd and 3rd on Iowa Street. You remember. Come on. The dish store, for crying out loud. They were wholesale dealers in imported glassware and crockery.

Remember when Dubuque had two Great Atlantic and Pacific Tea Company stores? The bigger of the two was located at 100 West 13th Street, which today is part of the Walsh Stores complex. Remember the ramp the customers had to walk up to get inside the store? That ramp was left over from what had once been a garage for repairing automobiles and trucks. From there that same store moved to the northwest corner of 11th and Central where Carpetland operated for a number of years after the A & P moved out to the building where Leath's Furniture Store is doing business today. Now, while I've described three locations, the three were basically for the same store. Where was the other A & P? Well, it was a small neighborhood store that operated at 2700 Jackson Street, right next door to Albert Gepfert's Meat Market. Remember Freddy Spiegelhalter who worked there with the owner? Sawdust on the floor, just like every other meat market in Dubuque at the time. That A & P sold every product that the "bigger" store did, including fresh ground Eight O' Clock Coffee. I can even smell it now.

Here's a bunch of memory zingers that should help recall some of the items people used in the past.

Remember when in the late '30s and early '40s, before metal for toys became scarce and nonexistent, boys were able to have a toy PT boat made of metal? Real PT boats were made of plywood, but the toy was made of metal and had two metal tubes that could be filled with water. A small candle heated the water in the tubes and physics took over, the water expanding and turning into steam, moved the boat forward. It made a putt-putt sound that was pretty loud. Guess what? They're back. I saw one advertised in a magazine. It's only five and a half inches long, while I believe the original was between eight and ten inches long.

Following WWII, there was a switch in the thinking concerning toy boats that moved under their own power. Plastics were in and metal out for the most part. A small boat of about six inches in length was hollow and had two holes in it. One on top with a cork that looked for all the world like a life preserver and a tiny pin-size hole that acted as a jet opening. The fuel was vinegar, poured in the open hole on top and baking soda. The plug inserted quickly and the boat dropped into water. I had one. I didn't realize the jet hole wasn't big enough and the first go 'round in the kitchen sink, resulted in an explosion. After the kitchen ceiling was painted, the boat was relegated to the backyard and a tub of water and I--well, I talked my way back into the house--on a trial family membership basis.

Remember when older women, most notably grandmothers, wore their hair in a bun?

Remember when a house was not a home unless it had a rug braided of rags? Rag rugs were beautiful if the colors were right or sort of drab if they weren't, but they wore like iron.

Remember when, before electricity was commonplace on the farm, an Aladdin kerosene lamp was the epitome of light? They came out in 1908 and slowly began replacing the smoked-up glass-shaded lamps that used a fabric wick. Today they are a fond memory of not having to squint eyes to read the newspaper after a long day of work in the house or in the field. The incandescent light produced by that fabric mantle, just about equalled a 100-watt light bulb. Shades were available that clung to the slim glass chimney.

Remember when instead of music or a radio announcer's voice waking you in a gentle way, your peaceful dreams were interrupted by a harsh-ringing alarm clock? They became sophisticated in a way, over the years but the loudest were those that had the bells on top of the round clock and a small hammer whacked away at the pair, loud enough to raise the dead. My uncles on the farm used one to awaken each morning.

Remember when after a long day's work and the front porch swing was full of other family members, there might be a steel lawn chair sitting on the porch or grass? Springy and comfortable, they were as relaxing as a rocking chair can be. They were normally shell-back shaped and the one piece arms and legs (actually one piece curved down from the arms to the floor or ground, curved back and around and up the other side,) made the sitting sort of bouncy and very comfortable. I have two that need refinishing and after writing about them, I think I'll do just that. Refinish them.

Remember when your mother used bluing in her laundry to get the whites as white as fresh driven snow?

Remember when, before the days of permanent press pants, your mother would use pant stretchers to "iron" your dad's pants while they dried on the line? Those remarkable devices were adjustable to fit any size adult trousers.

Remember, speaking of laundry, when on rainy days, your mother dried the laundry indoors on a clothes drying rack? Made of birch dowel and flat pieces on the end to hold the dowels in place, they were a constant reminder that it was winter time or raining outside whenever the indoors "clothes dryer" was used.

Remember when a bedroom wasn't complete unless the bed was covered with a genuine chenille bedspread? Today, a person might find one in a catalogue someplace but I doubt very much if a person could simply walk into a store that sells bedding and walk out with one, after paying for it, of course.

Well, there they are. Memories of items used in the past. Of course there's a ton more.

A few quickies:

Remember when Kretz's Cafeteria offered food so delightful it was virtually impossible sometimes to make a choice. Zeno Tranel continued the tradition for years.

Remember the Victory Cafe that operated on Eighth Street between Iowa Street and Central Avenue? Was this the same little hole-in-the-wall that served as a home for Act IV at one time? It was about big enough for five people it seemed. If there was a conversation going on, maybe four people.

THERE WAS A TIME...

There was a time when people had to rely solely on their own ingenuity for entertainment, pleasure and had to be truly resourceful while doing so. What do I mean? Well, let's say the whole family--and by the whole family, I mean aunts, uncles, grandparents if they were still living, all of the children and their families--had gathered at the "old home place" for Sunday dinner. Now, I'm picturing this on a farm, so stay with me. They'd butcher enough chickens to feed the "masses of family members," perhaps have two or three table settings and to work off all that food, probably play a game of softball in a nearby pasture. Then, someone, and it could have been anyone, would yell, "Let's make ice cream."

Sure. Right away. If the family is that tightly knit, I've got to be talking about a time prior to World War II. And they're going to make their own ice cream? Right? Right!

Somebody would fetch the ice cream maker, a wood, bucket-like affair that was made of oak. A bracket on the top held a metal canister in place, one with a bottom and a top that clamped on or screwed on. Inside that metal container another piece, the dasher, fit. It had paddles and mixed the ice cream stuff. The bracket that held everything together had a set of gears and a handle that could be turned, thus revolving the paddled mixer inside that metal container. There was nothing but space between the oaken bucket and the metal container and in there, someone would dump ice and rock salt.

(At this point a person would almost have to believe the whole thing of "Let's make ice cream" was rigged since ice was not found that often on a farm before WWII.)

A mixture of cream (real whole cream) sugar, vanilla or chocolate, usually vanilla, was put inside the metal container and once the unit was put together, the work started--turning that crank. I found when it was my turn, (I was about seven or eight), that I could hardly crank the darn thing, it worked so hard. While the crank was turned by just about everyone there, except Grandma and Grandpa, something magical was taking place inside that metal container. More ice would be added and salt and after what seemed an everlasting eternity, someone would say, "I think it's ready."

Slowly, ceremoniously, the metal canister was opened and inside was the richest, creamiest ice cream anyone could ever hope to see much less taste. The dasher inside, which had all the paddles was taken out and given to a couple of kids to clean off for their share. The rest was evenly divided. I can honestly say I have never in my life experienced anything as smooth or tasty as home-made ice cream.

People living in town had to rely on other methods for relaxation. Sometimes a hot evening's entertainment might consist of an ice cream cone. That's right. It could happen on a Sunday afternoon just as easily.

Up until maybe 1960 or so, just about every drugstore had a soda fountain and sold ice cream cones, malts, milk shakes, sundaes, ice cream sodas, phosphates and anything else that could be concocted behind a soda fountain. Unfortunately, Dubuque doesn't have a soda fountain left in a drugstore.

(There is one in Bellevue and one in Strawberry Point and I believe one might be in Galena.)

There was Schneider's Drug Store on 29th and Central; Ragatz Drug Store on 1996 Central Avenue; Falkenhainer Drug Company at 1097 University; Hartig's Drug Stores located at 730 Main, 97 Locust and 2376 Central all had their treats; Haas' Drug Store at 2510 Central Avenue and those were only a few of the drug stores.

Every neighborhood grocery store had ice cream cones for sale along with ice cream bars such as Fudgesicles, Smoozies, Dreamsicles, Popsicles and so on. For a kid, whose parent had just said it was all right to have a cone, it was a thrill to watch the grocer's arm disappear into the depths of an ice cream canister to withdraw on his scoop a ball of your favorite flavor. Then he or she'd repeat the process. Two scoops for a nickel. Then for as long as a person-kid could make it last, he or she would slowly lick those scrumptious flavors until the tip of the damp cone was left and that was popped unceremoniously into the mouth to be devoured.

But it was those hot summer nights when people didn't have air conditioning in their homes and blistering hot Sunday afternoons when ice cream tasted the best. It was a sort of holdover from those days when people made their own. The whole family would pile into the old bus (car) and head out in the country for a cooling ride. They had no television and there wasn't too much on radio during the summer and families did things together as a unit. Yes. Even the teenagers who were 15, 16 or 17 would go along.

No matter which it might have been, a hot Sunday afternoon or a steamy evening, the whole family went, not to make ice cream, but to top off their motoring excursion with a mouthwatering ice cream cone.

Of course, most neighborhood grocery stores were closed at night and on Sundays. Most drugstores were closed except for maybe Friday night when that was the shopping night or Saturday when that day was designated shopping day. Monday would come into its own in later years but who cares today? Everything is open every night and every day now.

Well, if that was the situation, where could that ice cream hungry family go for their refreshment?

In no order of importance or ranking because I don't feel those places could be ranked, that family could go to the Dubuque Co-op Dairy Marketing Association at 1020 Central and get the lushest vanilla ice cream cone. But as good as the vanilla was, the other flavors were just as good.

The Oakland Dairy had an ice cream/milk store in Key West. Their chocolate was to kill for, to coin a phrase. Their banana was pretty darn good, too. Gosh, all their flavors were great.

For something different, the family could go to the Hillside Confectionary at 815 West Fifth. They served conical shaped scoops of ice cream that fit right into the cone. Most flavors were available. But the ice cream was factory made and the only unique thing about it was the shape.

Then of course, there was George Kruse's Grocery Store, which was only a front for the best (my opinion and thousands of others) ice cream in

Dubuque or any place else for that matter. You won't believe me, unless you saw it yourself--people standing five to eight deep along a counter perhaps 15 to 16 feet long with as many as eight to ten people dishing up ice cream cones, hand-packing pints, half pints and quarts of Kruse's ice cream. Sometimes a person might wait 30 minutes or more to get waited on but the wait was worth it.

Why? Well, George got the cream he used to make his ice cream, from Middleton, Wisconsin and it was 20% butterfat cream. No wonder it was so darned good. Of course, the word cholesterol wasn't in anyone's vocabulary at the time, not even a doctor's much less the dictionary. So now, at this late date, the secret is out, thanks to Bob Hantelmann, who worked there as a kid. By the way, Kruse's offered 60 different flavors. Of the 60 flavors, White House and Blue Moon were the biggest sellers, according to Bonnie Bigelow, who worked behind that memorable counter.

Kruse's had every flavor known to mankind, I swear. As best as I can remember, they even had licorice ice cream at one time. Tutti Frutti with all the different fruits, vanilla, strawberry, peach (awfully good), my personal favorite, butter brickle, chocolate and its many varieties' and on and on.

Oh sure, we have 31 Flavors today and Dairy Queen drive-ins and they're good, without a doubt, but sonofagun, back then, ice cream was a treat, a special treat and most people loved it.

A MEASURE OF SUCCESS

A Short Story

To my eleven-year-old eyes, my dad was pretty dull. Looking back I guess I thought he was actually boring. But what was a kid to do? In the '40s, a kid got one father, one mother. Parents stayed together through thick and thin rather than run off and see a lawyer at the first rough wave on the sea of matrimony. Besides, there was a helluva war going on all over the world and things were tough and complicated enough without trying to break up families anymore than the draft already had.

People referred to me as a late dividend in my parents' lives, but I didn't fully comprehend just exactly what that meant. But my Dad was too old for the draft--too old to play catch with me--too old to do anything I wanted to do. He wasn't too old to go fishing though, which I thought was a waste of valuable time. I did go with him on occasion. It's just that I would rather have been doing something else. He tried to get me to go hunting once but I wasn't that strong physically and my mother argued to keep me home. She won and I was glad. It seemed whenever he went hunting, the days were always cold and gray and damp. When he arrived home, I would have to help him clean the squirrels he had shot and it was a struggle every inch of the way to keep from gagging and throwing up all over the wretched, little beasts.

To me, Dad wasn't much of a hero. A hero to me was like those on radio and in the movie serials the guys and I went to see every Saturday at the State Theater. Their exploits filled our heads, but the movie things were totally impossible. and we had our war heroes like Colin Kelly who flew his badly damaged B-17 into a Japanese ship after ordering his crew to bail out. And Kevin Thompson, who had been an altar boy at the same church where I attended and served Mass. Kevin had been in the Navy and caught a head full of shrapnel. All of the altar boys at Holy Ghost were in attendance at the funeral Mass when Kevin's body came home. I thought it was unfair of the nuns at school to make us go visit his Mom the day after the funeral. We had no idea what to say and Sister Philomena, the "black ghost" who supervised the altar boys, did most of the talking. I think it was probably the first and only time the altar boys were glad she was around.

Then, there was Joe Foss from South Dakota, a Marine air ace. I mention him only in passing because he was from my cousin's home town and every time I got a letter from Freddie, he had to tell me all about the Jap planes Joe Foss was shooting out of the air. Well, we had guys in the service from my home town, too. Maybe not of Joe Foss' stature, but we had our guys.

Back to my dull dad. He worked for a farmer's supply company and sold livestock part time whenever he had a chance. His wages were frozen until the war would end or as they said then, "'til the duration," which meant the same thing. There were all sorts of extra rules that we had to endure in addition to living on an outdated income. Rationing--of gas--of meat--of sugar--of coffee--of tires--of anything and everything people needed. Those things a guy my age could have gotten on without, were in plentiful supply. Things such as school and Sister Philomena or as the guys called her, Sister Phil-the-mean-one and dressing up to go to church on Sundays when I didn't have to serve Mass.

In Dad's sideline business, he would buy a cow or horse from some farmer and sell it to another one who needed such an animal. Of course, in his work at the Farmer's Supply Company, he had lots of chances to hear of such surpluses and needs. I guess he laid out as little of his own cash as necessary and just gathered in the profits. It seemed all he could talk to my mother about was some deal or that a farmer neede a cow or a horse. God, he was boring.

Not the least bit like my Uncle Pete. Uncle Pete wasn't drafted because he was a farmer and because there wasn't anyone to take his place. He said he wanted to go--to help get it over with--he'd show those Nazi and Jap bastards what the war was all about. Chills would run up and down my spine whenever he got talking like that and I could just see him wading into a bunch of "dirty Nazi rats" or "Jap sumbitches" as he called them. Whenever he got going like that, I could see him in my mind's eyes, a .45 in each huge hand, a cigar butt clamped in his teeth, ass-kicking those he wasn't filling with lead from those fire-spitting automatics.

At any rate, Uncle Pete had some cows he wanted to sell. They'd gone dry, whatever that meant, and he needed some that would come fresh by spring--whatever that meant. See, in those days, a kid my age was seen and seldom heard. A kid would get whomped if he popped off too much and it only took so many whompings before a guy got smart and simply shut up and listened. Not everything made sense and sometimes I thought my parents and other grownups had their own language, which I guess they did. So, there were dry cows and fresh ones and I was in my late teens before I learned what either term meant.

Uncle Pete called my dad and asked him to come out to the farm. He was to bring my mother and the kid along for Sunday dinner. I realize today since all of this is in the past, Uncle Pete thought he might con my dad into handling the dry/fresh cow thing for little if any money if our entire family ate a big meal.

We arrived shortly before noon and Uncle Pete said that the cows would hold until after "we et." I wanted to correct him but I didn't want my one and only real-life hero to get ticked off at me, so I did what most kids did best then and kept quiet.

Aunt Mary, my mother's younger sister, made enough food to feed a gang of threshers. Fried spring chicken, so tender and well cooked the meat fairly melted in my mouth. Mashed potatoes with the smoothest light brown gravy spilling over them. Tender green peas, fresh from her huge garden and creamed cucumbers with onions, were all heaped on my plate. Fresh-sliced tomatoes, homemade bread and butter completed the banquet. Eating like that made my mother say something about forgetting the war and rationing. We had a garden in our backyard--most people had their own victory gardens of some size, shape or other--but there was no way we could raise chickens in our yard or plant enough potatoes or anything to make it worthwhile. When I thought I'd bust if I ate one more morsel, Aunt Mary brought in the dessert--hot apple pie with melting vanilla ice cream. Somehow, I forced myself to make room for it.

After we finished eating, Uncle Pete and my dull Dad left the house and, because I didn't want to stay inside and listen to woman-talk, I tagged after the men. They went to the barn and I followed them inside.

"All six of them?" my dad asked, appraising the cattle held in place by stanchions.

"Yup. And I need at least three fresh ones to take their places. What can I get for these?" Uncle Pete plucked a stalk of hay from the pile behind him and stuck it in his mouth, chewing on it.

I wondered what it tasted like and chose one of my own . Pretty bland after all the great food we had just devoured.

My dad walked around the animals, eyeing them up and after a few minutes said, "They'll weigh about a thousand or so apiece. That should--"

"They'll only go eight--maybe 900 pounds each," Uncle Pete broke in.

My dad flashed his dull smile and shook his head. "I don't think so, Pete. I'd say more like a thousand."

"Doubt it," Pete mumbled gruffly. "At the price cattle 're bringing, I'd be able to get three fresh ones for sure--maybe four. But they won't go that much. I know what I'm talking about."

"They weigh more than you think, Pete."

"What makes you say they'd weigh that much?"

"I'll bet I'm right," my dad said.

I spun around to look at him. Dad had said it in such a way that I felt he knew exactly what he was talking about. But why would he want to bet on the weight? I wondered if he really knew what he was doing. After all, Uncle Pete owned the cows and should know what they weighed. He dealt with animals every day, while Dad did it on a part time basis. How could he be so confident?

Uncle Pete snorted but said nothing.

"I'll bet I can tell within 20 pounds the weight of each one of these cows," Dad said.

Uncle Pete shook his head. "Be careful, you're getting sorta frisky. You got something in mind?" He stroked his chin, narrowing his eyes while he sized up his dull opponent.

I thought to myself that if my dad had any sense, he'd back down. Why run the chance of losing a bet? I had heard him and Mom talking about how tight money was, even though there wasn't that much to buy because of the dumb war. But he wanted to save something for my college education. which I thought was a little ignorant considering I'd only be in the sixth grade in September.

"Nothing much," Dad said.

I breathed a sigh of relief.

Dad's dull eyes took on a gleam. "How about I put up a dollar a pound if I'm wrong and you put up a year's supply of beef and chicken for me, the missus and the boy if I'm right."

I looked at my dull dad who had suddenly become stupid as well. If Uncle Pete were right, and the cows weighed 900 pounds each, and Dad said they weighed a thousand, Dad would have to pay out six hundred dollars. I don't think he made that much in three or four months.

"Within 20 pounds each?" Uncle Pete asked, firming the details of the bet in his mind.

"Right."

"Done and done," Uncle Pete said, thrusting out his huge hand to swallow up my dad's.

Somehow, I worried that the difference in the size of those hands was a harbinger of the future and Uncle Pete was going to gobble up my dull and recently-turned-stupid dad.

"How you gonna tell what they weigh without a scale?" Uncle Pete asked, trying to conceal a chuckle.

Without a word, my dad turned and walked out of the barn. He returned in minutes, a sly, cocky smile fighting to break out but he did his darndest to keep a bland face. When he approached the first animal, he shook something out of his hand--something that looked like a tape measure. He threw it over the back of the cow and crouched, reaching underneath to retrieve the loose end on the far side. He pulled it under and brought the end to the tape behind the animal's front leg.

"This one here, will weigh 990 pounds," he said and looked at Uncle Pete.

"Write that down."

"What you got there?" my uncle asked, his curiosity aroused.

"Weight measure. Never seen it fail. It's always within ten pounds."

Uncle Pete fumbled in his overall bib pocket and pulled out a pencil stub and small notebook. He jotted the figure into it and looked up.

"One thousand twenty," my Dad said after measuring the next.

The remaining animals were measured and their estimated weight recorded. The two men looked at each other for a minute before turning to leave the barn. I followed and for the rest of the afternoon while they talked about the war and rationing and Eleanor Roosevelt traipsing off to England again, I wondered if we'd be eating like kings the next year, or if I'd have to drop out of school and beg for a living.

The results didn't take long in getting to us. Uncle Pete and Aunt Mary showed up at our kitchen door two days later, loaded with frozen packages of steaks and roasts and chickens, telling my mother that she should just let them know when the supply ran out and they'd bring in more the next time they were in town.

Dear old dull-and-stupid Dad had been right. Uncle Pete had gotten his four fresh cows for the six dry ones. When Dad came home that night, he didn't seem surprised that his estimate had been correct and Uncle Pete's wrong. He later explained that he needed a foolproof way of estimating weight when dealing with strangers and that in a way he had taken advantage of Uncle Pete but no more so than my uncle was willing to take advantage of my dad.

The beef and chickens were sure good that year but the most important thing was, I had a new hero.

Whenever I looked at my Dad, I could see him in my mind's eye, cigar butt clamped in his teeth, a blazing tape measure in both hands, ass-kicking Uncle Pete and a whole herd of cows to kingdom come.

AUGUST

Remember when I mentioned the six high schools that once were in Dubuque? I had it pointed out to me by a friend that his wife recalled there had been a St. Mary's High School at one time. That's right, St. Mary's High School for boys was begun in 1906 and came to an end for whatever reason in June of 1929. At that time, the students who had not yet graduated, were transferred to Loras Academy and the parish helped subsidize their tuition. The school was located across the street from St. Mary's Casino at 1635 White Street . The Brothers of Mary from St. Louis staffed the school during its 23 years of existence. I would like to thank Monsignor Paul Steimel, who was pastor of Saint Mary's, for the above information which he was willing to give at a rather early hour one morning.

To clean up the high school issue, it is also necessary to mention the fact that Sacred Heart offered both ninth and tenth grade to their students and Holy Ghost (a fanfare for my grade school alma mater, please) offered ninth grade. I guess the idea of offering either ninth or ninth and tenth grades softened the blow of entering the different world of high school. I'll never know. I left after eighth grade to go to Loras Academy.

Remember when the *Telegraph Herald* carried such comic strips as "Ella Cinders" (that's Cinderella flip-flopped)? She had two unattractive sisters and a not-so-too-awful-pretty- stepmother. How about "Boots and Her Buddies?" Did she ever have a last name? Remember when she got married in the comic strip and the *Telegraph Herald* carried the announcement of the wedding, complete with the bridal gown description, members of the wedding party and so on, on the society page? Do you remember the society page of the newspaper?

For the action-hungry readers, there was "Wash Tubbs" and his pal, Cap'n Easy. Do you recall the tough, cigar-smoking woman wrestler who shared some of their adventures from time to time? What was her name? I'll tell you a little later. "The Adventures of Steve Canyon" was followed by quite a few readers as well.

Western fans devoured the stories of "Red Ryder" and for a little while, readers followed "Dick Tracy."

There were a lot more that I'll try to get to later.

Remember when there were 134 grocery stores in Dubuque? They were supplied by four wholesale grocers. There were nine bakers including Trausch Sweetheart Baking Company at the time. How about the 44 meat markets that furnished the town with meat? They were in turn supplied by two wholesalers plus the Dubuque Packing Company. When people wanted to go to dinner for a meal away from home, they had their choice of 44 restaurants. Afterward, if the spirit so moved the night-on-the-town diner, there were 133 taverns at his or her disposal. And since man does not live by bread (and beer) alone...

Remember when there were only 42 churches in Dubuque? Today, there are 58 churches of different denominations. That seems to be a big step in the right direction.

And it was Lulu Suggs who helped out Wash Tubbs and Cap'n Easy!

Remember when we discussed prices from the 1930s and 1940s and how much people were earning at those times? Well, here are a few more prices for you to long after: bananas, 10¢ a pound; weiners, 89¢ for two pounds; crackers as low as 29¢ for a one-pound box; bacon was only 69¢ a pound and a shopper could buy a dozen grapefruit for a dollar way back in the spring of 1967. That's right! Nineteen hundred sixty seven--a mere handful of years ago. And don't those prices seem attractive today? Especially when a lean pound of bacon can run over three bucks and bananas between 25 and 40¢ a pound. And grapefruit can be as high as half a buck or more apiece.

Remember when there were church theatrical groups in existence? The Uptown Players at Holy Ghost Church out on Central? And the Marquette Players at Sacred Heart over on Windsor and 22nd is another. Were there anymore? I know there were but I can't mention every one of them. The two mentioned used to put on some darn good plays. I can recall right off the top of my bald head two titles of plays they presented: *The Scarecrow Creeps* and *The Eternal Light*. Small orchestras used to perform before the play started and between acts. Sure, it sounds simple by today's sophisticated standards of entertainment, but the value and the quality of that entertainment was spectacular. Besides, there wasn't any television and by going, one was able to help out the particular parish involved, with the price of admission.

Remember when, during the summer months, something magical in the air began happening around 4:00 or 4:30, each afternoon. The smells and aromas of your neighbors' evening meals being prepared, wafted through your yard in every direction. Soups, meats, anything that had a scent, made a person's mouth water. Confidentially, I always liked baking days. They never seemed to fall on the same day for everyone and as a result, on almost any given day, the perfume of pies, cakes, cookies or whatever had the salivary glands working full time if not overtime.

And why did any of that happen? Simple. There was no air conditioning. Windows were open. Doors with screen doors stood wide open. No matter what you were going to have for your evening meal at your own house, the smell of Polish sausage, or spare ribs and sauerkraut, or roast beef or my particular favorite because the smell was so pungent and carried so far, pan fried pork steak or beef steak, would pucker up your taste buds and a bowl of mush would have tasted great after all those appetizing ethereal hors d'oeuvres. I'm sure not everyone had meat every night for supper or dinner, whichever, but as long as somebody had meat being prepared, a bowl of "depression soup" would taste mighty good, once the smell of meat had permeated your nostrils.

You remember depression soup, don't you? Potato soup with carrots and onions and anything else that grew in your own garden. With a milk base, it was good and I still love it. Another meatless meal that I still enjoy today is fried potatoes with soft boiled eggs mixed in. You burned the stuff right

off your fingertips, trying to scoop out the egg but that was part and parcel
of that meal.

Other soups that were economical to make were bean soup with
dumplings, pure vegetable soup without meat base. My wife makes a killer
vegetable soup. How about beef bone vegetable or noodle soup with barley,
tomato soup and French onion. The last sounds so uppity doesn't it when it
is considered to have been very economical to make with a beef bone just
like the vegetable soup. The onions were grown in the garden and cheese
back then wasn't all that expensive--not the way it is today.

Remember when after eating one of those depression meals, the front
porch was the day's reward and while the family sat there and recounted
the day's activities, the sun went down and dusk grew into night and the
fireflies blinked on and off over gardens and lawns? Children played until
dark and then came home. By nine o'clock or so, most everyone was ready
for bed and neighborhoods fell silent. Sure is different today, isn't it?

Remember when commercials on the radio were "built into" the script.
Harlow Wilcox would stop by Fibber McGee and Molly's house at 79
Wistful Vista and chat, always leading the conversation around to the
sponsor's product? Most of the comedy shows did that sort of thing while
the mystery programs and adventure programs had regular and boring
commercials at definite intervals.

Remember when it seemed as if there were enough kids within a
two-block area to field at least two baseball teams in the summer, and a
couple of football teams in the fall? And where did they play baseball and
football? At one of the playgrounds? If there was one close enough, say
across the street. Otherwise, the games were held out in the street, where
bases were designated as the front bumper on that car, that manhole cover
in the middle of the street for second base and that tree over there will be
third. Homeplate? Why any tin can that's been flattened would make a
great homeplate. It sounds insane today to say that games were played on
Washington Street and Elm Street. Francis Street and even Burden Avenue
had such games. How many other streets were converted into ball parks
and football stadiums can only be guessed at today .

Of course the reason such games could be played then was the fact that
not too many cars were around. Now, those were the good old days--when
there weren't three or four cars for every household. I can recall the cops,
the fuzz, the policemen, whatever, prowling the neighborhoods in their

squad cars, driving slowly, while the kids backed away to make room for them to pass. They'd slow but only to ask what the score was.

Remember when, if attending a church picnic, a ball game down at the old Dubuque Athletic Park on Fourth Street Extension, or even at a carnival, you might see a little red popcorn wagon, trimmed in yellow, with glass all around the bin where the popcorn was made. That was Andrew Angelos' Popcorn Wagon.

Andy made super popcorn and roasted peanuts. He even tried vending ice cream at one time, but according to his son, Jim, it didn't work. Andy would blow his peanut whistle, which was operated by hot air, and for blocks around, kids would yell, "Here comes Andy!" They'd go outside after begging the price of a bag of popcorn or peanuts off their moms and Andy would go to work, filling bags.

Jim and I had a great time reminiscing about such things when he called me one day.

Remember when the corner of Loras and University or to be precise 2117 University was home of the University Restaurant Inn? Better known as "The Goat's," it was for years, the most popular kids' hangout on the hill. Irving grade school was almost next door at 2155-95 University. What? You don't recognize the area? Westminster Presbyterian Church stands guard over the site today and has the same address as the old Irving School.

Remember when there were livery stables of which one was located at 18th & White Streets? I reminisced with the late Frankie Weiland about it who told me that his father, Doctor F.W. Weiland kept his horse, buggy and cutter there. If he had to make an emergency call, the livery stable would deliver his rig and team to his home, which wasn't too far away.

George Pape became an apprentice farrier sometime between 1908 and 1910 at Matz's Livery Stable at 18th & White Streets. Yes, that was the name of the stable. George was from Balltown and came to Dubuque to learn a trade. While we're on the subject, do you know what a "farrier" is? It's not a blacksmith but a person who shoes horses.

Remember a while back, I recalled a lot of radio programs for you? John Sloan contacted me and mentioned a couple of more. These were for the most part evening programs and Saturday morning programs. The programs he mentioned were: "Mr. Keane - Tracer of Lost Persons," or, when I was a kid, it was always referred to as: "Mr. Trace - Keener Than Most Persons." I believe Mr. Keane's assistant was named Denny.

"Counterspies," an Alfred Lord production, told of intriguing stories dealing with spies. What else? Peters, according to John, was the number two man. He also mentioned "Bobby Benson and the B-Bar-B." The action took place in the big bend country of Texas, and Don Knotts was one of the players on that program. The last one John mentioned was: "Silver Eagle," who was a Canadian Mountie. His sidekick was a French-Canadian named Canuck, who always exclaimed, "*Sacre Bleu!*"

Remember when "Straight Arrow" rode the radio waves? "Straight Arrow" and the sidekick we kids made up for him, "Bent Bow"?

Remember when in February of 1942, a Japanese submarine fired at Santa Barbara? Yes sir. They fired 25 shells at an oil refinery north of that city.

And do you remember when a part of the United States of America was occupied by the Japanese during World War II.

Remember when the Coconut Grove burned down in November of 1942 in Boston, Massachusetts and Buck Jones, movie cowboy hero, was one of the victims. He saved four or five people and died two days after the tragedy from pulmonary edema.

It was that fire that caused laws to be passed, providing for hinged doors on either side of a revolving door. The Coconut Grove only had revolving doors and the stampede of people jammed the door, keeping it from moving.

Remember when "zoot suits" were the "in thing" for a guy to wear? The broad-brimmed, low crown hat, the jacket with tremendously wide shoulders cut to a narrow waist, super-wide lapels and the backside that ended mid-calf? The pants that were tucked neatly in the proximity of the arm pits held up by suspenders or a thin belt. A key chain draped to the bottom of the pants leg from the super-high waist. Pointy shoes and--well all I can say is thank God World War II was going on and such "fashions" were "sacrificed" for the war effort. The material was needed for uniforms and such things as cuffs on regular suits and narrower lapels were another style change brought about by the war effort. Vests virtually disappeared. Can you imagine where fashions might have gone without World War II? Remember "Evil Eye" Fleegel of the "Li'l Abner" comic strip? He wore a zoot suit.

Remember when a growler was a necessary piece of equipment in the home? What's a growler you might ask. It was a pitcher or pail the man of the house could take to the local neighborhood tavern and have it filled with the foamy stuff . The pails were either a half gallon or full gallon and were tinplated.

Sometimes the kids got to go for the beer, and yes, they would receive a full container. Why? Where would the kids have gotten the money to buy something such as that? Besides, the bartender knew them.

A gallon of beer would be equivalent to a little more than 10 cans or bottles. The growlers were usually used by older men, who had worked hard and when it was hot during their declining years, wanted some cold beer to cool themselves off while sitting on the front porch or in the backyard under an oak, sycamore or elm tree.

I remember the first time I saw an elderly gentleman (I even remember his name but won't mention it) walking up our street, an apparently empty growler swinging to and fro from his side. He was probably on his way to the Stock Yard Tavern on East Street. After an hour or so passed, he came walking back down the block, his pail undoubtedly full since it barely swung on the handle.

Because my dad used to give me a taste of beer on particularly hot days, I thought how great it would be to get old and take my very own growler to the neighborhood tavern. And that was real beer, then, not light beer that contains a lot of water but a darker amber fluid that smelled of its chief ingredients: barley, malt, hops but not rice, thank you. Genuine beer.

My son-in-law brews beer as a hobby and experiments with different flavors. He knows I like a good dark beer and whenever he brews, he always brings a six pack over. I have to ration it out, not knowing exactly when his next batch will be ready. So, okay, it's not in a growler but by golly, I'll bet it tastes the same as that beer sold by the bucket back in the teens, '20s, '30s, and early '40s.

Remember when just about everyone had a garden of some sort? In the '30s, having home-grown vegetables, helped a lot of folks survive the depression. Having a "Victory" garden in the '40s during World War II, assured people that they would eat when everything else seemed to be rationed or in short supply. Butter, coffee, sugar and meat all took stamps or tokens to purchase along with money, of course. Fresh fruit didn't require rationing, but what a treat when you found a store that had some.

Remember when, if there was a bumper strawberry crop, families usually had to eat them fresh. No one had home freezers at the time and if a shopper could find some sugar to buy, would said shopper have enough stamps or tokens? Why sugar? To make preserves and strawberry sunshine.

Of course the gardener didn't have to worry about potatoes, which stored well in the cellar, as did carrots or apples, if the family had a tree. Apples stored pretty well, wrapped individually in newspaper and stored in the attic. Beans, beets, peas, corn and tomatoes could be canned. Cabbage became sauerkraut.

A lot of gardens lasted through the 1970s, touching into the '80s. Today, farmers seldom if ever have gardens, unless they're truck farmers and take their produce to the Farmers' Market. I guess they feel they can buy the same thing without back breaking work involved. And the work is just that.

My grandmother, Susan Heiberger, and later her son, my uncle Larry always worked a garden. My cousin, Al English from Sioux Falls, South Dakota, and I would "raid" Grandma's garden. There's nothing that tastes better than a fresh onion or radish pulled from the earth in which it grew. After shaving off the dirt with our pocket knives, we were ready to dine. A handful of pea pods opened and the succulent little peas popped into our mouths. Juicy tomatoes randomly picked so as not to tip off anyone that we'd been there, followed as dessert. We knew we could get away with our raids since we took the vegetables from different places, never picking two onions or radishes that grew next to each other. Naturally, we would have tipped our hand had we taken something noticeable such as a head of cabbage, which would have tasted great.

By the way we picked the vegetables, no one was ever the wiser--except maybe Grandma and Uncle Larry.

Remember when Lifebouy was a sort of watermelon color and a housewife could get three Pyrex bowls for 95¢ or a 10-inch Pyrex pie plate for forty five cents?

Remember when Doctor West's Vray the modern dental cream, was sold--in bottles? Produced by Weco Products Company, it carried a money-back guarantee if teeth weren't cleaner, brighter and better looking after *one* brushing? I wonder what was in it to allow them to make such a claim. Or did everyone want their money back and the company went broke ?

Remember when a kid could get a really big "chew" of "Dubble Bubble " gum? Recall who manufactured it? Fleers, that's who.

Remember when a person could buy a bug deflector for his or her automobile. Of course they wouldn't work today, since hoods are made of one piece of recycled metal. But back in the days of "high technology"' cars, the hoods were made of two pieces of real metal and were joined with a seam. What's that got to do with bug deflectors? Well, the bug deflector was clamped onto that seam. The deflector itself was made of plastic and had various designs of wings. The theory was that the deflector perched out in front of the windshield, a little way behind the hood ornament (remember those?), would create a slip stream and bugs that were planning on committing hari kari on the car's windshield, were merely swept aside. You know what? It worked.

And while we're on the subject of high tech gadgets for autos of the past, remember when a person could have the family bus equipped with sun shields? In the wintertime, without a lick of effort, it automatically became a snow shield. The shield was attached to both sides of the car toward the top of the windshield and was normally made of metal. A brace in the middle that attached to the divider of the windshield (two piece windshields, remember?) gave the heavy gauge metal real stability and never wavered while the driver tooled down the highway at Iowa's safe and reasonable speed limit. True. There was no speed limit--only safe and reasonable. Heading into the sun, the shield protected the eyes until, the sun was almost down for the night. During the winter, the shield kept most of the snow off the glass. Rain didn't hit the windshield very much either. So, you see what was given up for air conditioning in cars, a lot more efficient heating units and more efficient wipers? That must be what they call progress, right?

About a year ago I received a nice letter from "Duke" Langanis telling me about his father's restaurant. He brought a lot of memories to the surface for me and I'd like to share a few of them and a few more later on. So, here are a few "remember whens" from Duke.

Remember Joe Takos--former city councilman and mayor? Frank Karigan? Frank's family's restaurant on 7th and Main? The Hubba-Hubba Tap? The pool hall owned by Morris Flick on 5 West Eighth Avenue? And a few doors away Elroy Grashorn's barber shop? Next door to the Corner Tavern on Eighth and Iowa, Syl Lambert ran his Tire and Bike service. And across the alley from the Hubba Hubba was the Victory Cafe, which was owned by Duke's Father, Tom Langas. Tom served up one of the meanest chili dogs around. Another favorite dish of Tom's patrons (as well as yours truly) was beef liver and onions.

We'll take another walk down memory lane with Duke in further pages of *Remember When...?*

How about a few Burma Shave signs for a change? Grandpa's whiskers old and gray/Often get in Grandma's way/Once she chewed them in her sleep/Thinking they were Shredded Wheat/Burma Shave. And: Don't lose your head/To gain a minute/You need your head/Your brains are in it/Burma Shave. Then there was: Car in ditch/Driver in tree/The moon was full/And so was he/Burma Shave. And finally for this go-' round: Ben met Anna/Made a hit/Ben wouldn't shave/Ben-Anna split/Burma Shave.

Remember when girls (and sometimes boys) made necklaces and bracelets out of white clover? Clover crowns and ropes as long as the girls could make, would be woven and tied together. What a pleasant and peaceful way to spend a summer's afternoon.

Remember when your mother would send you to the meat market and once the order was filled, the butcher would give--actually give--you a slice of sausage? It was usually bologna or baloney or "ham" sausage, all of which were the same product only by different names. And that slice tasted the best of all. Why? Because it was free and because it was your reward for taking time out from your "busy" kid's day to run an errand for your mom. Kids, back in those days, had little they could call their own, particularly if dad was out of work or things were tough for some other reason. When a piece of sausage came a kid's way, it was something real special.

Remember when another prized possession, especially for boys a way back when, was a worn out inner tube from one of the family car's tires? What luck! When that sort of "windfall" came a kid's way, there was only one solution. All right, two solutions. The first thing that could be made from an old inner tube was a slingshot. A small rock could be "shot" quite a distance with a strip of inner tube tied to a stout "fork" from some young tree branch. There was hell to pay if a window--any window--was broken accidentally by a slingshot.

The other use for rubber bands cut from an old inner tube was the legendary rubber gun. Remember those? The first step was to nail a short piece of kindling for the butt of the gun, at right angles and at the end of a longer piece, which would be the barrel. A clip could be fashioned from another small piece of wood or snap clothes pin, which would be fastened to the back of the butt in such a way that it would pivot on a fulcrum and was held in place by an inner tube rubber band. The top of the trigger was held snugly against the top of the butt by another band. Your weapon was ready to be loaded. A third inner tube rubber band was hooked around the

front of the barrel and double snubbed into the trigger. When the bottom of
that small piece of wood was compressed, the second rubber band was
released and went flying for a short distance--maybe 30 or 40 feet,
depending on how long the barrel of the gun was and the amount of
tension the "ammunition" was under. By the time a band flew 30 feet it
was almost out of gas and if the target was hit, why there was no pain at
all. Nevertheless, you were "dead" in a game of rubber band war .

Kids could be awfully inventive if they had no other toys to while away
the hours of a summer day. Machine guns, repeating rifles and cannons
were constructed using the same principles just outlined. They were
wonderful and made a boy feel almost invincible--especially if the
neighborhood bully came around, trying to cause trouble.

Remember when the "Great BB Gun War" took place along the tracks of
the Chicago Great Western Railway in Couler Valley, and up on the hill
east of Unique Balance? "Bad feelings" of a sort were running deep and
something had to be done. And it was. World War II was raging and we
decided to fight our own battle. Paired off on chosen sides and shooting at
each other from behind bushes and rocks, would do the trick. It was just
like in the western movies down at the old State Theater. Or on the
battlefields of Europe. BBs would whiz by a kid's head and he'd duck--right
up to the time one didn't duck quite quickly enough and caught a BB in the
cheek. Then another got one in the arm. And another in an ear lobe and
another... Hey. That wasn't supposed to happen and the war was called off.
Carrying their trusty Red Ryder 1000-shot carbines (with genuine wood
stock) and their Daisy pump BB guns, those stung and wounded headed
toward home, crying their eyes out. Each one told the same story. "A BB
ricocheted off a rock and hit me."' That was the end of the BB gun war and
none too soon, I might add, some 50 years plus later and using a little
common hind-sight sense.

Remember when rubber guns and BB guns were out and Indian weapons
were in? Gosh yes. I remember those my cousin, Eddie Heiberger, made
using split tree branches of appropriate size for tomahawks and spears and
bows and arrows.

Shafts for hatchets and spears were split and blade and spear-shaped
rocks were jammed in, and tied in place. A coat of shellac and some "blood
red" paint dabbed on the blades finished the job. The arrows never did go
very straight and the bows sometimes broke and had to be replaced. But
they were fine toys and never once--not once--mind you, did the federal

government stop up on Broadway and tell Eddie to stop--that his toys were dangerous. Nor did they ever get wind of the other weapons such as slingshots and rubber guns. Thank goodness.

156   Remember When...?

A WALK DOWNTOWN

At one time in downtown Dubuque it was possible to go from clothing store to clothing store, and really do some shopping. I don't mean just two clothing stores since in 1942, by way of example, there were in excess of 15 such stores that sold women's and girl's and men's and boy's wearing apparel--and they were all on Main Street. I'm not counting Roshek's or other stores that weren't on Main. Those stores, actually 18 of them, thrived on each other's competition just as those places of business, which are located in shopping malls and centers, do today.

But which of the two situations is really the more convenient? Most malls, other than big ones, generally try to boast of one of each type of business thus protecting the rentor and forcing the shopper to drive from center to center for the purpose of comparing products and prices. Granted, this is not true of large shopping malls but of the small seeking the services and products as offered by their tenants.

If the thought of 18 different clothing establishments tends to blow your mind, try this one. In 1942, and throughout most of World War II, there were exactly ten ground level stores that were vacant between Fourth and Main and Thirteenth and Main. That's an average of one per block.

In addition to a thriving business atmosphere and stores that were busy, busy, busy, there were those entrepreneurs who thought of the shoppers' stomachs. Over 40 years ago, there were 21 restaurants or establishements on Main where shoppers could quench their thirst or have a snack if not a full meal. And they were within ten blocks of each other.

In a hurry and want a quick hamburger? The Swiss Sandwich Shoppe was the place to go in Dubuque. It nestled among its neighbors, right next to a building, which housed at one time a bank, and served the best darned tasting hamburgers.

The Tri-State Motor Company Used Car Lot protected the shop on the north. That's right--a used car lot on Main Street! Back then, those tasty sandwiches cost all of a dime . I remember when the price went to 12, then 15 cents. Inflation! But the owners quickly offered two for a quarter and business continued thriving.

Inflation also struck the two Coney Island hot dog places. I have fond memories of "oinking" down quite a few hotdogs. A secret recipe of "herbs and spices" that went into the steamed ground beef that made the chili dressing, which in turn topped the weiner, created a sandwich that was out of this world. I haven't had one that tasted like those that came out of Dubuque's downtown for years. And we had two such restaurants. Ten cents a piece. Then, eight for a dollar was a great buy and eventually, urban renewal wiped out the possibility of having any more of them.

Naturally, prime time eating was available at Kretz's Cafeteria and at Diamond's Cafeteria along with the Triangle Cafe and the Hollywood Grill.

Probably the strangest name for a restaurant anyplace--not just in downtown Dubuque--had to have been Anna Hoppman's Euqubud Cafe. Dubuque spelled backward, but forward thinking service, friendliness and great tasting food. Incidentally, the Euqubud was located at 623 Main and the telephone number was--are you ready? --403. In those days there were lots of provincial things such as two and three digit telephone numbers.

Of course, if you just wanted a snack, something on which to munch while perusing goods and wares in different stores, there was always Browne's Popcorn Stand nestling under the metal steps that ran up the side of the National Tea Store at Ninth and Main. The popcorn came with or without hot butter and those fluffy, white kernels fairly melted in your mouth. Old "Orv What's-his-face" would have been jealous.

Mention of the National Tea Store brings to mind the fact that at one time there were seven--count 'em--seven grocery stores on Main Street. Beck's Food Market was the only one of them not to lie within the afore mentioned ten block area. However, Buehler Brothers meat Market, the National Tea Store, Michael Pusateri, Jacob Schwietering, Jack Solomon and Lloyd Wertz all successfully operated retail grocery businesses for many years. In fact, Wertz' red front with gold letters is as fresh in my mind today as it was forty years ago simply because it matched the S.S. Kresge store front.

Kresge's lasted the longest of the three "five and dime" stores. Actually, their price range was greater and they advertised five cents to one dollar. Recall the other two? F.W. Woolworth was one and eventually moved to Kennedy mall before leaving us all together. Neisner Brothers store, the third, was situated on the corner of Seventh and Main.

For years and years, the stores were open "downtown," or "uptown," depending where you lived, one night a week and never, ever on Sundays. The only activity on Sunday afternoon, other than at some of the restaurants, could be found at the movie theaters of which Dubuque boasted seven, some forty years ago. Of that number, four were located on Main Street--the RKO Orpheum, the Avon, the State and the Strand. The Grand should be mentioned since it was only a half block off Main. Do you remember the other two?

Of course getting to the business district was as easy as walking along an icy sidewalk that had been "cindered" or "sanded." Salt at the time was used mainly on food. Buses ran from about six o'clock in the morning until almost midnight and the city residential areas were pretty well serviced. As a result, if someone wanted to go shopping on Saturday night, public transportation was readily available. Then it changed to Friday night, then Monday night, then Monday and Friday night. Naturally, in those glorious days, there were no such things as parking meters and people seemed more willing to walk a few blocks if a parking place couldn't be found directly in front of their destination. There were no parking lots and ramps available and still, somehow, we all managed to survive. It's interesting to note that a rather well known Dubuquer mentioned to me at the time the first parking ramp was being built, that it seemed as though they were trying to discover a cure for an illness that didn't yet exist. Well, the cure is still with us but the illness never did quite materialize, did it?

Today, the city fathers are considering replacing the downtown mall and opening the streets. What goes around, comes around, I guess.

Oh, before I forget, the other two theaters were the Varsity and the Capitol.

THE BIG EVENT
A Short Story

According to my older brother, Jerry, "the big event" meant a new baby was going to show up real soon. Jerry was ten years old and our sister, Maureen, at fourteen, was the resident expert-in-everything. Because I was only seven, I didn't know anything according to her and she knew it all. Living on the farm made it pretty difficult to have friends, other than my own brother and sister, and still I felt that if they thought I really didn't know anything, I was a lot better off being by myself.

Papa had told us to get him out of the field when Mama would need him. Old bossy Maureen walked around the house, telling us to be quiet and to go outside and keep out of the way. She had things to do. I had no idea what she had to do other than call the doctor when Mama said Maureen should, and then send Jerry after Papa. Jerry was to drive the team and cultivator back to the barn and feed the horses while Papa would come directly to the house.

Ignoring her own orders about keeping quiet, Maureen yelled at Jerry when we walked out of the kitchen. "You stay close by the house so I can send you to the field to get Papa. Y' hear me?"

"Yeah," Jerry said quietly.

"What's going on, Jerry?" I asked once we were outside.

"Big Event."

"What's that? "

"Gosh, you ' re dumb. "

"Tell me . Please? " I climbed up on the house yard fence .

"Mama ' s going to get a baby. "

"A baby? "

"Then you won't be the baby anymore, Joey." He grinned.

"But how do you know? I didn't hear Mama or Papa say nothin' 'bout a baby comin' to live with us."

"Maureen got the cradle down from the storage room two days ago. Who's it for?"

I shrugged.

"Well, it ain't for you. It's for the new baby."

"Oh," I said, trying my best to sound as if I understood everything. But one thing bothered me. If what Jerry said was true, where did the baby come from? I asked Jerry.

"Why, the stork brings 'em, of course."

"What's a stork?"

"A bird with a big, long bill. See, they bring 'em and then fly away."

"Really? D'you ever see the stork? Did the stork bring me?"

"I didn't see it when you came to live with us, but Papa said the stork brought you . and, papa's always right."

I nodded, trying to take all of what he said in but decided I needed more information. I hadn't heard any talk about a baby, but i had noticed somethin' else. How come mama got so fat, Jerry?" I asked climbing down from the fence.This time it was his turn to shrug. "Mamas do that, I guess. "

"How come papas don ' t? " Another shurg. "Maureen says the doctor brings babies, but I don't believe it. Papa's never wrong about anything. 'Sides, Maureen's only a girl and what do girls know?" Jerry laughed.

I grinned. "Nothin'."

Off in the distance, we could sewee a ball of dust building on the horizon and Jerry ran to the fence where he climbed up on the corner post to see better.

"Bet it's the doc." He jumped down and ran to the kitchen door. "Maureen? The doc is comin'."

"Shhhh. You'll bother Mama. I already called the doc a while ago. How do you know he's comin'?"

Jerry pointed toward the cloud approaching our farm. By now, all of us could see the black Chevy coupe. Sure enough, Jerry was right.

"How come you didn't tell me to go get Papa, Maureen?" Jerry glared at her.

"Don't waste time askin' dumb questions. Get goin'. If Papa thought we had forgotten, he'd never trust us anymore."

The coupe turned into our farm and Jerry bolted out of the yard to get Papa.

The doctor hurried into the house and Maureen told me to stay out and not to "make any noise, for heaven's sake."

It wasn't long and Papa came running up to the house and dashed inside. I almost cried 'cause he didn't pay any attention to me like he usually did.

When Jerry came back to the houseyard after taking care of the team, he said, "What's wrong with you?"

I told him how Papa had run right past me and didn't say nothin'.

"Don't be such a baby, Joey. 'Sides, you won't be the youngest much longer."

I didn't know if I liked that idea or not. I enjoyed being held on Mama's and Papa's laps, although I did have to admit that lately, Papa's had been a lot more comfortable. Mama's stomach stuck out too far and during the last while, she claimed to have a backache and said she couldn't hold me.

"Come on," Jerry said, "let's watch for the stork."

"Hey, Jerry, how come the doctor comes way out here if that old stork brings the baby?"

He shrugged again. "I don't know."

"You suppose maybe Maureen is right? I mean about the doctor bringing 'em?"

"Did you see any baby when he went in?"

I thought for a minute. "No. All he carried was a little bag. A little black bag."

"See? What do girls know?"

"What if the baby was in the bag?"

Jerry laughed. "I suppose it's all folded up and has to be blown up like a inner tube."

I felt foolish. I guessed Jerry was right all along. After all, Papa had told him about the stork.

Then, we heard it. A cry. *A baby's cry.* We had a new baby in the family.

"Did you see the stork?" I asked in a hoarse whisper, scanning the cloudless skies at the same time.

Jerry shook his head. "Darn thing is pretty tricky, huh?"

"I guess so." I inwardly marvelled at the fact that a bird big enough to carry a baby could come by and get away without being seen. Maybe Maureen had something in what she thought, after all.

She suddenly showed up at the kitchen door and called us inside. "You can go in and see Mama for a minute and take a look at your new baby sister."

"*Baby sister?*" Jerry and I said together. Although we hadn't talked about it, I think we both wanted a brother. We never once thought it might be a girl. Another girl. Another Maureen? Oh boy!

We went into Mama and Papa's first floor bedroom and tiptoed up to the side of the bed. Mama looked tired but she was smiling like she usually did on Christmas morning. The doctor left and Papa went with him to the kitchen.

Mama sat up a little and pulled the blanket back from the baby's face. Boy, was she ugly--all wrinkled and red. But at least she wasn't crying anymore. Maybe Jerry *had* solved the mystery of the way the baby got there. Darn old Maureen was probably right about the doctor bringing the baby and Jerry had hit the solution as to where it had been when the doctor arrived. In the little bag, all folded up, waiting to be inflated like a tire on Papa's Model A.

"What do you think of your new sister, boys?" Mama asked softly.

"She's real nice, Mama, " Jerry said, staring at the little red face .

"Joey? What do you think? "

"She ain't very pretty for a girl. How come you didn't get a boy, Mama?"

Mama smiled at me and then I happened to notice something. Mama wasn't very fat anymore. what had happened? How could that be? I saw her earlier in the morning and she still had a big fat stomach. Now her frontside was almost flat. What could--? I stopped.

Jerry took my hand and led me from the room. I pulled back for one more peek at Mama. Could the baby have been in-- Naw, that was impossible. Besides, how could it have gotten in there? And how could it have gotten out?

I went outside and watched Doctor White's car turn onto the road. I swore never to tell Jerry or Maureen what I had thought about in the bedroom. The last thing I wanted was to have them laughing at me. I know they would have.

The Chrysler Airflow of the '30s was too much of a change for the times. (Author's collection)

Maggie and Jiggs' little-known son "Sonny". (Author's collection)

The Illinois Central's "Land of Corn" carried many students home for Easter vacation. (Author's collection)

The author sold "Collier's Magazine" and won the Sentinel Junior First Aid Kit. (Author's collection)

One of the great baseball teams formed by Dubuque players. (Contributed)

Duke Zalenski was at the throttle of the train that brought the Liberty Bell to Dubuque. (Author's collection)

Soldiers left for WWI from all the passenger stations, including The Chicago Great Western's. (Author's collections)

View of the Ice Harbor from the Hotel Julien's roof. (Author's collection)

SEPTEMBER

Remember when there were quite a few hotels in the "Key City"? There were no motels as we have today, but there were a few cabin courts nestled around the city limits, offering individual cabins to weary travelers.

While we have four bonafide hotels today, Dubuque in the past sported no less than 14 hotels. At various times in the past, there were probably more, but half a century ago, there were 14 such establishments .

Other than the two carryovers from that time, The Julien Motor Inn and the Canfield, the Colonial offered a home-like atmosphere at 883 Bluff Street, where the offices of the *Telegraph Herald* are today. In some ways, the Colonial was more of a rooming house, but it was still advertised as a hotel.

There were others that had just as impressive names. The Bel-Marr Hotel at 323 Main Street and the Shea Hotel at 401 Locust Street come to mind. Blum's Hotel was at 524 Central Avenue and the Park Hotel did business at 84 Main Street.

The Iowa Hotel carried a similar address at 84 Locust Street and the Garfield Hotel, located at 511 Garfield Avenue, stayed in business for quite some time. The Page Hotel at 75 East 4th Street stayed in business for a long time after 1942 and its restaurant, the Back Page, offered great food.

The Brunswick Hotel at 3203 Jackson Street, eventually became more of a boarding house and then converted to apartments while a tavern on the first floor continues to do business at that site today.

The wrecking ball got the Central Hotel and Drive Line stands in its place at 1006 Central Avenue. Near the end of the gone-and-probably-forgotten-forever list of hotels in Dubuque is the Merchants Hotel. It hung in there longer than most of them and went out of business not too long ago. Finally, there was the "infamous" St. George Hotel that had the "friendliest" little bar in the back room.

Remember when most of the movie theaters were in downtown Dubuque? And there were actually two neighborhood theaters that did a thriving business until the one-eyed idiot box came into its own in the late 1950s?

Of course the question is, "Do you remember their names?" Another good one is, "Do you remember what happened to each one of them?" To start out, we'll mention the Grand and the Orpheum (the latter at one time was called the Majestic) because they're still around--not as movie theaters but as legitimate theaters. That in itself is a gigantic plus for the city.

The most recent to be removed from the scene, was the Strand. The Strand started life as a church and was converted (pun?) to a theater under which guise it did business as a second-run movie house on the corner of 12th and Main Streets. It burned in the '80s and was never rebuilt. Today, a parking lot has taken its place.

The State Theater was the haven for Saturday afternoon matinee fans and was involved in the fire that took out a lot of the 900 block on Main Street's east side. The Avon, which stood between the American Trust and Savings Bank and the J.C.Penney's store on the west side of the 800 block of Main Street and was originally called the Princess, had a few first run "A" movies but specialized most of the time in "B" movies. Its space was absorbed by the J.C.Penney store when that establishment expanded.

One of the two neighborhood theaters was the Capitol on the corner of 22nd Street and Central Avenue, where the parking lot for a drug store is today. The Capitol was a fun place to go for its double features. In fact, with the exception of the Grand Theater, all of the movie houses in Dubuque offered double bills most of the time. The last theater was the Varsity, and until the new complexes were built on the west side of town, it was the newest motion picture theater in Dubuque. Today, people do their laudry in a laundromat where the Varsity once welcomed movie goers. At one time, the Dreamland Theater was in the old Hollywood Grill and matinees started a 5 cents and there were others in the distant past.

Remember when is going to take a look or better yet, a listen to some sounds from the past that are heard infrequently today. In some examples, they haven't been heard at all for many years.

Remember when there were certain noises all around you, if you happened to live in the city? The sound, for instance, of a circular "buzz" saw, which was powered in most instances, by a Model T or Model A auotmobile engine. The saw blade, which seemed huge to a kid of eight or nine, was about three feet or so across, and was used to cut firewood for the approaching winter. Old railroad ties, fence posts, and anything else that would burn and needed cutting up to fit in the furnace, wound up as fodder for the saw blade. Those many teeth would zing into a piece of old wood and whip through it like a hot knife through butter on a warm July day. Several nieghbors would join together, hire the man who owned the "saw rig" and gather the wood that was to be cut. The song of that blade accompanied the shouts of children playing many a summer evening.

Remember when screen doors squeaked? That was one of the friendliest sounds imaginable. The spring would be pulled tight and make that lovely yet objecting, squeaking sound. When it was released, the door slammed shut, punctuating the coiled spring's serenade.

Remember when houses had front porches and those same front porches had swings, large enough for two or three adults? The heavier the load the sweeter the sound of protest from the hooks embedded in the porch ceiling and the chains that held the swing itself. There was another sound that accompanied the swing's groans and moans. Talk. People, neighbors usually, carrying on conversations about this, that and the other thing. Both sounds are seldom heard today and that is unfortunate.

Remember when kids called for one another? They'd stand in front of the house or near the back door and yell--it was really more of a calling moan, "Baw--ob? Baw--ob?" or whatever the name was of the resident kid. Someplace, somewhere, the rule governing that behavior, was written and protected until the day of television intervened. Sections of this rule clearly stated: "Do not approach the house within 20 feet or call ahead on the telephone. Do not knock and ask for whoever is being summoned for some fun outside." Of course, a lot of families didn't have the telephone. No matter. The law was the law and it had to be obeyed.

Remember when deep-throated toots came from the many river boats plying the waters of the mighty Miss with their barges? No claxtons on board those beauties, thank you very much--just beautiful sounding three to six toned steam whistles .

Remember when before air conditioning became so readily available, the summer wind would moan around the corner of your house and whistle through screened-in windows and doors? Seldom heard today because of our creature comforts.

Remember when a Model A Ford would rock and roll down the street to the accompaniment of its "burping-to-sewing machine," four-cylinder motor?

Remember when kids roller-skated on steel wheels along the sidewalks of neighborhoods? There's a sound that's been gone for many years.

Remember when an inventive boy or girl would take their one remaining skate ("I don't know what happened to the other one, Ma, really. I don't. It' s lost. ") and make a skate scooter? The frame of this sidewalk vehicle and sometimes in-the-street vehicle, was nothing more than a hunk of 2 x 4 lumber about two and a half to three feet long. The skate was taken apart and the straps and heel and toe clamps removed before the two halves were nailed, screwed or bolted to the bottom of the frame. The top was a wooden orange crate that was nailed in place and fitted with two wooden handles on top. There isn't another sound on earth that begins to match that one and I doubt if it could be duplicated unless all the necessary components were available. The orange crate was the secret. The metal wheels with ball bearings made enough noise just like skates, but amplified through the orange crate? Wow! Believe me, a saint would have had a hard time getting through to heaven praying with that racket blasting through the neighborhood. Concentrate for a minute. Can you hear one coming down the sidewalk, going hell-bent for leather? Picture if you will, a kid, maybe ten years old, pumping with one leg, propelling that noisy contraption along the sidewalk. If you can, more than likely you did the same thing. Maybe that kid you're mentally envisioning, is you.

Remember when school would start and your mother would drag you down town to get a few new clothes and school supplies? No sir. There were no grade school uniforms way back then. Not in the '30s and '40s. Those who were going to attend any of the Catholic high schools, found themselves confronted with the problem of uniforms or let's-all-look-alike and try to be the same. No. That's not fair. The uniform complicated the lives of those who had to wear them in a very small way. Those guys electing to attend Loras Academy found themselves being told: No jeans in your freshman year. Slacks and shirt and good shoes." Well, there were some who could afford that and those who couldn't. The high, high tuition in those days at the Academy ran to somewhere around $42.50--per semester--and that was for the privilege of wearing an R.O.T.C. uniform. Cry because of inflation today, but sometimes that price of $42.50 prevented a boy from going to Loras Academy and chose instead Senior High School. There--ah, heaven--there were no uniforms. Still, there were forages made to downtown Dubuque for new clothing for the high school student attending Senior as well.

The only reason I know the tuition, is that I own a City Directory from 1942 and the ad that Loras College ran that year pointed out the cost. I don't recall at this moment, what the tuition was on the second hill at the college, but it wasn't much by today's standards. More on that later.

Remember when, during the first day of school, you saw kids you hadn't seen all summer? It was like a family reunion of sorts. Then, too, there were actually new kids or "the new kid" in your room in grade school. It was fun to meet someone from someplace else.

At any rate, I can remember meeting Bob Knopp, who today, is still with Medical Associates, when we were at Holy Ghost. Today, we're still friends. Then, too, I recall when Bob Hantelmann moved into Holy Ghost School. It sticks in my mind that he and his family came from St. Columbkille's school and parish. That was in second grade. And yes, Bob and I are still friends today. The two Bobs may deny it, but... My longest friendship is with Fred Uthe. Fred and I go back to 1937. To someone sixty or so, it's a lifetime.

Remember when, during the last few days before school was to start, you'd go fishing? You'd use something I haven't seen in quite a few years. Bamboo cane poles. Now there was up-to-date equipment. But, what difference? They worked. If you went with your dad or family, the poles were tied onto the car, depending on the appendages that stuck out here and there. Usually, they were tied to one side of the car, the left, since then, only Dad had to get in from the right-hand side and climb over to the driver's seat. Besides, it was safer getting out on that side in the event an emergency stop had to be made along the road. The butts of the poles were tied to the rear bumper and the middle of the poles were fastened to the protruding door handles. Remember how they stuck out? Then, the tips were brought around to be tied to either the headlight or the bumper. About 1936, '37, Ford models in those years and in the years to come, had their headlights built into the front fenders so the bumper was used. Chevrolets and other makes followed suit, but not until around the beginning of the '40s.

Now a cane pole might get you something in the Mississippi if you were lucky but cane poles, in my estimation, belonged on the backwaters of the river. Little streams that fed the Father of waters, had plenty of fish in them.

Bullheads, catfish or flatheads, blue gills, an occasional perch and bass. caught something for the table. Coming out of the depression wasn't all that much fun. During the '30s, times were tougher than old shoe leather. As a result, if the kids of the family went fishing and brought home a "mess" of bullheads or what-have-you, it was usually more than appreciated by their parents.

And isn't that an interesting expression--a "mess " of bullheads . Of course "mess" in the Armed Services, deals directly with food: mess hall, mess sergeant, mess kit, mess and so on. Whoops, wrong subject. That stuff belongs in "What's the Difference?" a syndicated word column I used to write.

Remember when, as a young man, you were all slickered up for a date with a girl? You were going to a movie or dance and you wanted to present your best face and appearance. Even way back then, we were told to make sure our breaths were fresh and agreeable. So what was the last things the guy did before knocking on the door? He rubbed each shoe on the back of his pants leg, to make certain the leather was at its highest shine. Then he dropped his attention to his front. Yup. The front of his shirt was tucked in, and the zipper was in place. Then, he dipped into his shirt pocket and pulled out an envelope not much bigger than a couple of postage stamps in size. He tore off a corner and shook out several tiny squares of something and popped them in his mouth. Ah, yes. Sen-sen. It would make certain his breath was sweet all evening . Inside, the girl was probably doing something quite similar. Weren' t those the days?

Remember when there were one-room schoolhouses dotting the countryside? While I never attended one, my wife, Kathy, did and when she reminisces about her years there, I feel envious. In country schools, there was one teacher for all nine grades. Enrollment varied according to the number of eligible school-age children in the district and a school could have anywhere from just a few to as many as perhaps twenty.

There was no running water and in some instances the students brought their own supply from home. If there happened to be a well of sorts on the school grounds, that water was used. There could be a water cooler made of baked and glazed clay that had a spigot or it might just be a simple crock that held the daily supply. Since there was no running water the way we know it today, there was no indoor plumbing, which meant there were twin outhouses to the side or in the back of the schoolhouse itself.

A potbellied stove stood somewhere close to the center of the small building to give heat to each corner--as much as possible.

Being a teacher in a country school meant more than just teaching . In addition to seeing that lessons were learned and homework finished, the schoolteacher also had to be janitor and see to it that the fire was going long before the students arrived to make certain the building was as warm as possible before school started. She or he also made certain that games were played during recess and the noon hour. Nurse and cleaning lady or man rounded out the job description.

There was no such thing as a hot lunch program and food was brought by each child from their home and eaten during lunch times. Usually, lunch was carried in gallon-sized tin pails. On occasion, a raw potato was included and then baked on the coals of the fire in the stove.

Those were the days of homemade bread sandwiches, slathered with home-made butter and a hunk of home-smoked ham or beef or jelly between thick-cut slices.

Other than the homeyness of such a school, the thing that impressed me most was the ability of the teacher to "float" from one grade to the next without missing a tick. The older children helped the younger ones, while the teacher would be engaged with a third group. That's a brand of togetherness that is seldom found today in any walk of life--most especially in schools. Today, a child should almost be armed in some communities, if they hope to reach home safely.

There were no school buses, and children walked or maybe in some rare instances, rode a horse. A few might have been given rides, but all things considered, it made for better people.

Those who received their elementary education in such schools have memories that no one else has or can ever have. Once they're gone, the memories are gone forever. That's a shame. In many ways, life in America began changing when the one-room schoolhouse went the way of the dinosaur. Whether it changed for the good or not still remains to be seen.

Was the quality of education good? When my wife was in the eighth grade, her teacher wanted her to go to the National Spelling Bee Finals that were held in Washington, D.C. That should prove something.

Remember when there was a playground where the "old" city garage was located? The "powers that were'" at the time, built a swimming pool on that block where the correctional facility is located today. But, the "powers" goofed royally and the drain for the pool wound up below the level of the sewer. Well, nobody in their right mind wanted to swim in that mess. Yuck!

Remember when a penny could buy a whole lot of sweet flavor? I'm referring to penny candy, which depended for the most part, on the momentary generosity of the grocer or druggist in question. If he or she were in a good mood, the child pressing a runny nose against the glass case, might get a couple of extra pieces for that penny.

Remember when there were such things as two-holers? While they disappeared first in the cities, they existed on farms into the '30s, '40s and '50s. There was nothing worse than a call of nature in the middle of the night in January and the temperature might be hovering around zero or even lower. The routine was simple. Get up. Get dressed. Put on your coat and boots or galoshes. Light the lantern, if it were dark outside, and there was no moonlight reflecting enough off the snow to show the way. Run through the darkness. Do what you went for and return as quickly as possible to bed. If you were fast enough, and remembered to pull the bed covers up, your spot might still be a bit on the warm side.

Remember when there were such things as chamber pots? Those could be used in certain instances rather than going for a midnight ice-cold run outside. Of course they had to be cleaned the next morning. Now, aren't you thankful for indoor plumbing? Remember the Sears, Roebuck and Montgomery Ward catalogues used for tissue in those outhouses? And newspapers, as well. I'm sure no one would want to return to those outdoor privies for any reason. I do know of one in Galena, that was a two-story, six-holer, that was built onto the back or side porch of one of the houses there.

Remember when a lot of house yards, both in the country and in town were enclosed with decorative wire fencing and gates?

Remember when some garages that had dirt floors also had grease pits dug into them so the owner could change his own oil and grease the car without jacking it up. Ours had one when I was a kid.

Remember when most houses in town had a wood shed? Lessons were, on occasion taught there when a youngster stepped out of line too far and wouldn't listen to reason or his or her parents. For the most part such children turned out to be pretty darn good citizens.

Remember when Dubuque had no regular garbage pickup in the '30s and '40s, and the city officials gave out contracts to Dubuquers and farmers to pick up the garbage? True. I recall different contractors going through our alley, picking up the garbage. Why? They fed the garbage to their pigs. The city did pick up the trash or rubbish, whatever you want to call it. See, in those days, we didn't have regulations regulating regulations to make certain the regulations wouldn't hurt, harm or bother anyone. Things then were a lot simpler, a lot slower and a lot less regulated and we all survived.

Remember when Frith's Rendering Works operated north of Dubuque in Couler Valley? The smell was not much to be sought after and could really be offensive at times--especially when a northerly breeze floated through Dubuque. Now that's a memory nobody will enjoy recalling, I'm willing to bet. But it is a memory of Dubuque, nevertheless.

Remember when it wasn't against the law to raise chickens in town? Quite a few people, including my grandmother, Theresa Butlett Tigges, had a small flock. She picked up eggs twice a day from her three dozen chickens or so and had regular customers for fresh eggs.

Remember when it was customary to go to one of the bakeries in town? You could choose from Humke's, Holsum, Reinold Dietzold , Jungk's , Moes', Schute's , The Stop and Shop Bakery, Sutter's and Trausch's Retail Outlet. Those places were busy on Saturday mornings, especially when sweet rolls were going to be on the breakfast menu after church services, the next day.

Remember when families would go on picnics? Not in the city parks so much as going out into the countryside and finding a shady hillside. Spread a blanket and bring on the cold, fried chicken and the rest of the trimmings.

Remember when I mentioned that the B-25 bomber used in World War II, was different from every other plane used by the United States. The question was: How was it different? Well, and you might know it would be a former B-25 pilot who wrote to me and said that, it was the only plane named for a person--Billy Mitchell. Mitchell had been a general in the fledgling U.S. Army Air Corps and proved the experts wrong when a squadron of bi-plane bombers of the fledgling Air Corps, blew a captured German battleship out of the water. Mitchell was so far ahead of everyone else in his thinking, in the late '20s and early '30s. He predicted that Japan would attack the United States and that it would be Hawaii that would be bombed from the air. Lot of good that warning did. The Army hierarchy decided General Billy Mitchell was a troublemaker, tried and court martialed him and, well as they say, the rest is history. The former B-25 jockey is Ray Dominy. He also flew the B-17. He racked up 150-200 hours in B-25s at Columbia, S.C. Air Force Base.

Remember when the subject was A&P stores? Well, several people from the hill area around Nativity Church, gently reminded me that there had been an A&P at 1085 University prior to the 1930s (before my time, by golly). Subsequent businesses that followed were Kalmes ' Tavern and Moes ' Bakery, a deli and on and on.

Another person asked me to mention "Fishhook" Henry who was a ragman. Fishhook would buy rags from housewives and a lot of other junk. To let the women know he was in the neighborhood, he carried with him a long horn and would blow it every once in a while.

Remember when during World War II, any family with a son, husband or brother in the service would look forward eagerly to the arrival of the mailman. If there was a letter from overseas, it was not the same type letter a person could expect to receive from say a cousin who lived in Weed, New Mexico. The letter would be a V-mail letter. I'll try to explain.

To cut down on the weight of all those letters being passed back and forth over the two oceans, someone used their heads (and isn't that a refreshing thought when one considers that the someone was in the employ of the government?) and suggested photographing mail and instead of tons of letters, there'd be only pounds of film. It took a specially designed envelope that opened with four flaps, one on each side of the writing page. The letter would be written and the flaps closed, the address added, and then mailed. The address was photographed, the envelope opened and the letter photographed, the letter discarded and on to the next one. When it reached the United States, the film would be developed, a picture of the letter enlarged, the address applied to the sealed letter and sent on its way to the recipient. People writing to their "boy" or "girl" overseas could buy V-mail envelopes at most retail outlets and dime stores and do the same to communicate with their loved ones.

And while we're dwelling a bit on World War II, remember when "Woolworth carriers" were used. Woolworth whats?

Can you name the Intercity Bus Companies that operated through or out of Dubuque in the early '40s? Answers later.

Remember when a good solid education didn't carry astronomical fees and tuitions? Would you believe a semester in the early 1940s at Loras Academy cost $42.50 or $85.00 a year? That was $340.00 for four years if you graduated in 1946. Then, if the spirit was willing and the money available, an Academy grad moved up to the next hill. There it cost $87.50 per semester or $175.00 a year at Loras College. When he graduated in 1950, his college tuition would have run $700.00. With the previously mentioned $340.00, all of $1,040.00 was the total tuition. That much today would get maybe an activity ticket, or a couple of weeks (maybe) at a private school. And state-run schools aren't much better today considering living costs and such. Oh, well. It was just as tough to come up with $1,040.00 for eight years in the 1940s as it is the thousands and thousands of dollars today's crop of college-bound kids have to face.

Remember when streets were virtually deserted for lack of cars and kids could play in a neighborhood street? Nor was it a big deal walking to school.

Remember when Duke Langanis, who has maintained the original Greek spelling of his family's name, wrote a lot about his father in his 1996 letter to me? Tom Langas opened the Victory Cafe sometime in 1944. He apparently took over the building when George Petrakis, who operated a cafe there earlier, moved to a bigger location. Tom's cafe had eight or ten stools, two tables and a booth in the center and four to six booths on the side opposite the counter. Tom cooked and Duke's mother, brothers and sister tended to the rest. The Victory Cafe closed in late '57 or early '58.

Duke also mentioned that their chili dogs were so popular with the Hubba Hubba tavern patrons on Friday and Saturday nights, that the Langases could hardly fill the orders. On those nights, Johnny Kane hired Harley Grant to liven up the place.

Tom Langas was the type of man who could never say no to a hungry person and fed many who couldn't pay. When George Arvanitis, who later owned the Busy Bee Cafe, came to the United States from Greece and settled in Dubuque, Tom always made certain he had enough to eat. Duke stated in his letter that: "...in those days, no one ever went away hungry." Duke served in the Navy during the Korean Police Action and when he separated, enlisted in the Army. Today, he's retired.

Remember when Belsky's Buick/Cadillac dealership was across Eighth Avenue from the Victory Cafe?

Remember when there was a very small restaurant at 817 Central. It was very small, very tiny and called Minute Lunch. I'm not certain if Minute referred to the span of time it took to be served or to the size of the operation.

Remember when, while walking through one of the downtown five and dime stores such as Neisner's or Woolworth's or Kresge's, a silver-tongued salesman or saleswoman on occasion, would enrapture a small gathering of potential customers from the ranks of the casual shoppers and hawk a new brand of silver polish or furniture polish or scratch remover or spot remover or floor wax or some gimmick that would revolutionize the lives of every living breathing human being on the face of the earth? Lordy, how they could talk. Normally, and without being aware of it, kids from maybe seven to 12 years of age would crowd around the counter and be in the first row. The adults--the potential customers, were held back by innocence for a while until the sales person got peeved and ordered the kids away. If some of them had their parents standing behind them, a possible sale was immediately driven away. Served the huckster right. But that's an aspect that has disappeared from the business place forever--I hope. Instead, they're on television today. And not in just 30 second or 60 second spots. They're called *infomercials*, and last 30-60 minutes. And don't you hate people who screw with the English language to that extent. Does anyone ever watch those things?

Remember when we did the Burma Shave signs. Want a couple more? I'm glad you agreed. Within this vale/Of toil and sin/Your head grows bald/But not your chin/Burma Shave. Another? Why not? Are your whiskers/when you wake/Tougher than/A two-bit steak?/Burma Shave. And finally one for the road. (I know it's corny and has been used before but it fits these darn things!) A silky cheek/Shaved smooth and clean/Is not obtained/With a mowing machine/ Burma Shave. Besides, that would hurt like all get out.

Remember when drug stores and grocery stores sold mysterious boxes wrapped in plain brown or gray paper with a "K" or an "M" scribbled on them? Kotex and Modess sanitary pads were not to be flagrantly displayed, lest children be scandalized or husband embarrassed if "forced" to purchase a box for "the wife." Today, take a look at the blatant advertising on TV for the similar myriad products. Have we come a long way, or what?

THE GREAT CIRCLE ROUTE

"Dad, there's a sock hop Friday night at school. May I have the car and ten dollars?" If there are teenagers in your house, it's certain you've heard that request or will shortly in the event they're just learning to drive. If you have teenagers of your own, it's absolutely certain you've been one yourself at some, cloudy moment in your past life. If you were a teenager during the late '40s and early '50s, you know for a fact there were no sock hops then. There were mixers, however. And, there were no places like Alakazaz, Tale n' Ale, or the Super Market. But, there was Diamonds--The Triangle--and the Hollywood Grill.

The differences between a teenager then and being one now, are myriad. Most parents, at one time or another, will have a particular memory triggered by a request their children may make of them. The above question could be answered with, "You know, when I was your age, I walked. I wouldn't dare ask my dad for the family car just to drive downtown to do whatever." Then follows a tirade of what was done for entertainment "when I was young," which is supposed to make the young adult entering the plea for the family automobile, fall back and re-evaluate his entire life style and all of the mores which have developed in the last 40 years or so. Most parents know it is to no avail but they like to relive their own memories.

Let's go back to those mixers. That expression will probably have to be explained to those teens not familiar with it. It was a dance, usually sponsored by a school or church, whose sole purpose was to mix together teenagers of the opposite sex in a situation where they could learn the niceties of social dignity, decorum and aplomb. Probably the best and most current mixer in the '40s and '50s was the Friday night NYO dance put on under the auspices of the Nativity Youth Organization. There were certain, unwritten rules for the teens of yesteryear to abide by and made about as much sense as any set of laws purposely written on paper by a committee of idiots.

The first rule was simplicity itself. It destroyed the reason for the dance. Remember? Mixing? Rule one: The boys stand on one side of the hall and girls on the other, the middle is definitely a no-man's land where dancing may be conducted after several hours of scouting the field. To an outsider who was unaware of rule one, it would appear as though he had just walked in right after a big brawl between the sexes and the opposing sides had fallen back, regrouping to take inventory of the wounded and so on. It's been said the same rule applies in certain instances even today. Do you have any idea who thought it up?

Rule Two was a little more complicated: Always scout a prospective partner for at least 20 to 30 minutes before approaching and asking for the next dance. Circle the floor and study every angle or curve as the case demanded. It seems to be an inborn trait in humans to mistrust their own eyes when beholding something. Rule Two was usually conducted something like this: First a guy would spot a young lady across the darkened hall. The room was kept dark for a reason because the sponsors wanted to hold down the overhead as much as possible and used as few as three light bulbs--a 40 watt at each end and a 100 watt at the door to make certain the admissions were collected. The other expense involved, was the record player blasting at one end of the hall.

The young swain would spot what he thought was a likely candidate and would study her at long distance for the required length of time. The girls were smart, since they did not turn in such a way so every aspect could be viewed from one angle thus causing the GREAT CIRCLE ROUTE to be invented. The route entailed the young man walking nonchalantly around the perimeter of the hall so he could, unobserved, casually pass by his future dancing partner.

The girl, meantime, was not idle. She would be standing with her back to the boys' wall but usually had a girl friend standing in front of her who would keep her apprised of the boy's actions. The very guy who had selected her out of all those other beauties was also being watched by his chosen one's friend.

When the young man neared, the girl's friend would tell her of his progress and the two of them would turn, thus keeping the target's back to the hunter. This little game would continue until he would enlist the aid of several buddies who would then approach from different angles. Defeated, the girl would settle back and wait until the guy got the reports from his friends as to appearance, smile, eyes, and anything else important. Then, armed with the knowledge that she was perfectly acceptable as a dance partner, he would approach the young lady. Which brings us to rule three.

Rule Three: All girls from good looking to beautiful must hang around those poor, unfortunates who are categorized from not-so-good-looking to YEEECH!

The reason was obvious when the two girls would be compared. However, the one barrier which seemed to be completely insurmountable was the better-looking half of the duo would insist she could not leave her not-so-attractive partner standing alone. Therefore, she would not be able to dance with the boy asking her until there was someone available to swing her partner across the floor .

Rule Four: Be persuasive, inventive and devious in solving any problem, such as Rule Three, by any and all means at your disposal. The most logical thing to do when Rule Three reared itself, was to find a partner for the lesser beauty. But that usually presented a problem since most teens at the time did not know the meaning of the word masochist. The best solution was the stag line which was comprised of boys who came every Friday night, leaned against the far wall at the spot of their choice, watched the evening's proceedings, helped by circling a prospective partner for a friend, if asked, and going home alone. Only on rare occasions would one of those wall supports get up the courage to ask a girl to dance--usually in their senior year in high school--after three years of leaning. There were spots on the wall where the paint had been worn off by steady customers.

With a fair amount of asking, probably termed more properly, begging, and in some rare instances, if the girl was particularly unattractive, bribery, a partner was obtained . Then, rule three having been adhered to, the dance was consummated and all would end well.

What did the young people of the '40s and '50s do on Saturday or Sunday afternoons and evenings or after a basketball or football game? Why go to Diamonds or the Triangle or the Hollywood. What else? Since Urban Renewal saw fit to remove those edifices of loafing, those monuments to "coke days," those memory-filled piles of brick, their locations should be mentioned in passing. Diamonds' Cafeteria was located where The Book Nook was established, on the corner of Ninth and Main and where AAA Travel Agency once operated, had dark, wooden booths which could hold six easily and there were occasions when as many as eight squeezed into one. It was a perfect place to meet the "gang." The Triangle Cafe was a couple of doors north on the same side and, although the cafe was brighter, it had some dandy little two-people booths for that private tete-a-tete. Four blocks to the south, again on the same side of the street, stood the Hollywood Grill. The Hollywood sort of fell in between the lighting of the cafeteria and the cafe. It, too, had some two people booths but if there were more than six in a party, and if you were ever in such a group, there was the big horseshoe booth right in front by one window. Remember? Today, nothing is on the corner of Fifth and Main but grass growing. Imagine, not even a marker--or is that really what the "Continuum" was supposed to commemorate?

Cokes were 15¢ plus a penny for the state. An order of French fries was 20 cents. For half a buck, a guy could order his date a coke and they could split an order of fries. If a young suitor could talk two bucks out of his father, he could afford to put between three and four gallons of gas into the tank of the family car, one fourth of it into his and his date's mouth and go home with half a buck.

Today, the modern counterpart probably has a job and doesn't have to mooch off his father. But, if he does, two dollars won't do it. It'll take five bucks or more to get the same amount of gas and a lot more to buy as much coke and fries. If he wants to go home with an equivalent amount of "bread" today as his father did way back when, he'll need at least one picture of George Washington and a little change.

So in case your teen will be asking for the car and a little traveling money soon, be prepared to fork over a ten spot.

Can you imagine what your grandchildren will ask of their parents?

"Dad, there's a barefoot stomp Friday night at school. May I have the car and 30 bucks? "

AN ACT OF KINDNESS
An Apocryphal Tale
As written by
John Tigges

They were a nice old couple, and they reminded me of everyone's idea of grandparents. The Lowes lived next door to my new home where I lived with Marcy, my wife and our great Dane, Grendl.

Mr. and Mrs.Lowe were good neighbors, and by that I mean they didn't bother us and we didn't bother them. Oh, we spoke whenever we saw one another but we didn't visit back and forth the way we might have, had we been closer in age.

Marcy and I had been married for only three years and our house, the last one on the lane, was an ideal place to raise children. Another year or so and we'd start our family. The Lowes were childless and I had seen them many times, fawning over their pet rabbit, Fluffy. I always felt sort of sorry for them whenever I saw them playing with it. And of course because of the rabbit, I usually kept Grendl chained to a long wire run, so he could exercise all he wanted.

My life sort of changed the day Mr. Lowe came over and knocked on our door. When I opened it, he said, "I was wondering if we could ask you a favor, Phil? My wife and I are planning on going on a few trips and we wondered if you' d sort of watch our place. The people you bought the house from, always did and we watched their place whenever they went on vacation."

Well, they had never once bothered us in any way and because they were a nice old couple, I said, "Of course, Mr. Lowe. Marcy 'n' I'll be happy to do that. When you leavin'?"

"Tomorrow morning--early--before the sun comes up. We always like to get a good start 'fore the traffic builds up too much."

"Sure, I'll watch your home. No problem."

"Oh, gosh. I almost forgot. You'll have to look in on Fluffy, too. She'll be in her hutch in the backyard. You won't have to feed her or anything. I've filled the hopper in back and the water pan, so it'll be enough to take care of her 'til we get back. But she's getting old and likes a little company."

"How long will you be gone?" I asked, suddenly wondering about being a rabbit sitter.

"Only a couple of days. We'll be back the day after tomorrow. Then in another week or so, we'll be going for about a week or ten days. Maybe you can watch the place then, too."

"Sure. No problem," I said. "Have a nice trip."

"Thanks, Phil. Say 'hello' to Marcy."

"I will."

He turned and left.

I told Marcy what was happening and she thought it was a good neighbor policy to watch each other's place when going on vacation or whatever.

Early the next morning, I heard some noise from next door and then subdued voices, and after another while, their car starting and leaving.

At 6:30 our alarm clock went off and it was then I heard the growling and snarling. I jumped out of bed and ran to the window. I suddenly thought of Grendl and the fact he might have gotten loose, or worse yet that some smaller dog or a cat had gotten too close to his run area and the Dane had grabbed it.

I was both wrong and right. No other animal had gotten close, but Grendl had gotten loose somehow and I could hear him snarling and growling, but I couldn't see him.

I hurriedly dressed and called Marcy. She got up and slipped into her robe, while I ran to the kitchen and looked out. There was no sign of Grendl. My heart skipped a beat and I ran outside. The sounds were coming from next door--from Lowes' back yard.

I hurried to the wooden fence that separated the two yards and looked over. I wanted to scream. The door to the hutch stood open and that stupid white rabbit had gotten out and Grendl, sensing it moving around, fought to break loose and succeeded.

Grendl had Fluffy by the back and was shaking her for all he was worth. Her legs and head flopped this way and that. There was no way the rabbit could still be alive. I hurried around to the gate and let myself into the yard.

I managed to get Grendl to drop the rabbit, and Marcy took him home. I picked up Fluffy . Amazingly enough, there was no blood, but Grendl had sure done a number on her. Her white coat was all dirty and black. What a way to die--being shaken to death .

Then I thought of the Lowes. What would I tell them? How *could* I tell them? They treated Fluffy almost like a child. Why hadn't they taken the darn thing with them?

I carried the dead rabbit home and asked Marcy, "What are we going to do?"

She shrugged. "I don't know. This is awful, Phil."

I looked closer at Fluffy. It was amazing all right--about the lack of blood, I mean. Grendl's teeth hadn't broken the skin. He was simply playing with a new toy. That was why there wasn't any blood. I pointed that out to Marcy.

Her face brightened. "I've got an idea."

I looked at her. "What?" What sort of idea could she have that would solve our awful problem?

"Let's shampoo the rabbit until it's as white as it normally is. We can blow dry it and then put it back in the hutch. The Lowes'll think she died a normal death--of old age."

I kissed her right then and there. What a wonderful, ingenious idea.

We set to work. In minutes we had one soggy, dead rabbit, but at least it was white. Marcy got her blow dryer and in a few more minutes we had a beautiful rabbit corpse.

"Looks perfect," I said and bent Fluffy's legs to make it look like she was just sort of sitting there when she passed on.

"It surely does."

"Now what?"

"Take it over and put it in the hutch. The Lowes won't be any the wiser."

"It surely does."

"Now what?"

"Take it over and put it in the hutch. The Lowes won't be any the wiser."

We watched for the Lowes' return but they didn't show until real late the next night, and Marcy and I were already asleep. About 11:00 p.m. we were awakened by a screech which was followed by a woof from Grendl. We sat up in bed.

"What was that?" Marcy asked.

"Darned if I know. Maybe a cat in heat. It doesn't seem to have bothered Grendl too much."

"You're probably right," she said and lay back.

In minutes we were both sound asleep.

I saw the Lowes' auto in the driveway when I got up and thought it best to wait a while before going over to "hear about" Fluffy's untimely demise. Before I could get dressed, I heard their car start and saw Mr. Lowe back out of their driveway and leave.

I decided it would be better if he were there when I went over. I sure didn't want to face Mrs. Lowe and have her crying and carrying on all over the place.

A little after sunset Mr. Lowe drove up alone and got out of his car. I knew I had to get it over with. I was about to see what sort of actor I was.

He saw me coming, and I thought he looked like death warmed over.

"Hi, Mr. Lowe. How was the trip?"

"Trip was fine, but we had an awful homecoming."

"How's that?"

"Well, sir, the morning we were going to leave, we went out to say goodbye to Fluffy and found her dead. Poor thing died of old age. I took her out to the back of the lot and buried her. When we got home, my wife found her back in the hutch. Mrs. Lowe couldn't stand the shock and--well, she's in the psychiatric ward at the county hospital."

OCTOBER

Remember when your mother would "build" a set of silver-plated flatware and other necessary pieces, from Betty Crocker? Betty Crocker gave the pieces away through coupons in her different flours and other items "she" sold. Today, however, some of those same salad forks that your Mom sent away for and Betty mailed to her, go for as high as $14.00 a piece. Knives can be between $16.00 and $18.00, while a tomato server is forty-two dollars. Who would've thought...? Obviously, not Betty Crocker, that's for certain.

Remember when it was a lot more economical for the family to "make" ice cream sodas at home than it was to go to the store and buy them? A quart of bulk pack vanilla ice cream and your favorite bottle of pop was all that was needed. Orange Crush or any flavored soft drink--root beer, Seven Up--one of the colas. Remember the huge and I mean huge advertising campaign that went on for years with Doctor Pepper? There were three times a day they suggested that a bottle of Doctor Pepper would hit the spot. Remember what they were? Sure you do. Ten a.m., 2:00 p.m. and four p.m. Ten, two and four.

Remember when we recalled certain sounds that are for all practical purposes, gone from our earshot forever. Things like a buzz saw cutting fire wood for a group of neighbors to see them through the cold winters of the thirties. Squeaking springs on screen doors and front porch swings moaning under the weight of two or more adults. Kids calling for one another and river boats galore belching out their calls on deep throated steam whistles. Wind moaning around the corner of a house and the peculiar sewing machine sound of a four cylinder Model A Ford' s engine. Roller skates on sidewalks and skate scooters and their attendant noises were "played back" in our memories.

Well, there are more.

Remember when, on a farm, roosters would greet the rising sun? Throughout the day, they continued their crowing, calling attention to their strutting sense of importance . And the hens paraded around the farm yard, "visiting" among themselves or bragging in satisfied cluckety- cluck-cluck-cluck-clucks about laying another egg? Very seldom heard today--even on farms--unless one goes to a chicken factory and--. Well, let's let it stop right there. It's just not the same.

Remember when, again on the farm, the pigs would eat all night long at their "automatic" feeders. They'd lift one lid with their noses, thrust their snout and whole head in and eat to their hearts' content. When they left that particular feeding station, the steel lid would fall, making a loud banging noise when it struck the steel base. If a farmer had 100 or 150 pigs and owned several feeders that had 16 to 20 feeding stations, the chow-down-all-nightlong-food orgy continued until right before dawn. Those sounds are never heard today considering there have been all sorts of advances made and pigs are fed on a timed basis.

Remember when, in the springtime, kids would meet in alleyways and any place where there might be bared dirt--clear enough to draw a circle on the ground--and shoot marbles? The gentle clicking of glass balls and clay ones or mibs, would be the only sound heard while the sharp-shooting, eagle-eyed boys and girls took aim. And they usually played for keeps.

Remember when, if you lived in the country and at a certain time each day, the sound of an airplane could be heard? The mail plane . Going from somewhere a way off to some other place--a way off. Mail planes followed railroad tracks and highways and well marked by-ways, making their appointed rounds. A person could really feel lonely, if that plane crossed over shortly before the sun went down and the day's work was finished, the evening meal's dishes washed and put away. It seemed as if you were the only person on the face of the earth. You and the pilot--and he was up in the air, sort of mocking you.

Remember when trains were pulled by steam locomotives? Their whistle, late at night, wailing through the countryside, like some unseen banshee, would filter through the dark for miles until it reached your open bedroom window. Somehow, that sound, however loud close up, when muted by distance, seemed to assure you that things were all right after all--that God was in his Heaven, and all was well with the world.

Remember when you were a kid, and the high point of any fall season was Halloween? I truly feel sorry for today's kids when they come to our front door and sing-song: "Tricks or Treats, money or eats." Why? Well, for one thing, don't ever tell them that you would prefer the tricks because they wouldn't have a clue as to what you were talking about. They do their little chant without listening to the words and as a result, 25 percent of the rhyme is wasted. Oh, they get their treats all right and it is usually money or eats and just how healthy is all that candy?

Remember when, while you were out doing the neighborhood for Halloween, you would do the same little verse about money or eats before you performed a trick or two? The whole idea was to earn your handouts. Remember? Sure you do.

You also knew that those six words could be turned to your advantage if the person on whom you called, didn't play the game. While today's little kids are taught to be more mercenary in their approach to Halloween, we were more or less left on our own and we concluded that a little revenge against the person who didn't give you a treat or money or eats, had a trick coming their way that would better educate them for the next year's romp through the black and terror-filled night.

Remember when the terror that came out of the night on Halloween came from you and was directed at those who didn't support your cause? Sure, that was the "two-edged sword chant" at work. If the people you called on didn't want to see you perform a trick, they asked for it anyway, since they weren't about to give you any rewards for doing nothing. All we wanted was a simple request. "Show me how high you can jump. " "Can you move that rocker on the porch?"

Remember when some of the tricks perpetrated as your mark of revenge-- a handful of corn thrown at someone's window just when they were about to settle in and resume listening to the radio or pick up where they left off in that novel they were reading, would unsettle anyone's nerves . It sounded like the window had smashed into a thousand pieces. Only the strong of heart would not react. And the weak-of-heart would sometimes swallow their gum or whatever. Served ' em right, too. The next time they'd know better and give to your cause. In time, bean blowers replaced the corn. In the days of the outdoor-plumbing outhouse, all it took were two or three husky sub-teens or teenagers, and over it went. Gates were easy targets and many wound up in someone's tree or on someone's garage or woodshed roof. In later days, the whimpy idea of soaping someone's windows came into vogue. Today, even that fun is denied the children for the most part.

Remember when you wore a home-made Halloween costume? There were girls dressed like boys and boys dressed like girls and women. There were more hoboes on the road on the night of Halloween than any other. Rarely did one see a store-bought costume. At least not in our neighborhood. Who could afford such frivolity?

Masks? Sure, the type that covered just the eyes and nothing more. No molded faces from Mars or someone's nightmares.

Remember when you worked hard on Halloween night to get your share of the wealth? By that I mean, the loot that was being passed out at the front doors of your neighborhood. There were no small Snickers bars or Baby Ruth or anything like that, which had been miniaturized just for Halloween. Then, since they were easy snacks, the companies in charge of dental cavities, decided they should be available the year around, and that's where we are today. But back then, you might get a rare nickel Baby Ruth or full size Snickers or Mars bar handed to you, and they were big then. No. My hand wasn't small by comparison. The candy bars of yesteryear were bigger for a nickel than the 50 cent jobs are today. But the main fare at the doors was more likely to be an apple or an orange or a banana. In the event traffic was heavier than usual, the fruit might be gone but you'd still get something.

I remember once, receiving a Pecan Log, which was a luxury as well as a very large hunk of candy, from a neighbor. I was late in getting there and they were out of everything and offered the Pecan Log to me. Did I refuse it? Did my parents raise any dumb kids?

Well, other than the smells of a cool autumn eve, when the ghosts and goblins were about, there wasn't much more to the Halloweens we had as kids, other than the parties we might be invited to or give. They were good days and nobody got hurt.

I still wonder who ran the fake ice cream cone up Holy Ghost School's flag pole every Halloween? The cone came from across the street at MacDonald's Ice Cream Shoppe. Every November 1st, Mac and Ben Roth stood muster, saluting a papier mache ice cream cone, flying at full mast.

Remember when there was a slough called Rafferty's? I know I've written about this earlier in the book, but if you're in your '50s and lived in Dubuque when you were a kid, you should remember the ball diamonds that existed where Sears built their store on South Locust back in the early '60s. Prior to 1935 or thereabout, the area was pretty much a backwater of the Mississippi and was home to a large dumping site that was inhabited by thousands of rats . Maus Lake is all that's left of the backwater area today. The rest had been filled in, in the late ' 20s and early ' 30s. Once solid ground was had with good f ill, the city recreation department built several ball diamonds on the site currently occupied by Eagle ' s new store and the old one, as well as a few other businesses I won' t take time to mention.

Down by Maus Lake, Moore's Mill stood against the bluff near where the new four-lane freeway is today.

Remember when Kerrigan Road was two lanes, and was called "the new road"? Why, you might ask? Well, Southern Avenue was the "old road" that wound up through the valley toward Grandview Avenue and ultimately to Rockdale and the Old Military Road . Another name for that particular street, was "Whiskey Hill," in reverent and irreverent memory (depending on one' s drinking habits at the time) of an incident involving a horse-drawn wagon loaded with full whiskey barrels and a loose end-gate. I shouldn't have to paint word pictures on that one, but the inevitable and the unthinkable both happened at once and residents of the area, depending again on their imbibing or non-imbibing nature, were out there with cups, bottles and anything else that would hold that amber-colored liquid. Whatever, it' s a nice story and a lot of hills, called Whiskey Hill, " with similar legends, are located throughout the country."

Main Streets had been a movie theater at one time? It was called "The Palace" and earlier, I believe, it was named "The Dreamland." Of course it carried a nickname delast sounds so uppity doesn't of the cowboy shoot-'em-up westerns and cliff-hanging serials of the day--"The Bloody Bucket." In later years, once the Hollywood Grill came into existence, that particular nickname was spread to "The Capitol" movie theater on 22nd and Central Avenue, where the Hartig-Snyder Drug Store parking lot is today. I believe the Varsity

Remember when a person could polish their teeth with Doctor Lyon's Tooth Powder? Remember Teel? Sure you do. Teel. The red liquid that came in a strangely-shaped bottle that looked like an over-grown, inverted glass golf tee? A person dribbled a little of the liquid onto the tooth brush and in seconds, you' d have foam in your mouth while you brushed. I wonder what they put in that stuff to make it do that? I don' t go shopping with my wife much, when I do, I don't stand around the drug items and study labels, checking to see how many different kinds of toothpaste are on the market. Is Ipana still available? I was always concerned that I'd wind up with buck teeth like Bucky Beaver. Remember: *Brusha--Brusha* and so on? What about Pepsodent? *You' ll wonder where the yellow went when you brush your teeth with Pepsodent.*

And the Listerine folks still make toothpaste, and they still make the mouthwash but back a ways it was only natural that company would get into the toothpaste end of things that go in the mouth. Of course, they also make toothbrushes.

Remember when every backyard had a cistern, which caught rainwater through the down spouts from the house, and had a pump of some sort above, to bring that pure soft water up to ground level and into the house. A person couldn't beat that water for washing hair or washing out fragile sweaters or ladies' dainties. Naturally, a way back then, the rain was acid free and any bits of debris from the roof, sank to the bottom of the cistern. Crank-type-water lifts brought the water up in small metal cups hooked to very economical to make wiumps worked the way all pumps do, lifting the water through a suction and valve principle.

Remember when young married couples were given a "shivaree"? I 'm willing to bet money there are a lot of readers out there under the age of 40 or 45, who th a beef bone just like the ve. It comes from the French word "charivari" and means to serenade with a lot of noise. If the married couple could afford a honeymoon, the shivaree took place one of the first nights they were back. Pots and pans and bells of any sort, car horns and whatever made any sort of loud noise, were brought together, the perpetrators sneaking up to the front or back door, wherever the lights were on. Sometimes, the crowd would wait until the house was dark. On a given signal, all bedlam broke loose. Depending on the wealth of the couple involved, the younger shivaree participants were given money. But

most of the time, the perpetrators brought food and beer and an impromptu party was held right then and there. Today, it seems more likely for a group of people to get together and set up a pool to see how long the marriage will last--not the way it is today.
It's a shame that some of the simpler things in life have gone by the wayside.

Remember when one of the big moments connected with the Sunday comic strips for little girls, and I guess some big ones as well, was looking for "Boots and her Buddies"? Why? Because almost every Sunday there were cut-out shapes of dresses and swimsuits and a paper doll of Boots and on rare occasion, Pug, her kid sister. The doll was printed in a particular pose and the wardrobe would fit that figure. Small white tabs strategically placed, allowed the dresses to be put on the doll. If there was a bottle of mucilage or tube of glue handy, the doll could be fixed to a more firm piece of paper or thin cardboard and cut out again. Such clothing gimmicks appeared with "Jane Arden," "Tillie, the Toiler" and other comic strips.

By the way, congratulations to Jim Schroeder and the others who gave the names of the Aleutian Islands held by the Japanese during World War II. The islands of Attu and Kiska were occupied by the Japanese for a while. They decided that the elements and the islands that were already held by American troops were too much of an obstacle to overcome and quit.

I do like those Burma Shave sign rhymes. Spring has sprung/The grass has riz/Where last year's/Careless driver is/Burma Shave. See. They can be almost philosophical as well as entertaining.

While people sent rhymes to Burma Shave by the carload, Jazbo of old Dubuque made a ton of money with some of his "Quickies." Jazbo wrote:

KNOWLEDGE
Sooner or later
Each of us learns
No man can have life
On his very own terms!

And isn't that the truth.

Remember when way back when, if you lived on or visited a farro and it was Monday and the sun was shining, it was wash day? I remember awakening to the putt-putt sound of my grandmother's washing machine, which was run by a small gas/oil engine.

It smoked and it belched and burped while it continued running until all of the bed sheets and white shirts and underthings were finished before the colored clothes went in. Last came the shirts and overalls that had seen a lot of dirty work during the week.

The clean clothes were hung on wire clothes lines and propped up with long saplings that had a small fork at the end to help sustain the weight of the wet clothes. Those clothes would snap in the wind when it blew. I can't come up with anything that smells better than laundry that's been washed and dried outside.

And what did they do in the winter? The same thing, with one exception. Most of the laundry was pretty stiff when it was brought inside to be ironed with a gas-powered iron.

Remember when I asked if anyone knew what a "Woolworth carrier" was? I had a couple of tries but no one knew. During World War II, some carriers were built to perform escort service. They weighed between 7,000 and 12,000 tons and were limited to 20 knots in the speed department.

They were built using the prefabrication method and carried 20 fighters and torpedo bombers. The "Woolworth carriers" were also used in landing operations as aircraft transports and as tankers. United States shipyards erected 115 of these carriers between the summer of 1942 and Japan's capitulation in 1945.

THE NIGHT AMERICA PANICKED

Six million people listened that night and one million of them believed every word of it. Edgar Bergan and Charlie McCarthy probably won a larger audience, but Orson Welles' "Mercury Theater On The Air" certainly had a bigger impact on the country October 30, 1938.

America wasn't ready for the dramatization of H.G. Wells' "War of the Worlds." At least not in the way it was presented. Machine-gun style reports from Grover's Mill in New Jersey, Princeton University, New York, Chicago and other places sounded too real to the radio audience.

Those people who had tuned in from the beginning of Wells' program, realized that it was only that--a program and nothing else. But many listeners that night, listened to the "Chase and Sanborn Hour," which starred Bergan and McCarthy from 8:30 p.m. EST. When that program was over, they began "going around the dial" to see what else was on the radio. That was when they tuned in to hear about the invasion of Earth by Martians.

Despite disclaimers that stated the audience was listening "to a dramazitation of H.G. Wells' "War of the Worlds" many were too already disturbed to think clearly.

The result? Panic.

Today, it is difficult to find anyone who will admit they heard the program and actually believed it. Americans in the '30s were quite unsophisticated and naive as a people. The only exposure to science for most, was Buck Rogers, Flash Gordon, Brick Bradford and Alley Oop in the comic pages of America's newspapers, and movies and serials of the same theme. Their worst fears were being realized when they tuned in to the Mercury Theater that Sunday night before Halloween.

In New York City, for example, tenants in apartment buildings poured out into the streets, running blindly for wherever. If they owned cars, they could ride to wherever in comfort. But *where* could they go?

A man in Pittsburgh came home to find his wife in the bathroom with a can of poison ready to commit suicide. "I'd rather die like this," she told him, "than die like that." No one ever learned what "dying like that" exactly meant.

A woman, who was never identified, ran down the aisle of Indianapolis, Indiana's St. Paul's Episcopal Church screaming, "The world is coming to an end." The congregation was hastily dismissed.

In Toledo, Ohio, three persons fainted at their telephones while trying to call the jammed lines of the police department.

In Chicago, people ran out of restaurants without finishing or paying for their meals.

Needless to say, hysteria ran wild. And not only in the east. Similar reports poured in from all over the country, from coast to coast, from gulf to border and beyond. Canadians panicked as well.

And what of Dubuque? Well, Monsignor Casey, Pastor of St. Raphael's Cathedral, opened the doors to the church around 7:30 p.m. CST and it filled in minutes. Other churches in the city followed suit. Parents took their children. Even sick people were dressed and taken to be "near God at the end of the world. "

Corinne Moravec of Dickeyville, Wisconsin lived a couple of blocks from the Cathedral when she was a girl. "My grandmother, Priscilla Devaney prayed a lot of rosaries in her lifetime but really ran the beads through her fingers that night." Moravec's mother, Margaret Casey had a sense of humor about most things. If someone played a joke on her, she would, in time, be able to laugh at her having been taken. But not that time.

Mrs. Casey seldom wanted to even talk about it years later. When she did, she said such enormous and monumental sensations passed through her that she was absolutely stunned. Thoughts of Hitler's ranting and raving in Europe and the depression being so real and still so much in evidence, paled by comparison to the threat of a Martian invasion, that night. When the disclaimers were read, Mrs. Casey knew it was nothing more than a radio play but nevertheless, she bought it hook, line and sinker, according to her daughter. "She could laugh off most things but this one, she never did. She couldn't," Moravec said.

Roy Schmeichel, retired Dubuque paint store owner, said, "I heard the program from the beginning and knew it was just that--a radio program." Schmeichel grew up in Sheboygan, Wisconsin and said some of the people panicked but not enough to draw national attention.

Schmeichel's wife, Katie, who grew up in Elkader, Iowa, said the people of that small town didn't buy the idea at all.

The late Joe Rand, Key City entreprenuer, originally came from Wisconsin.

"I tuned in about ten or 15 minutes after the "War of the Worlds" started, but I knew it was a radio program," Rand said. "I listened and enjoyed it."

Gordon Kilgore, retired KDTH radio announcer, came to Dubuque, from Randolph, Ohio. He also knew from the beginning that it was a program, but other Randolphians took it in a serious way and went house to house alerting those who hadn't heard the program. They called others on the telephone. "Even though I knew it was a program, I still had a reaction to it," Kilgore said.

While churches had been opened and virtually filled in Dubuque, not one person took time to call the radio station carrying the broadcast. The late Vaughn Gayman, one time announcer emeritus of Dubuque, worked at WKBB at the time and was on duty that night. "Not one call came in," he said. "People's attitude at the time was, 'if it was on the radio or in the newspaper, it was true."

"War of the Worlds" did more for establishing Orson Welles, who was 23 at the time, as a national celebrity than anything else he ever undertook in his lifetime.

And radio grew up that night as well. It seemed as if "War of the Worlds" was a dress rehearsal for the real war that was about to begin within months, the following year.

Radio brought news flashes concerning World War II to the public within minutes of receiving them. Edward R. Murrow put the finishing touches on Welles' style and radio was forever established.

While the furor died down within two or three days, there were demands for "a full investigation into the situation with corrections," from elected officials. But nothing happened. By Thanksgiving, it was beginning to be nothing more than a memory and when recalled, brought on an embarrassed laugh. But as stated earlier, it's hard to find someone today, who will admit they had the junk scared out of them that night.

ALL HALLOWED EVE
A Short Story

I opened the door and entered the front hall of our home on Elm Street. After dumping my plastic garbage bag with my door-to-door, tricks-or-treats loot, I took off my eye mask and looked in the mirror. The Zorro mustache and sideburns makeup, which my mother had put on me, still looked good. At the age of 11, I hadn't really wanted to go out and take part in the age-old routine, but my folks convinced me I would regret it in later life if I didn't do as many kid things as I could, while I could.

When I opened my bag and spread the candy and fruit on the kitchen table, my mom and dad came in. They looked worried for some reason.

"What's wrong?" I asked.

"Your dad's father has taken a turn for the worse. We've been waiting for you to get home. We have to go to the hospital but we haven't been able to find someone to sit with you."

I fumed inside. I was 11, going on 12 and they wanted to get me a *baby sitter*. The only one I would want was Cynthia Fredricks who lived down the street. Cynthia was 14--not all that much older than me, and a real knockout. She baby sat for a lot of the neighbors. I wondered if Mom would call her if I suggested her. What the heck. I'd take a chance. I had nothing to lose.

"Did you call Cynthia?" I crossed my fingers waiting, hoping. She was so beautiful that I could sit there most of the night and look at her and think.

About what? You know. Man/woman thoughts, that's what.

"She was the first one I tried and she's already working tonight."

I mentally snapped my fingers. Easy come, easy go.

"Hey, look, Mom--Dad, I'm 11 and I can take care of myself. You don't have to spend money to get a babysitter. I'll be all right. I promise."

My mother looked at me in a skeptical way and glanced at Dad. "What would you do?" she asked, fixing her "let's have the truth" stare at me.

"I've got all my homework done. I'll probably listen to the radio a while, eat some of my candy and go to bed at nine o'clock the way I always do."

"And once you were in bed?" she asked, as if she were cross-examining a witness on one of her "soaps."

"I've been reading *My Friend Flicka*. I found the book in the school library. I'd probably read it until I got sleepy."

"If you promise to do all those things, we'll let you take care of yourself tonight," my dad said.

Dad looked real worried and anxious to go. "I really will. I promise. Shouldn't you get going?"

Dad nodded to me and then mother. "Come on, Charlene. We've got to go. Let's trust Eddy. I know he can do it."

Any thoughts I might have had about having a little party for me, went out the window when Dad said that.

My mother slipped into her blue sweater and walked to the door. "Behave, Eddy. This is no time for you to act up."

"I won't, Mom. I promise."

When they were gone, I looked at the candy on the table and picked out a few Tootsie Rolls and headed for the living room. I twisted the dial back and forth about 15 times and settled on listening to the end of "Counterspy." I turned off the Stewart-Warner and headed for the kitchen to pick up my Halloween candy and put it in a mixing bowl.

I figured I might as well head up to my room and get ready for bed. I could read lying in bed and fall asleep. At least I wouldn't be trouble for Mom and Dad while they worried about Grandpa. I wondered for a moment what had gone wrong with him. He was pretty old, and old people were supposed to die, I guess. Maybe it was his time. I didn't know. Geez, what can I say? I was only eleven.

I left a lamp on in the living room and went up to my room, counting the 14 steps and noting each one's different-sounding squeak or groan. We lived in a two-storied house in a sort of middle-class neighborhood. I turned off all the other lights and when I reached my room, I opened the door to the bedroom next to mine.

Once I scrubbed the makeup off my face and brushed my teeth, I climbed into bed, leaving the ceiling light on as well as the lamp on my bureau . I had asked for a reading lamp that would attach to the headboard so I could read more comfortably in bed. Maybe I'd get one for Christmas.

I opened the library book clutched in my hand. After finding the place where I had been reading, I quickly lost myself in the story about Kenny McLaughlin and his mare, Flicka. Flicka had been sick or something and was in a sling out in the calf pasture . See, Ken had found her lying in the cold stream, with a raging fever and he'd slipped in beside the mare to comfort her. He'd caught pneumonia and was in bed at the ranch house and his father was on his way to put Flicka out of her misery. When he entered the pasture, he checked the filly and found the infection in her leg improved and built a fire to keep watch over her, his rifle across his legs .

Now, there had been a mountain lion in the neighborhood and wouldn' t you know it, that big cat started stalking Flicka and Kenny's Dad. The lion gets to within a few feet at the edge of a small outcropping of rocks and Kenny's old man is dozing off to sleep. "Wake up," I wanted to shout, but gosh, it was only a story. The cat moved closer and--The lights went off in my room.

What the heck had happened? A power failure? My eyes slowly adjusted to the dark and I could see the outline of the windows in my room and the next bedroom through the tan shades. It couldn't have been a power failure if the street light in front of the house next door was still on. A fuse must have blown. I had watched Dad change them enough to believe I could find the bad one and put in a new one. All I had to do was get the flashlight from my parents' bedroom and I was in business.

I had been reading, propped up on my right elbow and hadn't moved since the lights went out. I still held the book and decided my plan of action would be to throw back the covers with my left hand and grope for the hunk of paper to mark my place in the book.

I was just about to put my plan into action when I heard a noise. The first step creaked. I froze. That step only did that if someone stepped on it. I tried to move but I couldn't. The next step groaned. *There was someone in the house with me.*

In rapid succession each step sounded off and whoever was in the house was on the second floor with me--maybe 15 or 16 feet away.

I could feel cold sweat pouring from my forehead and just about every other pore in my body. I tried to move. I couldn't. I tried to pray and couldn't remember any of the words.

What was I going to do? Some fiend had broken in and was going to chop me into little pieces of Eddy West. I had an overwhelming urge to pee in my pajamas but somehow managed to control that.

I fixed my eyes on the windows in the next bedroom. If the murderer was going to come for me he might come through that way and I'd see his shadow flit across the light-colored shades. At least I would be ready for him. Sure. Of course, when I couldn't move a muscle. I was really paralyzed with fear, I guess.

Then I saw it! A shadow moved past the first window--then the second. It moved right toward my open door. The threshold always squeaked when someone stepped on it. It squeaked. Whoever or whatever had invaded our home was in *my bedroom.*

There were two windows in my room--one at the foot of the bed and the other to the left. The shadowy form slipped past the first window at the bottom of my bed.

I waited. Nothing happened. Then I could hear breathing. And it wasn't mine.

A bluish light started glowing in the corner between the windows and a dim outline of a figure--a man--took shape. The blue color grew stronger and eventually lighted the man's face. *It was my grandfather.* What was he doing there in my room? He was supposed to be in the hospital--maybe dy----

"Good bye, Eddy," he said and the light and the figure vanished.

The next thing I knew, my parents were shaking me and I opened my eyes, blinking in the bright light of my ceiling fixture . I was all mixed up. Where was I? Why was I propped on my elbow, holding a book?

"Eddy? What ' s wrong? " my mom asked .

"I--I--, " was all I could manage.

"Are you sick, son? " my dad asked .

When I realized who they were and what they were asking, I said, "Did you put a new fuse in, Dad?"

He had no idea what I was talking about. "Fuse? What fuse? We came into your room to kiss you good night and found you wringing wet. What' s wrong? "

"You'll have to get up, while I change your sheets and covers, " Mom said. "You' d best take a quick bath and warm up. "

I obediently got out of bed, thankful I could finally move, despite my cramped muscles from holding that position for so many hours. I glanced at the clock on my dresser. Two thirty a.m. It really *had* been a long time.

After I toweled off and put on clean pajamas, I went back to the room. Mom and dad were waiting for me.

"Your grandpa died tonight," my dad said, a tear glistening in his eye.

"I--" I almost said, "I know," but caught myself in the nick of time. If they didn't believe a fuse had blown, they sure weren't about to believe Grandpa had come to say goodbye to me. Tears came to my eyes and rolled down my cheeks when I fully realized that Grandpa was really dead.

"Dad?" I said.

"Yes, Eddy."

"You sure there wasn't a fuse blown?"

"No, there wasn't. We walked in and turned on the lights. We did the same when we came into your room. Why do you keep asking about it?"

"Well, the lights went off and I--" I stopped when Dad interrupted me.

"Probably a power failure. That's all."

I nodded and crawled into bed. Power failure? Sure. Especially with the street lights on. They kissed me good night and, Dad, being the last one to leave, turned out the light, but I noticed something he didn't. When he turned the light switch up, the light went off. After they were gone for a while, I slipped out of bed and went to the switch.

I moved it down in the "off" position and the ceiling light went on. When I moved it up, to the "on" position, the light went out. That switch worked backward from that night on until we sold the house and moved.

I wonder if anyone else has ever noticed the sign my grandpa left to show he had come to say goodbye to me.

NOVEMBER

I have learned one thing doing research: The more things change, the more they seem to stay the same.

I know others have said the same thing, but ask any one of my teachers from the dark ages, and you will find that Tigges had to learn things for himself, the hard way. Take for instance, the matter of highways.

Remember when there were no hard surface roads leading into Dubuque? Don't say a person would have to go back into the 19th Century to find that time. T'wouldn't be true. As recently as 1922, according to an old map of Iowa that I have, the road west from Dubuque, which is now U.S. 20, was a two-lane gravel road. And that, folks, was the best of the lot. The road to Anamosa was graded, which meant that the first good rain turned it into a quagmire. The road south, our U.S. 61 today, wasn't even built as such nor was the north way out of town, U.S. 52 and Iowa Three. Oh, the trails were there, marked by wagon ruts and tire tracks of the more adventurous auto drivers of the day, but they were little more than trails. Talk about being isolated. Of course, the railroads were operating, thank you.

So, the next question is: Do you remember when highways were named and not numbered? I can remember my dad saying: "I'm going out on the 'Hawkeye' today," or "So and so lives south on The Mississippi Valley (Highway)."

I learned from little on, that the "Hawkeye" was a road, but I hadn't thought of that fact for a long time. Then, one Christmas, I received from my son-in-law, Carey Lewis, a history book titled *Transportation in Iowa*. In that book, along with other maps and topics, was a supplemental map showing the registered highway routes from 1914 to 1925. There were 64 named routes throughout the state and no less than seven of them utilized routes into the Key City. I know this sounds like I'm contradicting myself, but read on.

"The Burlington Way" and "The Mississippi Valley Highway" entered Dubuque from the south on what would eventually become U.S. 61. "The Red X Route" wound through the hills and over them where U.S. 151, the Old Military Road, would when the route was numbered.

"The Hawkeye Highway," "The Rainbow Trail" and "The Washington Highway" headed west toward Manchester and points west, along what was to become U.S. Twenty. The aforementioned "Mississippi Valley Highway" passed through Dubuque and continued north toward Elkader.

These routes came into being when the 1913-formed Iowa State Commission began registering routes by name and gave right to use certain route names, color combinations and designs for route markers for roads of 25 or more miles.

Remember when there was a Dubuque Club? It came into being April 17, 1902, and was formed as "...an association or club, fraternal, athletic, social and political in character, for its members...and for the advancement of the civic and political interests of the City of Dubuque." Some of the signees and first officers were people whose names became pretty well known in Dubuque's history.

William Lawther, J.T. Carr, J.F. Stampfer, H.E. Tredway, and Frank J. Piekenbrock were the first officers. The membership read like a who's who in Dubuque's history as well. I was impressed when I read the roster. Eventually, "The Dubuque Club" became the Dubuque Chamber of Commerce.

Remember when Frank Weiland operated his D-X station on 2nd and Locust?

Remember when Eddie Cantor sang: "Tomatoes are cheaper! Potatoes are cheaper!"?

Remember when the lady of the house, your mother or mine, would turn on the radio and listen to different programs while she did her housework? There was the "Breakfast Club ," with Don McNeill. Shortly thereafter,

"Breakfast at Sardi's" aired with host Tom Brenneman. In time, the program became the "Tom Brenneman Show," or something like that. Later in the morning, "Welcome Travelers" aired . But it was shortly before noon that the "real good stuff" came on. The soap operas.

Remember when you had to stay home from school because of a sore throat or cold or something, and you had to be very quiet so Mom wouldn' t miss a single word of "Helen Trent"? Then came "Our Gal Sunday." After the news with Vaughn Gayman on WKBB or the news from that new station, KDTH, the soaps came one after the other . "Myrt and Marge, " "Portia Faces Life, " "Mary Noble, Backstage Wife," "Bachelor's Children," "Ma Perkins," and yes, we cannot overlook "Painted Drees." Who was the central character on "Painted Dreams"? Why Mother Monoghan, of course.

Remember when Shirley Temple charmed the whole nation with her 56 curls (actual count) and deep, deep dimples, singing, "On The Good Ship Lollipop"?

Remember when a kid could buy a Christmas present for his or her best friend for a nickel? What could possibly be had for five cents? A Big Little Book for a boy or girl, would fill the bill quite nicely and it always gave the giver a great feeling, being able to do something like that for a friend.

I have several Big Little Books in my collection that have been inscribed. For example, in the front of my Big Little Book entitled *Jimmie Allen in the Air Mail Robbery*, it is inscribed: "Max from Gene, Xmas 1936." My 1933 *Dick Tracy Out West* Big Little Book carries the following: "Merry Xmas from Lloyd Mizner," and my *Buck Rogers in the 25th Century* has "Wayne Olson, Denver, Iowa, Dec. 25, 1933" written in the front.

Remember when, back in the '30s, how hard nickels were to come by? Well, no matter how difficult it may have been, friends, even among children, were and always would be a precious commodity. Sure, nickels were valuable way back then, but friendships were much moreso, especially to youngsters. It was always great to give a gift and to receive one from a friend, even if it did only cost a nickel.

How about a Burma Shave roadside ad that you can recite under the mistletoe at Christmas time? Before I tried it/The kisses I missed/But afterward--boy!/ The misses I kissed/Burma Shave.

Remember when it usually snowed sometime prior to Thanksgiving? And it seemed as if the snow stuck around until somet ime close to the first of March.

Remember when you were in grade school or high school and classes were finished on the day before Thanksgiving? Sometimes the teachers or nuns dismissed the classes a little earlier than they should have. I guess they wanted a little extra Thanksgiving vacation away from us as much as we did from them.

Remember when your mother got up before everyone else and was busy in the kitchen by the time the rest of the family got up and came down stairs? The bird was already in the oven and pies were being prepared for baking, if they hadn't been made the day before. And all those other delicious, traditional foods. Yams, candied or otherwise, mashed potatoes. The smell of turkey dressing mingled with the aroma of the roasting bird. Hot vegetables. Tangy cranberries simmering.

Remember when, if you were lucky, your mother also baked her own bread and biscuits? Of course, being a dumb kid, I always wished for "store-bought" bread and would have considered myself very lucky if my mother had brought home a loaf of Sweetheart Bread along with the other groceries. Sweetheart was always so nice and soft. Thank God, I married a gal who, on occasion, whips out some homemade stuff. Today, I know I'm lucky the way I was lucky back then. Yeah.

Remember when, speaking of Sweetheart Bread, the cost went from 10¢ a loaf to eleven cents? Wow. People were fit to be tied. That was a ten percent increase. Prior to the dime a loaf cost, the price had been even lower. Nine cents.

Remember when, the day after Thanksgiving was the first official day of the Christmas shopping season? Everybody, and I mean everybody, converged on downtown stores, fighting for whatever parking places were available. Back in the '30s, '40s and '50s, there were no parking ramps, no huge expanses of parking lots. There might have been one or two small lots but parking places were at a premium.

Remember when building-to-curb sidewalks were filled with building-to-curb people who were doing their shopping, jostling each other? "Merry Christmas," seemed to be on everyone's lips. They may not have had much money but they had the true spirit of the holidays. Cross words were seldom, if ever, exchanged.

Remember when J.C.Penney's store, Stampfer's, Roshek's and Montgomery Ward's (Monkey Ward's) department stores were loaded to capacity? Kresge's, Neisner's and Woolworth's were no different. The Hub, Graham's and Edwards' were filled with shoppers to the brim. And it seemed as though the stores were never below capacity or the number of people who showed up that Friday after Thanksgiving. Here is an about face of sorts. Rather than recall a local memory most of the readers could conjure up, the subject of early day television will probably enlighten most of you with a brand new tidbit of memory or should it be trivia?

Remember when there was a DuMont Television Network? On March 10, 1949, a new program, featuring the song and piano stylings of one Delora Bueno, premiered. It lasted until May 5, 1949. However, ten days later, "Flight to Rhythm," was premiered and this show, which was set in "Club Rio," a Brazilian nightclub, featured Miguelito Valdez's Orchestra. Starring as vocalist, was none other than Delora Bueno. No memories yet, huh?

To finish this little escapism of yesterday's TV efforts, let me quote from a TV magazine of the day (1949) concerning Miss Delora Bueno: "This 25-year-old South American beauty was actually born in Dubuque, Iowa." Now, you got the connection.

When Delora was three years old, her Brazilian father resigned from his position at the University of Dubuque, and returned to his South American home with his American wife and daughter. I checked in my own reference books and by golly, Dubuque had a television star in 1949.

Remember when Campfire Marshmallows were the best, the very best on the market? Whatever happened to them? They were a little different from those available today. Their outside had a sort of skin and weren't the least bit mushy. When a person toasted a Campfire Marshmallow over a campfire (where else?) or over a fire in a fireplace (again, where else?), the outside would brown slowly and the inside got all goopy and gooey. If one-was over cooked, the skin might break but that was a rarity.

Remember when... No. Let's make this a trivia question. What was the original name of the newspaper for which Clark Kent worked, in the comic books that starred Superman? It wasn't *The Daily Planet* but *The Daily Star*.

Speaking of comic books, remember when there were ads on the back covers or inside the back covers advertising toys and other gimcracks . If you don' t know the word "gimcrack, " look it up and it will save me a lot of explanation and you'll learn a new word. Among the more prominent items a boy could buy was a stick and tissue model of a Stinson Reliant airplane. It's wingspan was five feet and had a length of 38 inches. It weighed all of eight ounces when built and cost a gigantic one and a half dollars. If a kid couldn't afford $1.50, there was always the Stinson Reliant Jr. version. It had a 24 inch wingspan and cost a quarter. Postpaid, mind you. No shipping and handling charges.

Among the other items were one tube pocket radios, midget radios, wireless transmitters, electric phones and crystal radios. For the girls, 35¢ would buy a blond wig and there were dolls available as well. One could become a ventriloquist for one thin dime while a ventriloquist's dummy cost a dollar and thirty five cents. Twenty five cents bought a live chameleon and field glasses, telescopes and cameras were available for under a buck.

For mere pennies, a boy or girl could become a musician. An ocarina cost 35¢ while a jaw's harp cost ten cents. There were nose flutes available as well and I have to stop and think about that one. What the devil was a nose flute? Could it be played if the musician had a head cold? For 15¢, a grade schooler, assuming he or she had 15¢, could start his or her own five piece hillbilly band. The five pieces included a harmonica, a flute (for the nose or mouth I have no idea which. It wasn't explained in the ad.) a warbler(?), a round hum-a-tone and a kazoo.

Remember when a person could answer an ad and start your own Home Recording Studio with six blank records and all the equipment necessary to make your own recordings for two dollars and ninety eight cents? Even big band leader Charley Barnet used one, or so the ad claimed.

Remember when around 1940 or so, a school kid could sell 40 packets of Christmas seals at 10¢ each and earn "valuable prizes"? Each packet contained 96 sparkling seals. If the young door-to-door vendor sold just one order, 40 packets, that is, he or she could get a Marx windup train or a Daisy Red Ryder Carbine, 1,000 shot repeater. Electric movie projectors and lots of other prizes were available. The 40 packets must have been a difficult item to sell since the most a salesperson had to sell to get any one of the items, was ONE ORDER. Makes a person wonder, doesn ' t it?

Remember when a kid's prized possession might be a Superman Krypto-Ray Gun? It looked very much as if it came from another planet or at least from someone's imagination of what such a gun would look like if it did come from another planet. At any rate, the Krypto-Ray Gun, projected still pictures of the Man of Steel, doing his thing, on any flat, light-colored surface.

Remember when Gus Zuccaro peddled fruits and vegetables from the back of his wagon, which was drawn by a horse? Gus covered the city and knew just about every neighborhood in town. He gave up the horse and wagon about 1941 or so and went to an International Harvester pickup truck, which was colored a sort of deep red. When he bought it from the "world's greatest salesman," my dad, John G. Tigges, he didn't know how to drive and Dad taught him. That qualifies Dad as the greatest salesman. How many salespersons do you know who could sell a car to someone who couldn' t drive?

Remember when I asked for the names of the bus companies that operated out of Dubuque in the early ' 40s? We had a winner, not that she won anything, in Elinor Workman. She worked at the Union Bus Depot when it was at 303 Main Street. The companies were: Hiawatha Stage Lines, Interstate Transit Lines, Jefferson Transportation Motor Company, Northland Greyhound Lines, River Trails Transportation Company, The Orange Line and Black and White Transportation Lines.

Remember when Fishhook Henry was mentioned earlier? I received a nice letter from his grandson, Mike Henge. He told me that "Fish Hook" was a tree trimmer, not a rag and junk buyer. The rag/junk buyers were Sampulskey (sic) and Orval Bess (sic) according to Mike. Sampulskey was a big guy and drove the horse and wagon while Orval, who was little and had a high-pitched voice, did all the work. That's life. Mike also asked about the TV commercial concerning the Hoffmann--Schneider Funeral Home . The store front he and his friends can't identify, was Martin's Wallpaper and Paint Store at the corner of 15th and Central--1499 Central, which had been The Hoffmann Mortuary until 1940 or 1941. At that time, Al Hoffmann moved his business to 1640 Main Street, where it is known today as The Hoffmann-Schneider Funeral Home. Problem solved.

Remember when your mother used to use a sprinkling bottle to dampen her wash when it dried too quickly before she finished ironing? The cap was made of tin or aluminum and had cork around the bottom of it to make it water tight. The metal part flared out to a head about an inch and a quarter across. Little holes covered the top. Usually the sprinkling cap was stuck in an old pop bottle such as the 12 ounce Pepsi Cola bottle. (Pepsi Cola hits the spot/12 full ounces/that's a lot./ Twice as much for a nickel, too./ Pepsi Cola is the drink for you.) Remember?

Remember when some automobiles had the heater under the front seat? The back seat got just as much warmth as did the front. Not all of them had that setup but a lot of GM cars did, as I recall .

Remember when Armour and Company sold butter, poultry and eggs under the name Cloverbloom?

Remember when Nesbitt's California Orange drink was *the* orange drink? Of course Sanitary Dairy's was just as good but wasn't nationally advertised the way Nesbitt did their products.

Remember when Kolynos Tooth Powder offered "a double your money back if the product didn't clean a person's teeth or refresh the mouth?"

Weren't those the days?

Remember when the United States had two Thanksgivings? That's an interesting memory and points out the fact that there really is no such thing as a national holiday. Each state must, through legislative enactment or executive proclamation, appoint the day on which each holiday is to be observed. Because Thanksgiving is the "kick off" for Christmas shopping, some states made an effort to gain an extra week of business and celebrated Thanksgiving on the third Thursday while others celebrated on the fourth . The "double " holiday lasted for three years until 1942, when World War II brought the reconsolidation of Thanksgiving and it has remained that way ever since. Maybe I shouldn't have mentioned this. Some money-hungry merchant might try to set our day of Thanksgiving on October 1, and have some 11 weeks for Christmas shopping. Perish the thought.

THAT FIRST THANKSGIVING

Most everyone has a picture in their memory bank as to what the first Thanksgiving was really like in 1621. Pilgrims wearing their quaint costumes--the men their strange looking hats, women their little bonnets sitting around long tables filled with a cornucopia of food: turkey and pies, fruits and vegetables, potatoes and cranberries. The Pilgrims were so overjoyed and proud of their success at growing food in the New World, that they invited the Indians to join in their feast of Thanksgiving. Right? Wrong on every count other than the fact the first such feast took place in the 17th century, but not in 1621.

While the idea is picturesque, that particular concept of Thanksgiving has been passed down from generation to generation, from grade school teacher to grade school teacher and perpetuated in such works of art as J.L.G. Ferris' painting "The First Thanksgiving," which depicts pretty much the same sort of picture as the vignette of the first paragraph.

If that isn't a correct interpretation, then, what really did happen? Let's settle the year first. The first feast of Thanksgiving was held in 1610, in Jamestown, but it wasn't a feast. The thing those settlers were thankful for was the fact they had lived through the winter. The spring of 1610 ended what they called "the starving time." Jamestown started with 409 colonists and had been reduced to 60 survivors by that spring. They had no food and had no idea as to where they might get any. When a ship loaded with food and supplies arrived from England, they had a religious service to give thanks. Interestingly enough, the colonists who survived did not commemorate that particular year--and who could blame them? Who wants to remember almost starving to death?

On December 4, 1619, 38 colonists arrived at a place they called Berkeley Hundred. In essence, they ordained that "the day of our ship's arrival...in the land of Virginia, shall be yearly and perpetually kept holy as a day of Thanksgiving to Almighty God." On the first anniversary, they fasted and prayed. And that was the last celebration, since by December 4, 1621, the colonists were all dead--massacred by the neighboring Indians.

Well, at least we've gotten up to 1621, the date everyone uses for the "first" Thanksgiving . The Pilgrims, or Saints, the name they used for themselves, arrived in 1620, a bit off course . They were supposed to sail to Virginia but wound up in a place they called Plymouth Colony. There wasn't a farmer among the Saints and that first winter they darn near starved to death, kept alive only through the generosity of the local Indians, a much nicer group of people than those in Virginia. With the help of Tisquantum, whom the Saints called Squanto, as an interpreter, they accepted the foodstuffs from the Wampanoag Indians and followed their instructions the next spring when it came time to plant. Naturally, that was done Indian style and corn was planted around trees and so on, rather than disturb the native plants.

Though the Saints were a hardy bunch, life was difficult at best. Many had died throughout the winter and only five, that's right, five women were around that fall to prepare the first feast. They had a bumper crop, for those times, and the colony's Governor William Bradford invited Chief Massasoit and his brother to join the feast. Wouldn' t you know it? The Chief took advantage of the invitation and brought along 88 hungry braves. And remember there were only five women to serve the total of 145 diners!

The Saints embraced Puritanism and a Puritan day of thanksgiving was one of fasting and solemn prayer. For example, such days were declared following the end of a drought or if a battle was won. Failing to observe it, was a crime the same as taking part in a sporting event on the Sabbath.

I know, you're thinking about the football games played on Thanksgiving in the 20th century, right? Times have changed, haven't they?

The first feast of Thanksgiving was not just a one day affair. It was a three day Harvest Home celebration which was an ancient tradition, and those poor women--well, all 90 Indians hung around the whole time, making it three days of feasting for 145. The idea behind it--the governor's idea to boot--was that the best way to preserve food for the winter was to "pig out" and put on a lot of body fat. Bradford's idea behind inviting the Chief and his brother was to stay on the good side of them and keep their friendship going. But 88 extra for dinner? Certainly a *faux pas* even in 1621 .

Referring to the first paragraph wherein some of the supposed foodstuffs were listed, I beg to differ. Let's take a closer look. If there was a turkey or two on the table it was a wild one brought down by some lucky Saint with his blunderbuss. The poor thing was probably half blown apart.

Anyone who has hunted turkeys is fully aware of the species' wariness. So it would have been luck more than hunting skill, considering the fellow on the butt-end of the blunderbuss. Since the Saints had not grown any wheat, there wasn't any flour for pie crusts, so that takes care of dessert. There wouldn't have been potatoes on the table because they were still considered to be poisonous in 1621. And since there wasn't any grain grown and no flour there weren't any biscuits or rolls either. No cattle meant no beef and no butter .

Well, then what in the name of Mylanta did they have on the menu? Venison for sure. There were a lot of deer in the area. Wild fowl in addition to the one or two turkeys mentioned earlier. I know there could have been more but bear with me. Shellfish, lobsters, eel, corn which was boiled to a mush-like consistency since the kernels were tough and nothing like the sweet corn available at Farmer's Market and dried fruit. Sweet potatoes, squash and pumpkins were available along with cranberries and other wild fruits but no apples, which meant no cider, or oranges, for that matter. All of that was likely washed down with homemade wine, made from wild grapes.

Originally there were about 110 people who landed at Plymouth. Half died those first ten months. The five surviving women probably would have demanded that they be taken out to a restuarant the following year, if there were any such places around at the time. Alas there weren' t. Besides, the women wouldn't have had a thing to wear, since their simple costumes were probably all tattered by then. And it isn't really known if they commemorated that first Harvest Home feast or not. They probably were concerned that the word was out that every Indian in the territory was welcome if they celebrated again and so voted to forget the whole thing. Instead, they more than likely held their traditional day of thanksgiving and prayed and fasted.

Well having thoroughly destroyed your idea of that first Thanksgiving, I hope that you and yours have a good one and that you have much for which to be thankful. Watch the pro football games on TV and don't eat too much turkey. However, do bear in mind that we are what we eat.

DECEMBER

Where were you when they bombed Pearl harbor? Our whole family was together that Sunday in a rather unusual setting. My father, John G. Tigges, a "colonel" in the then thin ranks of local auctioneers, was listing a farm sale while my mother, Madonna, sister, Phyllis, and I waited in the car. We had the radio playing in the '36 four-door Chevy Standard, waiting for the news to come on. Afterward, the radio would go off until Dad finished and we'd be on our way home. A few minutes before the local newscast was to begin, a network announcer came on the air with a bulletin,"The Japanese have attacked Pearl Harbor and. . . "

That's where I was. Where were you? As with the assassination of John F. Kennedy, most people recall exactly where they were when they received word of the "sneak" attack, if they were around at that time.

I believe that, in retrospect, the most overwhelming part of World War II, was the fact that the United States was so ill-prepared for war. Caught with our pants down, the greatest industrial effort ever in the history of man, even through today, was made. Automobile factories, farm machinery plants and just about any type of manufacturing process were converted to the war effort. While I don't have the exact figures, the number of fighter planes and bombers produced for the different branches of the service, along with ships of every kind, tanks and other types of land vehicles, is staggering. And it was done without complaint from anyone for the most part, and with the cooperation of just about every man, woman and child in the nation. See May chapter for exact figures.

Keep some of that in mind while we commemorate the anniversary of Pearl Harbor.

Remember when going shopping in downtown Dubuque was an adventure? Parking was virtually non-existent except for unmarked places on the street --no parking ramps or meters either. It always seemed like the accomplishment of a lifetime to find a space big enough for the family bus to squeeze into, so that the family could get out and "go shopping."

Remember when department stores had toy train layouts? The biggest of all was in Roshek's Department Store. For years, the toy department was on the second floor in the southwest corner. At Christmas time the department e-x-p-a-n-d-e-d and became a virtual Christmas wonderland.

The toy train layout was a knockout. Depending on the current manager at the time, sometimes two, three and even four trains might be running at once. In the late '30s, when money was scarce, there were still people buying much needed and necessary items as Lionel trains.

During one trip to the store, I watched, envy dripping from my lips, while my 8-year-old face and eyes turned absolutely lime green when a customer was shown the large, Lionel scale Hudson locomotive, the biggest, best locomotive the firm ever made and one that was half its size but just as detailed, just as beautiful. The man was actually going to buy one of them. He'd take it home and I'd never see it again. I stood there, mouth agape, while the salesman rattled off the advantages of both sizes. I don't remember if the purchase was made or not.

But in one way, I did gain satisfaction where that toy department was concerned. While going to college, I was hired by Charlie Laird, then-current manager of the toy department TO RUN THE TRAIN LAYOUT! By that time, I had trains of my own, but there was still something magical about being in charge of that particular layout.

Remember when the usual refreshments served at Christmas time were wine, cookies and fruitcake? Most of the time the cookies and cake were homemade and some of the time, the wine was too. The kids would get lemon-flavored soda.

Remember when Christmas time was the time for visiting relatives? Aunts and uncles and their children, your cousins, would come to your house and visit. The cousins would play with your new Christmas toys and games. Then, a few days later, your parents would take you and your siblings to visit them. It was your turn to play with someone else's toys and games and that opportunity was always welcomed. Why? Well, I guess nothing was absolutely boredomproof, even in those days.

Remember when dickering over the price of a Christmas tree was also a highlight of the season? Of course, extra branches had to be included to improve on Ma Nature's artistry. Did you ever have a tree so overbalanced, it had to be tied to the wall with black thread?

Remember when Radio Flyer wagons were a prime Christmas gift that a boy or girl might hope to find under the Christmas tree? A wagon could be red or blue with silver hubcaps on the white wheels. Nice memory.

Remember when, in the late 1960s, aluminum trees with a handful of ornaments, and a spotlight with rotating color lenses off to one side, became the vogue for a "modern" Christmas? Gone, and forgive me for bringing up the memory.

Remember when a child might hope for a pedal car--one in which an eight year old and under might get into and actually drive? Wow! Of such things were dreams made of in the past. A convertible. A fire engine. A truck. Today, they are collectors' items and demand a three figure price tag. How times have changed .

Remember when Mercury Theater of the Air would present Lionel Barrymore as Ebenezer Scrooge in the drama-adapted-to-radio, "A Christmas Carol"?

Remember Amos of the "Amos 'n' Andy Show," explaining to his daughter, Arbadella, thoughts of Christmas by explaining the prayer, "Our Father"?

Remember receiving Tinker Toys or an Erector Set or a set of Arkitoys for Christmas? The things that could be built were amazing.

Remember when, if you were a girl, how you anticipated getting a Shirley Temple doll or book or cutouts? Or one of the many Dionne Quintuplet products that were around in the 1930s. I remember a book we had at home on those five children, and Doctor DaFoe, who had delivered them. How about a Jane Withers doll or book of cutouts? Do you remember Jane Withers?

Remember when you had a doll and no buggy, and prayed every night that Santa would bring a new doll buggy for you?

Remember when, if you were a boy, how you longed for and lusted after a real, genuine Lionel train? Or an American Flyer? Or even a Marx train?

Remember when you tried to convince your parents that a chemistry set would help you in school and, once you received it, the only thing you contented yourself with producing was an occasional stink bomb and invisible ink?

Remember when, once you had your doll and buggy, you began wishing for, and working on getting the small metal refrigerator, stove and sink/cabinet that had actual running water?

Remember when your mother would make home-made fruit cake? Made correctly, this is one of the best tasting treats around. The secret is the wine that is added--and added--and added over a two to three month period. We make my mother's recipe every other Christmas. Yes, it was and still is delicious, and wou'dja believe tha's the honesh-to-goo'ness trut'?

Remember when, because there was a shortage of ornaments, either because of the economic times or because of war shortages, a Christmas tree could be decorated with a few ornaments, cranberries and popcorn strung on thread and multi-colored paper chains?

Remember when the mail men had to make two and sometimes three and four deliveries a day to make certain all the Christmas cards and packages were delivered on time?

Remember when Midnight services in Dubuque's churches were actually held at the magical hour of 12:00 midnight. That just made the occasion that much more mystical and holy.

Remember when everyone stayed home on Christmas Day to be with family? Besides, there wasn't a darn thing open, other than the movie theaters.

Remember when a Tom and Jerry, made with home-made batter, was about the sweetest thing to flow down one's gullet?

Remember when you'd overeat on Christmas candy? Hardtack, not the bread but the small candy pieces in various shapes and colors that were sucked, chocolate in a million shapes, peppermint canes, fudge both white and dark, white-chocolate-covered pretzels, nuts, peanuts and on and on and on.

Remember when time was allowed on Christmas morning to make quick visits to the neighhorhood kids to see what they got for Christmas? Then, they'd visit your home.

Remember when Christmas shopping season started the day after Thanksgiving? Who of you remember hearing Christmas carols being sung in October on radio, with offers to buy some collection or other of Christmas carols and songs? Today, on television some of the edge is taken off the season and gets rid of that warm glow a person can experience when the spirit of Christmas should be in your system.

Remember when you shopped at J.C.Penney and they had the little baskets that carried money over the network of rails and cables? Your money and the written receipt were stuffed into the little conveyance (I always called them little cars) and hung onto the track. The cable zipped your money away, up and over the store to the cashier's area, where addition and taxes were verified, and the proper change made. The receipt and change, if any, was put back in the little container and it flew across the store at a pretty fast pace, right back to where it had started. The one thing I could never figure out as a kid, was how did the little "car" know where to go on that return trip?

If I remember correctly, The Hub had an arrangement something like that but it was much more simple. One basket for the entire store. The money, change for items and so on were put in the basket which memory tells me was about a foot or so long, maybe eight or ten inches wide and zipped up to the mezzanine office where change was made and so on. Made a lot more sense to me then, than did Penney 's.

Those little "cars" were zooming all over the place--from the mezzanine and the second floor and the basement and naturally the main floor to the office and back. To a kid, it was fascinating and especially during the Christmas shopping rush, when there was so much traffic. The interesting thing was, they never once collided.

Remember when Roshek's Department Store (downtown that is) had the train that kids could ride on? It ran almost the full length of the building, not quite, but almost. Santa Claus would sit on his "throne," and hold court. One year yours truly played that role. While it was a sad job of miscasting, my slim figure (yes, I actually was slim at one time) was puffed out with appropriate padding and I never had so much fun.

Remember when it seemed that giving was more important than receiving? What has happened to that spirit of Christmas? It has gotten so commercial, I can understand a lot of the resentment that people have for the holiday. I have a Thanksgiving season picture of a farm, turkeys, and the farmer and his son are heading toward the axe, which was stuck in the stump of a tree, to keep the blade clean. Next to that lovely picture, I had commercial, I can understand a lot of the resentment that people have for the holiday. I have a Thanksgiving season picture of a farm, turkeys, and the farmer and his son are heading toward the axe, which was stuck in the stump of a tree, to keep the blade clean. Next to that lovely picture, I had three old Thanksgiving cards, which people used to send to one another during that particular season. One of the people in my Thursday's novel group which meets at my home, said, "How did the greeting card company ever let that idea get away from them?" Good question. But there 're cards for everything else.

Does anyone remember the Spacelander bicycle that came out in the 1950s? It was designed by Ben Bowden in 1945 but not built until a few years later. What a thrill it would have been to see one of those beauties standing near the Christmas tree. That bike was as streamlined a bicycle as ever conceived by the mind of man. Other than the handlebars and wheels, there were only three pieces to the body. The body proper and the rear fender, which also encompassed a double-sided chain guard, along with the housing for the fork and double headlights were all in one piece. The seat and the front fender were the other two pieces. I have no idea what those babies were priced in the ' 50s. There were only 522 ever produced and there are 38 bikes known still to exist today. One in good condition recently was sold at auction for--are you ready--fifteen thousand dollars. A bit beyond the normal household budget for a Christmas gift for one of the kids. Right?

Remember when, if a family couldn't afford store-bought gifts, they made their own? The same for ornaments and just about anything else a person can name today. Back in the '30s, many people had to do without, when it came to a special Christmas dinner. But, whatever they did have, they thanked God they had it and probably enjoyed it more than those who had a "normal Christmas dinner," whatever that might have been. Ham, chicken, turkey, roast pork and all the appropriate trimmings. They still celebrated the birth of Christ.

Remember when, if you were a boy and wanted a train set for Christmas, you would lie in bed and picture that wonderful toy. Girls, leaned toward dolls and their accessories back then and with reason. It was the times and the way children were brought up then. Even if the doll was not an expensive one, the little girl would always love it as if it were her own child. Naturally, that depended on the degree of imagination she might possess.

On the other hand, if a boy received a Marx train set, when in reality he had hoped and prayed for a Lionel or American Flyer (later Gilbert) set, he could still play with that little, tin toy train and run it until one day he could own a Lionel or American Flyer. Sets of Marx trains sold for as little as $3.55 for an engine, tender and three cars, plus a loop of track and a transformer in the 1930s. Wow!

Remember when instead of electronic games that cost up to $200.00 and more, Christmas toys were actually toys? Marx Toy Company of Girard, Pennsylvania led the way in wind up toys such as the model of the old car with an off-center axle on the rear wheel, which limped across the floor after it was wound up. An elephant on a tricycle, scooted across the floor, spinning the ball on it's uplifted trunk, tassels flaring out after it was wound up. Note the fact that both were wind-up toys and used no batteries. While the elephant is not a Marx product, the car is and one thing a kid could count on was the reliability of Marx toys to work. I have acquired a few Marx trains (oodles of, wife's comment) in my time and every locomotive, regardless of age or condition would invariably run after a few minutes of freeing the wheels. And all of the Marx trains I have are made of tin.

Tonka was another producer of excellent toys, all metal again, when our children were young. No batteries. No electricity. Just well constructed toys. We had a policy in our home when the kids were small--toys only at Christmas time. But we bought the best we could, so they would last. And last they did. Remember when little girl's toys included dolls, available from a much larger choice. No Barbie dolls of infinite variety or G.I. Joe dolls.

Remember when during World War II and there were no metal toys, nor plastic toys, but cardboard toys by the hundreds. Cut out dolls, dresses and furniture and whatever could be printed on cardboard. There were punch-out Army vehicles and soldiers for the boys, punch-out dolls and dresses-- three dimensional punch-out comic strip characters--The Captain and the Kids and all their supporting cast; Li'l Abner and his family and neighboring Dogpatchers; Popeye, Olive Oyl, Wimpy and Sweet Pea and that peculiar little animal, Eugene the Jeep . And those cardboard toys had to do the job . Why, even Lionel Trains produced a cardboard freight train to keep train-loving hands busy. A.C. Gilbert at one time produced a cardboard circus and a cardboard farm as accessories to their American Flyer train sets.

Remember the little navy ships that were available during the war? Boys and girls had to assemble them using tiny pieces of dowel and preformed cardboard bottoms, decks and super structures. Battle ships, destroyers, submarines and aircraft carriers about two inches long were the result of hours of work.

And since metal was not available to the A. C. Gilbert Company for the erector sets that are such hot items as collectibles today, wooden construction sets, such as Tinker Toys and Arkitoy (red and green pieces of varying length wood with holes drilled in them to accept small bolts and fastened with tiny nuts) took their place. Of course Art Nagle and I are the only ones who remember Arkitoy sets.

Remember when, if you received a Flexible Flyer sled for Christmas, there was no such thing as boredom during January and February as long as snow covered the ground? They were the epitome of sleds and a ride down any hill on one, was a thrill kids seldom experience today. The runners slicing through the snow, the rider changing direction whenever he or she wanted, maybe another kid sharing the sled if it were long enough--picking up speed, the cold wind in your face, your nose snuffling, your mittens soaked and your hands cold and body chilled through to the bone. When the ride was over, the long trek to the top of the hill to do it again--and again and again. Then home for some hot chocolate. Yeah. That was living for a kid.

Remember when Christmas wasn't quite so commercialized? Oh, it's always been to some degree, but it hasn't always been as much as it is today. In the past, it seemed as if those merchants involved with selling Christmas items still remembered what the whole season was all about: The birth of a baby who would grow up and do marvelous things and wind up crucified on a cross, paying for my sins and yours. All the season's greetings and glitter and glamour, as thought of by Madison Avenue, pales when the Christmas spirit is thought of in its entirety. It's truly the season of love.

Regardless of the manner in which you think of the Christmas holiday and regardless of how you may celebrate it, have a blessed and merry one. Try recalling the days when you were a child--and thought like a child--and acted like a child--and magically, your holiday will take on the old glow that the season used to have.

Whatever your belief might be, worship in your own way and do remember that the "good will" promised is really a promise of "peace on earth *to men of good will.*" So we have to earn that peace, by treating one another the way we would want to be treated. Just think, if that were actually done, we might attain world peace.

I wonder if we could handle that?

THE GOOD THIEF
A Short Story

The streets of Jerusalem lay dark, deserted. The boy, puffs of steam
jetting from his nostrils, moved stealthily through the night, staying in the
shadows while he made his way along the broad avenue. He didn't have far
to go and once through the gate, he knew he'd be safe.

A loner ever since he'd been orphaned at five, the other homeless street
urchins avoided the ten-year-old when he made it clear he wanted to be by
himself

Hugging the cold wall, he peered around the corner. Two guards huddled
around a small fire near the open gate . He could smell burning wood and
imagined how comforting its warmth must feel on such a chilly night. Cold
as he was, he was even hungrier. For three days, his usual sources of food
had failed and he couldn't find anything of value to steal for bartering.
Stealing was his way of life and he always swiped food and clothing to
sustain himself . Then, he had foolishly taken the sandals . He'd been seen
and chased and thought every Roman in Jerusalem was alerted to arrest
him. Walking down a street in broad daylight would be impossible without
being chased by a soldier. All he could do was go to another town where he
wasn't known.

Checking the guards, he went back to an alley he'd passed. The narrow passageway curved between the buildings, opening at the opposite end close to the gate. After making certain the alley was open all the way and that no one was around, he picked up a discarded staff and went back to the far end where he inched closer to the boulevard opening. Pounding the staff on the wall next to the street, he shouted, "Roman slowpokes! Can't catch me!"

The soldiers turned and seeing it was only a boy, shook their fists at him. When the ruckus continued, they reluctantly set out in pursuit, leaving their warm fire.

The boy darted back into the alley and dashed along his route of escape once the guards took up the chase. His pursuers were quickly left behind and once he turned the final corner, found the gate unguarded. When the sentries rounded the corner of the boulevard, the boy leaped over the fire and disappeared into the night through the portal.

His feet barely touching the ground, he raced toward the south, through the darkness. A pile of boulders loomed ahead and he made his way there. Ducking behind the largest one, he waited to see if anyone followed. Peeking over the top, he could see the gate but no soldiers. He was safe.

In time, his breathing returned to normal and lying back, he studied the stars. There were so many. If he knew how, he ' d count them and then he'd be the only one who knew. He sat up and stretched. The next town wasn't too far and he wanted to reach it before sunup.

Of a sudden, a huge star caught his attention. He couldn't remember seeing it before when he had looked upward. It was gigantic. It had to be the general of all the stars. The beaming light dimmed, then shimmered, brightly pulsating.

Night still darkened the countryside when he stood on the last hill. Below, the village nestled in the valley. The bright star, higher now, hovered over the little town glowing brightly. How could a star move around like that?

Cautiously moving toward the outskirts, he stopped short when he heard voices behind the first building. Easing forward, he held his breath and glanced quickly around the corner. Soldiers. *Roman soldiers.* They'd probably been sent out to watch for him. The gods were against him.

Quietly retracing his steps, he wondered what he should do. He'd have to find a hiding place close to town, one where he could sleep and rest. When he awakened, he could find food and leave for another town. When he stood clear of the buildings, he made his way toward the hills on the far side of town. A spot, blacker than the rest of the hillside, appeared as if it might be a cave and he hurried toward it.

The pungent smell of manure passed almost unnoticed when he approached. He'd spent many cold nights in animal shelters and if this cave was used as a stable, he'd be able to make a bed of hay.

He pulled back, when he saw a small fire burning in one corner. Pressing against the outside of the cave, he waited, breathless .

Then, a baby cried.

What would a baby be doing in a cave? No soldiers were around and his curiosity overcame him. He stepped inside, toward the fire. A young woman lay on a makeshift bed of hay, while a man, probably her husband, held a naked baby.

The boy coughed to announce his presence and moved into the dim light. The man turned. "Who--who are you?"

"I'm-- Whatcha doin'?"

"My wife has just given birth to a baby. What's a youngster like you doing out so late at night?"

"I ain't got no home 'n' I was gonna sleep here. What is it? A girl baby or a boy baby?"

"What?" the man asked absently, caring for the infant. "Oh, a boy baby. A fine boy." He held up the crying, wriggling baby for the youngster's inspection.

"He sure is scrawny 'n' ugly," the boy whispered, his eyes widening.

The man smiled at the candid remark but said nothing . Instead, he went to his wife' s side."Mary? Are you awake? The child is hungry and should be fed."

Mary opened her eyes and smiled weakly. "I'm very tired, Joseph, but I can feed him." She turned to the intruder. "We didn't think he'd be born so soon and planned to get a room at the inn tomorrow after some of the people left. We'll have to keep him warm by the fire until morning."

The boy shook his head. "He'll freeze by then. I got an idea." He went to the back of the cave and came back leading a donkey . " Is this yours? "

Joseph nodded, a questioning look on his face .

"I've slept in mangers lots o' times and animals' breaths kept me warm. The more animals, the better. " He tied the donkey close to the woman and her baby and returned to the other side of the cave. He pulled and prodded a stubborn ox and when the man stepped forward to help, the animal grudgingly moved and was soon tethered next to the ass.

Mary smiled gratefully and pulled the shivering baby closer to her. The boy was right. It was too cold and unless they got something to cover the infant, he might well be dead by morning. She looked at the boy, a silent pleading in her eyes.

"Maybe I can stea--or--er--borrow something," he said, turning to leave.

When he was outside, he shook his head. What was wrong with him? He had enough to do just caring for himself. The image of the ugly baby formed in his mind. He had to help.

Running down the hillside toward the sleeping village and to the back of the first house, he found its court empty of anything he could use. The next was the same. Behind the third building, he found cubits and cubits of narrow muslin strips draped across some rocks where they'd been left to dry. Scooping them up, he ran as fast as he could, back to the cave.

Breathless, he entered and handed the material to the man. A tear of gratitude rolled down the man's cheek, disappearing in his beard. Joseph turned to his wife who stood weakly, and helped wrap the child. Together they knelt by the manger and tucked the baby in snugly.

The boy looked about. Somehow the cave seemed brighter. He turned and looked out and saw the dark sky. It'd be at least another hour before sunrise. Facing the manger again, he found the infant glowing and no longer ugly and scrawny.

"Well--I--ah--gotta go." If the guards he'd heard, saw that strange glowing light that filled the cave, they might investigate.

Mary stood. "I don't know how to thank you. I don't even know your name. What is it?"

The boy stared at the floor. "I--I don't like my name. I never use it. "

"Such a thoughtful child would have a good name. Our son's name is Jesus."

"How come he glows like that?" he asked, pointing a dirty finger at the child.

"Jesus is a king and one day will free God's chosen people."

The boy stared at her. The woman must be nuts or something. A king? A king indeed--in a stable. Of course.

"You've done something nice for Jesus and perhaps one day He can do something nice for you. Won't you tell me your name so I can tell Him who it was that clothed Him when He was born?"

didn't know it. There shouldn't be any harm in telling the lady. When he reached the entrance, he turned back to look at the man and woman and infant. A light, blindingly radiant, filled the cave. Squinting for a moment, he spun on his heel and ran down the hill, full tilt.

"It's Dismas," he called over his shoulder.

Legend tells that the Anglicized name of one of the robbers crucified with Christ on Good Friday was Dismas. He belonged to a gang of Judean robbers, who as a boy, allegedly helped Mary and Joseph and the baby Jesus during their flight to Egypt. The inspiration for this short story came when I wondered from where the swaddling clothes had come. --Author

"One of the criminals who were hanged railed at him saying are you not the Christ? Save yourself and us!' But the other rebuked him, saying, 'Do you not fear God, since you are under the same sentence of condemnation? And we indeed justly; for we are receiving the due reward of our deeds; but this man has done nothing wrong.' And he said, 'Jesus, remember me when you come in your kingly power.' And He said to him, 'Truly I say to you, today you will be with me in Paradise.' "   Luke 23:39-43

INCIDENT ON HARTNESS STREET
A Short Story

Tommy Wayne hurried to the kitchen. "Papa's home."
The windows on the porch rattled when the door slammed, continuing their noise while Mike Wayne stomped his boots free of snow. The door opened and he stepped into the warm room.

"I was beginning to worry about you," his wife said. "That storm is a bad one."

"The bus was running late, Clara," Mike said, shivering while slipping from his mackinaw. "I don't think it'll let up all night. Hi, Tommy." He smiled at his son.

"Hi, Papa."

"Wash your hands, Mike," Clara said, "and I'll dish up."

When the kitchen was clean, the family went to the parlor. "Can I listen to the radio, Papa? "

"What's on tonight?"

"'Gang Busters' ! "

His mother stepped in the doorway. "I don't want you listening to that stuff. It only puts bad ideas in your head. "

Tommy knew she always said that, but usually--

"Now, Clara, " Mike said, "I like that program, too. "

"My, look at the time," Clara said. "I think if Tommy wants Santa to come, he should go to bed now so Santa knows Tommy's good and not naughty like the McMann boys."

"Now, what did they do?" Mike waited for his wife ' s report on the neighbor children .

"Oh, nothing really bad. But they were throwing snowballs again today and hit Tommy in the face. "

"Was he hurt? " Mike asked, sitting up.

"No."

"Well, then, what's the problem?"

"It's just the idea. He could've been. They should stay on Hartness Street where they belong."

"I could have fallen on the way home and froze to death," Mike said.

"What's that have to do with it?"

"If you worry about something enough, it sure might happen."

Clara ignored Mike's philosophy. "Off to bed with you now, Tommy. Your father and I will be up in a while to say good night."

"Good night," Tommy said, slowly starting for the hallway and the steps.

He wanted to hear what they'd say about his friends. Tommy knew the boys hadn't meant to hit him. Sitting on the bottom step, he listened to his parents talking.

"Mike, I don't want those children playing with Tommy."

"Clara, Tommy's a big boy and he knows right from wrong. I feel sorry for McMann and his family. He's been out of work ever since they moved in on Hartness and that's a year now. Raising a family with this damned depression is bad enough but to not have a job? What they got? Five boys and no work and Christmas the day after tomorrow. I'm just glad I've got my job at the Post Office. How'd you like to be in their shoes?"

"You know I wouldn't. But the point is those boys are roughnecks."

"Maybe they're roughnecks because they haven't got any other way to get rid of their energy. No toys or games to play with, and they probably know how tough things are for their folks. Kids're smarter today in '36 than when we were growing up."

"I know I'm being unreasonable but I was afraid Tommy was hurt. I do feel sorry for them."

Tommy walked into the room.

"Why haven ' t you gone upstairs, Tommy?"

"I overheard you and Papa talking, Mama. What are we having for Christmas dinner?"

"Turkey."

"I heard Mrs. McMann say they *might* have meatloaf."

Clara glanced at Mike. "I see. Does that bother you, son?"

Tommy thought for a moment. "Yeah."

"Why, Tommy?" Mike asked.

"Well, I guess because we've got everything we need and they don' t seem to have nothing."

"Why worry about them? " Mike asked .

"I don't know. Maybe because it's Christmas and I'll be getting presents, a big dinner and everything. And they ain't got nothing."

"Look, son," Mike said, "when you grow older, you'll find there are a lot of things wrong in the world. A person can't take on everybody's problems because they're there or because they make a guy feel bad."

Tommy looked away. "They're my friends."

"I know, son. But worrying about them and upsetting yourself isn't going to help them or you. You go to bed and I'll turn up the radio so you can hear 'Gang Busters' while you fall asleep."

"Okay, Papa." Dejected, Tommy left the room.

He walked up the steps and entered his room. While undressing, he wished there was something he could do for the McManns. Opening the closet door, he saw his blue and white striped pajamas standing out in bold relief against his dark winter clothes. He pulled the top over his head and stepped into the bottoms. Tying the draw string, he stared at his toy box. He closed the door and turned out the light.

The sheets were icy cold, and he pulled his legs up. Happy thoughts mixed with sad ones when he thought of the toy box in his closet.

"Why not?" He sat up. "I'll do it." He jumped from bed, tiptoeing to the hall closet where more toys were stored. Down stairs, the cacaphony of machine guns, police whistles, sirens and shouting voices filtered up the stairway.

Opening the door, he reached inside for the light. There were all sorts of toys.

He'd have no problem. He quietly closed the door, and hurried to his room. He felt good but, with sirens coming from the radio downstairs, he felt as if he had committed a crime. Jumping into bed, he took mental inventory of his toys. In seconds, he fell asleep.

The next day, Tommy brought out cars, trucks, games and puzzles . He cleaned and inspected each for damages that might make it no good. He quickly repaired those things he could and by noon, 15 items lay in the middle of Tommy' s bed--enough for five boys. He stood back to admire his work just when the door opened.

"What ' s going on in here? "

Tommy blustered, trying to think of an answer that would satisfy his mother, but couldn't imagine her allowing him to go ahead with his idea if she knew about it.

He stared at the floor and told his mother of his plan. When he finished, he looked at her and found her smiling.

"I think you should consider giving them more than just toys."

"What do you mean, Mama? "

"You know their clothes are ragged. You have lots of things you've outgrown. Maybe there would be some sweaters or pants we could include.

"Oh, Mama!" Tommy hugged her.

They worked feverishly to finish before Mike got home. They knew he'd be late again and there were other preparations to make for their holiday. When the parcel was wrapped with a big red bow, they hurried to finish their other jobs.

When told of Tommy's idea, Mike said, "I am not going to carry that over to Hartness Street. No sir! I'm not taking part in this at all."

"Why, Mike?" Clara asked. "Tommy's worked hard to do something nice for someone. Don't disappoint him."

"I don' t want to make McMann feel bad. What the hell will he think if an ordinary working stiff like me brings a whole bunch of junk to his house for Christmas?"

"All you have to do is put it on the porch and leave. They'll find it and never know who brought it."

The pleas of his wife and son overwhelmed Mike and he agreed to carry the box. Tommy insisted on helping.

Mike lifted the box to his shoulder and father and son made their way into the crisp, cold night. Quiet stillness pressed in on them, while overhead, glittering stars filled the heavens. Only their breathing, and the crunching of their boots on the snow-covered sidewalks disturbed the night.

At McMann's house, Mike tiptoed up the slanting steps, carefully placing the box.

When he returned to Tommy, the boy said, "What if they don't find it, Papa?"

"They'll find it."

"I gotta make certain. I'll go along the side of the house and knock. Then I'll hide in those bushes next to the porch."

"Where'll I be?"

"Come with me?"

"All right."

They carefully made their way to the hiding place and once in position, Tommy reached around the corner to knock sharply. They heard footsteps approaching and crouched behind the hedges.

Shouts of surprise told the man and boy the box had been found and they could hear the excited voices while they dragged it inside.

"Close that door! Don't let all the heat out," Mrs. McMann shouted.

When Mike and Tommy felt it safe to leave, they hurried to the sidewalk, and strode toward home.

They had gone a few steps when Tommy stopped, lifting his cap's ear flap. "What's that tinkling noise?"

Mike listened. "I hear it, too, son. I don' t know. "

They remained quiet for several minutes, trying to identify the sound. Peering up, they searched the sparkling sky but saw nothing out of the ordinary.

The silvery tones continued until a voice, filled with merriment and joviality softly cried out, "Merry Christmas to all and to all a good night."

JUST LIKE DADDY'S
Based on a True Christmas Incident

It's never been easy raising kids at any time in the history of the human race. And the truth was the same for my husband, Joe and me back in the early '60s when our twins were five years old. Some days they could be angels and other days the imps from hell. Any parent, will understand what I mean.

Looking back at those times, the young parents of today seem not to have that many financial problems when it comes to raising their youngsters. Oh, they probably do, but Joe was working at the John Deere plant in the office for about two years at the time of this incident. He made--gross pay, mind you--about $410 a month. The take home pay was about $330 or so, what with withholding tax and Social Security and believe it or not, we were able to save about $20 a month in the credit union. Our house payment was $50 a month and food ran somewhere in the vicinity of $125 per month. So we weren't really that bad off when it came to paying our bills and even going on a little vacation once a year for a few days just to get away.

Joe got bumped to the third shift and went into work at 11:00 p.m. and got off at 7:30 the next morning. He was 30 years old and I was 28 and besides our twins, Johnnie and Julie, we had Tim who was only 14 months younger and an October-born baby girl, named Tracey. As a result, Joe decided to get a part-time job over the Christmas holidays at a department store downtown--Rosheks. He knew the toy department manager, Charley Vance, and because he was still a big kid at heart, Joe approached Charley for a job.

Now Joe weighed about 170-175 pounds at the time and was pretty muscular. When he came home and told me he was going to be Santa Claus during the daytime hours of 1:00 to 5:00 p.m., I thought both he and Charley had lost their minds.

"I'll be wearing padding," he said when I settled down and wiped my eyes from laughing.

I started whooping again. My six-foot tall, narrow waisted, big-chested husband was going to make a pretty silly-looking Santa Claus--padding or no padding.

The time came for him to go to Rosheks' Department Store and be the little elf with the stomach like a bowlfull of jelly and cherry red nose and twinkling eyes. That I had to see. I burst out laughing again.

He came home about 5:30 and said everything went well, and he had really enjoyed it. He went to bed for another few hours sleep before he had to go to work at John Deere that night. The next morning, he would come home and go to bed and I'd get him up to go play Santa Claus and the routine was set.

The extra cash Santa Claus was able to earn helped greatly toward our family having a wonderful Christmas that year. While I still had some last minute shopping to do, I wanted to get at least the three older children to see "Santa Claus." The two boys, Johnnie and Timmy didn't seem too interested in going shopping, even though I promised they could see Santa and tell him what they wanted for Christmas. I called my mother-in-law and asked if she could take care of the two boys and the baby. She agreed and I told Julie that she and I would go to see him even if the boys weren't along.

We finished the little shopping I had to do and headed for the toy department at Rosheks. I wondered what would happen. From what Joe had told me, he made a pretty good Saint Nick. Would Julie recognize him behind all that white angel hair? Would she recognize his voice? I hoped she wouldn't.

She and I stepped off the elevator and walked around the toy department for a moment, more to build my confidence than my daughter's. When she saw Santa Claus sitting on his glorious, golden throne, she tugged at my coat and pointed.

"There he is," I said. "You do want to tell him what you want for Christmas don't you?"

She nodded a little hesitantly, because of the three oldest children, she was by far the most shy. Clinging to me, she walked up the steps and I released her mittened little hand. She was on her own. And so was Joe.

Suddenly Santa laughed, a deep hearty laugh and I wondered if it really were Joe behind all the white and padded belly.

Julie smiled tentatively and when Santa held out his arms to her, she stepped right into them. He swung her up on his lap and they began talking, her voice tiny and afraid, Santa's deep and soft spoken. When she said something that must have struck Santa funny, he laughed that deep laugh and Julie bounced on his "bowl full of jelly. "

She looked into Santa's face and grinned, suddenly very much at ease. When she finished, she slid off his lap and walked down the steps to me . We both waved good-bye to the beloved figure of Santa Claus.

"Merry Christmas, Julie and to your mommy," Santa said and waved with his red mittens.

Julie was quiet, which wasn't out of the ordinary until we got on the bus to go home. She turned to me and said, "You know somethin', Mommy?"

" What's that, darling?" I asked.

"Santa Claus has eyes just like Daddy's and I love him, too."

IN MEMORIAM
A Short Story

The neighborhood I grew up in was a typical, below-middle class type,
where wooden-framed homes housed factory workers and people too old to
work and who had grown crochety over the years. I was the only kid at my
end of the block but there was a boy on the other end who was about my
age of nine. We got together a lot and played, which was most of the
summer when school was out. Up in the next block the stork was a more
familiar bird, since there were dozens of kids living there.

Our close-by neighbors, most of whom had never had children were not
too much of a problem for me. I thought they tended to ignore me and I
paid little attention to them. The only time I ever heard from them was
when they thought I'd done something wrong and told my mother or father
about it. It was hell having that many people look out for my welfare.

Naturally, there were other people who lived on our street but the one
person who literally scared me everytime I saw him was old Ed Boden. Mr.
Boden lived on the other side of the Trellises, who lived next door to us.
Mr. Boden always sat on his front porch during nice weather and took to
shaking his cane at me or any other kid who went past his house that one
summer. There was a solid wall railing around the porch and all I could

ever see of him was his head. He always was looking down at something he was doing and only looked up to yell at me and shake his cane whenever I rode my bike past his house.

There wasn't much to do during the summer months, other than play Army or baseball with the kids from the next block whenever we could get enough players together to have a game. Once I had performed my weekly ritual of cutting the lawn and taking out the trash, I was my own man. I often wondered what Mr. Boden was doing on his front porch, since I could never see anything other than his head. He wore a white beard and had white hair and was skinny as anything or anyone I'd ever seen. He sure would've made a lousy Santa Claus. But then, I concluded he was too grouchy to even think about Christmas let alone be merry and happy.

I decided one sunny afternoon, late in August, about two weeks before school was to start, that I was going to find out what he was doing whenever he sat on the porch. I knew he wasn't reading because his head bobbed up and down as If he were doing something with his hands. His head would've been still if he'd been reading.

I plotted my mission. I'd go around our garage, through the alley and sneak through Trellises' yard and along Boden's house. There was only one window on that side of the Boden house and it was in the kitchen. If I made sure he was on the porch before I started my trek, I'd be safe.

I went into our parlor and looked through the south window. Sure enough. There he was, sitting on his chair, head bobbing up and down, all the while concentrating on something in his hands. But even from that higher position, I couldn't make out what it was he was doing.

Most kids during World War II, played a lot of "war games" with home-made weaponry, and I was no different. Whenever we couldn't get two teams together for a game, some of us would go on a "mission," cross the Chicago Great Western Railway tracks and head up the big hill a couple of blocks away.

Considering I was going on a solo mission I thought it best to take my Garand M-1 semi-automatic rifle along. Of course it was only a broomstick handle, but it would give me confidence while I stalked the enemy.

I went through our back gate and along the alley until I came to the Trellises' gate and entered their yard. That was the point of no return. I was committed. Easing along the Boden house, I hugged the wall to make certain no one saw me.

When I stood by the porch, I peeked under that solid railing and could see the enemy--Mr. Boden--sitting in his chair--whittling. Whittling for crying out loud! Was that all he had to do? Whittle? A pile of shavings lay at his feet and I decided the mission was a washout and was just about ready to leave when he turned and looked right at me. At least I thought he was. Could he see me? The little slot I was spying through and which was intended as a water outlet for the porch, was pretty narrow. I wasn't sure if he could see me or not. So, I did what any good commando would do. I froze--actually more from fear and the overwhelming urge to pee in my pants, than from instinct alone.

He stared at that slot for the longest time and then went back to his whittling.

I turned and raced back along my route and put my M-1 in the garage and went inside the house, just when the phone rang.

My mother picked up the receiver and put it to her ear, holding the candlestick phone in her other hand. "Hello?" I heard her say.

"How are you, Mrs. Oakes?"

Bessie Oakes? Fat, nosey Bessie Oakes? What did she want? Had she seen...

"He was?" My mother turned and looked at me.

I felt like melting. Something was wrong. There had been a fifth columnist involved in my daring plan.

"He did what?" She glared at me.

I was in trouble. No two ways about it.

"Don't worry, I'll take care of it, Mrs. Oakes." She hung up and turned to face me. "That was Mrs. Oakes, Jay."

"I know."

"Do you know what she said?"

I had a pretty good idea but I thought it was best to clam up and let the enemy torture me to get the information.

"She said she saw you in Trellises' yard and that you were bothering Mr. Boden. Is that true?"

What chance did I have with so many spies around. Since she had me cold, I felt it best to admit it and take the punishment. I slowly nodded.

Then, she surprised me, the way she did so often while I was growing up.

"People like Mr. Boden, when they get old and live alone, get sort of set in their ways. He doesn't have any grandchildren and his only son was killed at Pearl Harbor. He doesn't like to be bothered and you'd be doing me a favor if you stayed away from him."

I tried to explain about wanting to know what it was he was doing and she kindly told me it was none of my business. End of mission. No court martial. No stockade sentence. No firing squad.

I knew he had had a son and that he'd been killed in the sneak attack on Pearl Harbor. Still, I didn't think it gave him the right to scare me and other kids with that darned old cane of his whenever he shook it or yelled at us for going past his house.

School started and things were pretty normal. Halloween came and went and Thanksgiving came with a skinny turkey without much meat on it and whatever mom could scrounge up for that feast. There was a war on, you know. My dad, who was too old for the draft, said grace and after that day, I started counting the days 'til Christmas. I knew what I wanted for Christmas--a Lionel electric train, an Erector set and a Red Ryder 1,000 shot BB gun. When I looked through the Christmas catalogs that came to the house, I didn't see anything like those dreams anyplace in the toy section. It looked like everything was made out of paper or wood and there sure wasn't much of a choice where those things were concerned.

So I thought I'd take what came my way and wait for the war to end, to fulfill my dreams.

On Christmas eve, we were all set to go to Midnight Mass at Holy Ghost Church. When we walked out the back door, my dad kicked a box that leaned against the bottom step. Being a father, I guess he thought he had to act like one at that moment.

"How many times have I told you not to leave things on the steps, Jay?"

"I--I didn't leave--that's not mine."

"Oh, yes it is. It's got your name on it. Jay Rober... Hey!" He looked at Mom and then at me. 'This is wrapped like a gift--a Christmas gift."

"Well, put it in the house and Jay can open it when we come home from church," my practical mother said. "If we want to be able to sit together during Mass, we'd better get going right now."

Never before in my life or since, have I attended such a long mass. It dragged on forever. All I could think of was that box at home and what might be in it. And who had left it there? Finally when Mass was over and people were filing out of church, my very Catholic mother suggested we go up and see the manger scene and the Christ child. I wanted to explode, but what choice did I have? When we reached home, it was almost 1:30 in the morning.

When we walked into the kitchen, I grabbed for the box.

"I think you should wait until tomorrow morning, Jay, when we open the rest of the gifts," Practical Mother said.

"So do I," Agreeable Father said.

I didn't, but fat lot of good it would've done me to protest. So, we went to bed. Mother and Dad with visions of sugar plums and all that stuff in their heads, while I rolled and tossed doing my best to think of what might be in that box. Money? Jewels? An electric train? *Something! WHAT???*

When I awoke after falling asleep on guard duty, I jumped out of bed and raced to the parlor where the tree stood and our few gifts snuggled around its base. The mysterious box leaned against the wall. Could I open it first? I asked. No, they said. And I opened those gifts that Santa Claus had brought, and the gifts Mom and Dad had gotten for me and the gift from my cousins in Sioux Falls, South Dakota. Now, there was a biggie. They sent me a copy of Louisa May Alcott's *Little Men.* They signed it: Jay from Alfred and Stuart. Now there was something I was going to read right away before I took another breath.

I turned to my parents, who sat on the couch. "Now? *Now,* can I open the box?"

They both nodded.

I tore the plain dark gray paper off and saw a Campbell's Soup cardboard box that had held canned chicken noodle soup at one time. Maybe it still did. I ripped off the lid and there, before my very eyes was a wooden fire engine with ladders and men and everything--all in wood, a wooden steam locomotive, tender and two passenger cars. A tag attached to the locomotive read simply, "Merry Christmas to Jay from Mr. Boden."

I couldn't believe it.

Later that day, I went over to his house and thanked him. When he came to the door, our eyes locked the way I thought they had when I had spied on him in August. I suddenly saw the real Mr. Boden. His eyes twinkled and while he would've made a lousy Santa because of his skinny body, there was something about him that didn't seem scary anymore. I noticed he had not put up a Christmas tree or any decorations.

A picture of his son in his Navy uniform stood on a table in one corner. It couldn't have been too happy a day for him.

"Mr. Boden, sir? Would you like to come to our house for dinner?" I asked, not quite knowing how my mother would take my generous offer.

He looked at me for what seemed forever and finally said, "Did your mother tell you to ask me, Jay?"

I nodded. "Sure," I lied.

"What time?"

"I--I'm not sure. I'll run home and ask Mom and come back and tell you. All right?"

He nodded and I left.

Surprise of surprises, my mother and father agreed, saying I had done the right thing.

Well, that Christmas has stuck in my memory all these years and I still have the train and fire engine Mr. Boden carved for me. He died the summer following that Christmas but in those few months, he and I became good friends and I like to think that I was able to bring just a little happiness into his life. I always wanted to ask him why he had done it for me, but for some reason I could never get up the courage. It's probably just as well. I'd like to think he did it for me, in memory of his son.

ACKNOWLEDGEMENTS

I'd like to thank the people at BQW Publishing House for their efforts in putting out *Remember When...?* Without their help, it would not have become a book. I'll try to give thanks to those who have helped out with pictures or information. If I miss someone, I'm sorry. Here they are in no particular order or importance not even in alphabetical order:

Mr. and Mrs. William Decker; Mr. and Mrs. Dick Brandenberg; Ray Grutz; Roger Broessel; Norm Zepeski; Mr. and Mrs. Tom Breitbach; Mrs. Phyllis Roth; David Tschiggfrie; Mary Burris Post; Don Ahrendt; Damaris Brauer Eichman; Darlene Zahina Manders; Bob Gribben; Joe Wareham; Mary Keas; Elmer Schwers; Carey Lewis; Art Rooney; Al Birch; Sam Young; Bill Oglesby; Cy Behr; Carol Loetscher; Edward Heiberger; Mike Henge; Charles Berger.

And a special thank you to my wife Kathy. Without her, none of *Remember When...?* would exist.

This beautiful blonde sang with Leo Pieper's band when big bands were in vogue. (Contributed)

The author's dad, John G. Tigges and Topper, ready for a trot through the countryside. (Author's collection)

An Autocar panel truck from the late '30s. (Author's collection)

Dubuque's
All Girl Orchestra.
(Contributed)

Kretz's Cafeteria, later Tranel's.
(Contributed)

A moonlight excursion
aboard the steamer "Avalon"
gave more than enough time
for dancing and "sparking."
(Author's collection)

Cultivating corn
never harmed the land
the way
chemicals may
be doing today.
(Author's collection)

Author's dad's first automobile.
(Author's collection)

The Chevrolet Fleetline with
snow, sun and rain shield
above the windshield.
(Author's collection)

Remember the hours of pleasure from
chewing Fleer's Double Bubble gum?
(Author's collection)

A team of mules taking a load of shocks
to the threshing machine
(Author's collection)

The author's Uncle Leo leaving to peddle to the
country schoolhouse, where he taught eighth grade.
(Author's collection)

The author's childhood home.
(Author's collection)

The Frazer 4-door sedan...
with its astonishingly low price,
definitely the value leader
in the fine-car field for 1951.

How many cars on this page?

You see two, but actually there are three! Above is the luxurious 1951 Frazer 4-door Sedan. Below is the glorious 1951 edition of an original Kaiser-Frazer idea —the Frazer Vagabond.

It's really 2 cars in 1! For on a moment's notice, it converts from sedan to spacious cargo carrier with room to take with you anything portable for sports or business.

The other magnificent 1951 Frazer models include America's only 4-door Convertible, and two versions

of that stunningly smart Frazer original, the "hardtop". Aptly called the Frazer Manhattan, it comes with a "Convertible Look", solid steel top, either painted in gleaming metal, or covered with shimmering nylon.

All Frazer models are powered by the new Supersonic Engine! All have completely proved Hydra-Matic Drive at extra cost; all have *handcrafted* quality throughout. All are priced astonishingly low! All are *built to better the best on the road!*

KAISER-FRAZER SALES CORPORATION, *Willow Run, Mich.*

The handcrafted

1951 FRAZER

The Pride of Willow Run

The famous successor to the station wagon
...the 2-cars-in-1 Frazer Vagabond
converts in 10 seconds from luxurious
6-passenger sedan to spacious carrier.

© 1950 KAISER-FRAZER SALES CORP., WILLOW RUN, MICHIGAN

The Kaiser Frazer automobiles introduced in 1947 brought many innovations to the market, including the first "hatchback." (Author's collection)

Preston Tucker had to fight Detroit and the U.S. Government and lost before the Tucker "Torpedo" could be proven to be a "super car." (Author's collection)

Picking corn by hand.(Author's collection)

Boots of the comic strip
"Boots and Her Buddies."
(Author's collection)

Tillie and her mother
of the comic strip
"Tillie the Toiler."
(Author's collection)

Thanksgiving Day the way it was in the past. Is yours the same today? (Author's collection)

Big Little Books made a great Christmas gift for a friend since they only cost a nickel. The signatures are in the front of the two Big Little Books shown. (Author's collection)

Is she dreaming of a new doll for Christmas? (Author's collection)

There were only a
little over 500 of
these Spacelander
bikes produced
in the '50s.
One recently sold
for $15,000.
(Author's collection)

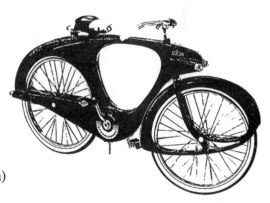

A boy could've received the above train set,
with track and transformer, for $3.95.
(Author's collection)